Adolescent Literature: Response and Analysis

Adolescent Literature: Response and Analysis

Robert E. Probst
Georgia State University

Charles E. Merrill Publishing Company
A Bell & Howell Company
Columbus Toronto London Sydney

Published by
Charles E. Merrill Publishing Company
A Bell & Howell Company
Columbus, Ohio 43216

This book was set in Palatino
Text designer and production coordinator: Mary Henkener
Cover Designer: Cathy Watterson

Library of Congress Catalog Card Number: 88–63534
International Standard Book Number: 0–675–20171–3
1 2 3 4 5 6 7 8 9—89 88 87 86 85 84

Printed in the United States of America

To my parents, Harry and Marian Probst.

And to my wife, Wendy, and my children, Geoffrey and Bryan.

Contents

Preface

Even in this scientific and technological era, literature remains a vitally important subject of the curriculum. It is our reservoir of insight into the human condition, the pool of perceptions and conceptions from which we draw our own visions of what it is to be human. Literature hasn't always served this role in the schools. Too often it has been reduced to merely the facts, figures, and terminology of literary history and genre—to be learned, remembered briefly, and then forgotten. Literature thus presented is not likely to matter very much to the student. It remains something apart, the object of exercises and tests, rather than a vital and shaping experience.

This book teaches that literature is experience, not information, and that the student must be invited to participate in it, not simply observe it from outside. Thus the student is very important—he or she is not simply a recipient of information, but rather a maker of knowledge out of meetings with literary texts.

Rosenblatt argued for this approach in *Literature as Exploration* in 1938. Contemporary critical theory is only now beginning to catch up and rediscover the notions she examined almost 50 years ago. The excitement in current criticism comes from renewed attention to what the reader brings to the literary work and to what the reader must do to enjoy and make sense out of it—central issues of Rosenblatt's work. That the reader's role should generate so much enthusiasm so long after *Literature as Exploration* was first published suggests that the critical implications of Rosenblatt's theories have not been worked out as fully as they might be.

Nor have we fully examined the implications of her ideas for the classroom. Textbooks and curriculum guides suggest that New

Critical and historical approaches to literature, neither of which have paid close attention to the problems and pleasures of the lonely reader, have dominated instruction not only in colleges but also in secondary schools. Yet it is in the secondary schools, where the whole population is represented—not just the serious student of literature—that attention to the individual reader is most important. Here the student can be led to organized and intelligent reflection on the great issues of literature, which are also likely to be the great issues of life. Literature might then serve both to give pleasure and to help in understanding the world.

This text suggests an approach to teaching literature in the secondary schools that pays close attention to the reader, which is to say, the student. Drawing heavily on Rosenblatt's work, it tries to see what it would mean to assume that literature must be personally significant, to respect the reader's responses to literary works, to insist that the reader accept responsibility for making sense of personal experiences, both literary and otherwise, and to acknowledge the influence of literature in shaping our conceptions of the world.

This book shares the fundamental assumptions of contemporary approaches to instruction in writing—that knowledge is made, not found; that making knowledge is a verbal operation; and that the business of making knowlege is not for professionals and scholars alone, but is everyone's task. Especially is this so when the knowledge is of the difficult philosophical and ethical questions that constitute the core of our literary heritage.

I thank Maia Pank Mertz of The Ohio State University, R. Baird Shuman of the University of Illinois, Jeffrey D. Caskey of Western Kentucky University, Jerry L. Sullivan of California State University at Long Beach, Alice Brekke of California State University, Alleen Pace Nilsen of Arizona State University, and Emerita S. Schulte of Ball State University for their thoughtful and professional readings of the later drafts of the manuscript and their valuable suggestions, and Margaret Conable for her conscientious editing. I'm grateful to Dr. Hiram D. Johnston, Chairman of the Department of Curriculum and Instruction at Georgia State University, for his support throughout this project. And I would like to express special appreciation to Dr. Mary H. Scott for her help in editing the manuscript, and, most important, for her steady counsel and encouragement during my years of work on this book.

PART I

The Logic of Response-Based
Teaching

The Reader and the Text 1

THE SECONDARY SCHOOL LITERATURE STUDENT

The pleasures that drew us first to literature were not those of the literary scholar. When our parents read us *Mother Goose*, we enjoyed the rhythms of the language without analyzing the political or social significance of the nursery rhymes. Later, we listened to "Little Red Riding Hood" not to identify characteristics of the fairy tale, but to find out whether or not the wolf had the little girl for dinner. And still later, we read *Catcher in the Rye*, not to investigate Salinger's style and trace the literary influences of his book, but to see how Holden Caulfield copes. These are the kinds of rewards most secondary school students seek in reading.

Most secondary school students will not become professional literary scholars. When they finish school, they are more likely to drive cabs, wait on tables, or sell real estate. To assume that they are interested in the same aspects of literature that interest Kittredge and Brooks and Frye is to make a rash leap of faith. If we begin to plan programs by investigating literary scholarship, cataloging techniques, and outlining a history of major writers and writings, we make that leap. Scholarly questions are not irrelevant, but other questions may take precedence; they have to do with the interests and satisfactions of the average reader.

What, then, are the reasons for reading literature, and why do we attempt to teach it? If, as we have suggested, students are unlikely to come to the literature class with a scholarly passion for information about the sources of Shakespeare's plays or the social context of the early American fire-and-brimstone sermons, they will nonetheless bring with them experiences, interests, and a lengthy agenda of ideas, problems, worries, and attitudes, all of which concern and

3

preoccupy them. If literature is enjoyable or if it touches upon some of those preoccupations, then students have a reason to read. They will read because they are interested in themselves, and because in the reading they may become the focus of attention.

In other words, their reason for reading is the same as that of an independent adult or a younger child—self-indulgence. That self-indulgence may take many forms. Its most common form is a harmless pursuit of diversion and simple pleasure, the escape into a good story that entertains and distracts us from other worries. At its worst, the self-indulgence is a search for confirmation of distorted visions, a vicarious exercise of hatreds and biases that cannot be safely indulged elsewhere in a civilized society. But at its best, it is an attempt to see more clearly who one is and where one stands. Great literature demands reflection upon and reexamination of one's own attitudes and beliefs. The unique claim of imaginative literature at its best is that it is about me, and, of course, about you.

When literature is *read*, rather than worked upon, it draws us into events and invites us to reflect upon our perceptions of them. It is not at that point a subject to be studied as an artifact illustrating an age or a product representing an artist; it is rather an experience to be entered into. "Entering into" literature, however, may be different from most of our other experiences. The literary work invites us in not only as participants, but also as spectators, giving us the opportunity to watch ourselves. It freezes events and holds them still for examination. Few other moments in our lives allow us that time for thought; events move too quickly and we are too deeply and thoroughly involved. Literature, however, allows us both to experience and to reflect upon experience, and thus invites the self-indulgence of those who seek to understand themselves and the world around them.

The adolescent, characteristically preoccupied with self, should be an ideal reader. That is not to say that he *will* read well, or even read at all. He may despise literature, the literature classroom, and the literature teacher, and express great pride in his inability to make sense out of the written word. But unless he is very unusual, he has the one characteristic essential for a reader—an interest in himself. He is concerned about his relationships with peers and parents and his gradual assumption of responsibility for himself. He is growing more aware of the important decisions he will soon have to make. He wants to understand work, love, hate, war, death, vengeance, responsibility, good, evil—in other words, he is interested in the themes of the literature that has established itself as worth reading and discussing. He is not, or at least we hope that he is not, someone beyond caring about those matters, whose most serious thoughts are of football scores, current hairstyles, and next week's episodes of the soap operas.

An adolescent should not yet be content with his knowledge and understanding of the world and of himself. He should not grow rigid and unchanging, working as hard to avoid learning as the young child does to learn. Literature should strike a responsive chord in him, offering the substance to keep alive questions and interests, feeding them so that continual reexamination is rewarded with some sense of growth or progress.

Preoccupation with self should make adolescents uniquely receptive to literature, for literature invites their participation and judgment. It gives them the opportunity to test perceptions against those of author, character, and other readers, and in that testing to see more clearly who they are and how they feel, react, and think. That opportunity is the purpose for teaching literature. Students read literature to know themselves, and—insofar as they each are a composite of their ideas, attitudes, beliefs, and emotions—to create themselves, for reading will enable them to refine and sharpen their conceptions of the world and the people in it. It is those conceptions that make them who they are.

PURPOSE IN LITERATURE TEACHING

To begin by discussing the interaction of reader and literary work may seem odd. Would it not make more sense to begin with the substance to be taught—the content of the literature course? We could list the appropriate works and compile the relevant information about authors, historical events, literary periods, and genres. We could identify the terminology that might prove useful in the classroom and specify the literary concepts that students should master during their secondary school years. Then, having laid this foundation of information about literature, we could discuss what we know about adolescent students and their interests, skills, inclinations, habits, and problems. We could analyze their psychological and linguistic development and consider the results of reading-interest studies. We could then make some assertions about what we wanted to teach—the literature—and whom we wanted to teach—the adolescent—and from those assertions we might expect a pedagogy to emerge.

This strategy has an undeniable appeal. Moving down the journalist's checklist from "what" to "whom" to "how," and presumably sooner or later to "why," it seems logical and manageable. Moreover, the lists of texts, names, concepts, terms, and dates it produces could be easily subdivided into units and lessons, the building blocks of the secondary school curriculum. Our list of literary genres, for example, might suggest that part of the curriculum be arranged generically: a few weeks on poetry, followed by a stretch on the short story, a drama unit, a couple of months on novels, and whatever time is left over on the essay. Literary history suggests a chronological pattern which is easily developed into a full curriculum, especially if we restrict our attention to the literature of one national group—the seventh century is followed by the eighth, the eighth by the ninth, and so on until either centuries or school days run out.

Such structures are reassuring. They give shape and substance to the work of the literature classroom, helping us both design instruction and evaluate our results. Starting with the literature itself, and following one of several cleared and marked trails until we have sufficient guidelines for a course, seems to be a rational and practical approach to teaching literature. To wander from those trails is to stray into unmapped regions with no assurance that we will emerge where we hope to be.

But that raises a real and fundamental question—where do we hope to be? What do we want the literature student to experience and learn in our classes? The question is neglected if we start with the accumulated body of information about literature and allow it to set directions. If knowledge of genres is the essence of the literary experience, it is difficult to argue with spending a year investigating the differences among the genres. If literary history is the model, we should certainly begin with the seventh century and dutifully work our way toward the twentieth. But the question remains—does genre study, literary history, or any similar approach create the experience of literature that we seek for students in the secondary schools?

The appealing strategy of using the knowledge accumulated over the centuries about literature to generate curriculum and instructional procedures has the virtue of efficiency, but it does not consider purpose. By failing to ask what we intend to accomplish in the secondary school English program, we assume that the goals of the professional literature student are also the goals of the secondary school literature student, though instinct, common sense, and brief experience in the classroom all tell us that this is not a safe assumption.

Literature is unique as a discipline. In a very important sense, it does not exist outside the individual reader in the same way as do the physical phenomena studied by scientists. A volcano is there, regardless of who sees it or fails to see it, and it will erupt or lie dormant whether anyone cares or not, but a literary work has no significance at all until it is read. The ink on the paper is nothing until a reader picks up the page, reads and responds to it, and thereby transforms it into an event. Slatoff, commenting on the uniqueness of literary works as objects of study, remarks:

> The objects we study are curious . . . in that they assume their full or significant form and being only in active conjunction with a human mind. To some extent, of course, this is true of all objects. Whatever one's theory of perception, one has to agree that some qualities of any object are dependent on human perception. But works of literature have scarcely any important qualities apart from those that take shape in minds.[1]

Literature, in other words, is written for readers. That does not mean that specialists cannot study it, but if they neglect to consider the fact that they are not the primary or intended audience, they stray from center. It is clearly possible to distinguish between Petrarchan and Shakespearean sonnet forms, to argue whether a certain Coleridge poem is one of his "conversational" poems, or to quarrel over the authorship of Shakespeare's plays, but it is unlikely that any of the authors planned their works as subjects for that sort of treatment. If the literature curriculum gives the students that misimpression, it does them a serious disservice, teaching them that they are not sufficiently prepared, that they do not have the background or the scholarly disposition to be readers. Shakespeare's audience, those standing in the pits munching oranges, would not have been so intimidated. They would have come to the play for the experience it offered, and would not have doubted their competence to enjoy it, despite their lack of professional literary training.

Literature is not the private domain of an intellectual elite. It is instead the reservoir of all mankind's concerns. Although it may be studied in scholarly and professional ways, that is not its primary function. In the secondary school especially, we are not dealing with an intellectual elite, but with a representative group from the local community. We must keep clearly in mind that the literary experience is fundamentally an unmediated, private exchange between a text and a reader, and that literary history and scholarship are supplemental. Studying them may or may not contribute to our understanding of the private exchange, but it cannot be substituted for that immediate experience. As Rosenblatt says:

> all the student's knowledge about literary history, about authors and periods and literary types, will be so much

useless baggage if he has not been led primarily to seek in literature a vital personal experience.[2]

When we substitute historical or critical questions for the direct experience of reading and reflecting, we are on the periphery. We are like baseball statisticians discussing batting averages—the discussion has to do with the game, but it is not the same as playing the game. No doubt some people will prefer the statistics to the game, but it is nonetheless important to perceive the distinction between the two and avoid confusing them in our teaching. The ball player and the statistician require different sorts of training. So do the reader and the literary scholar.

Our literature programs must provide the experience that the typical reader requires. If we can also satisfy those rare students whose interest in literature extends to literary scholarship, then by all means we should do so, but we must not neglect those who will simply be readers and not scholars. Such negligence has been a fault of most literature programs that evolve from cataloging information about literature. Applebee, in his history of English teaching, points out that "Teachers of English have never successfully resisted the pressure to formulate their subject as a body of knowledge to be imparted."[3] He continues:

> Part of the uneasiness which teachers have felt with attempts to define their subject matter as a body of knowledge results from an awareness, often unarticulated, that the goals which they seek to accomplish through the teaching of literature are ultimately not defined by such knowledge, but rather are questions of values and perspective—the kinds of goals usually summed up as those of a "liberal" or "humanistic" education. . . . Only rarely have they considered, however, the implications of such an emphasis for the way their subject should be taught, being for the most part content to assume that the humanistic benefits would follow naturally from exposure to the proper content. . . .[4]

Rosenblatt, many years earlier, criticized the results of that assumption:

> The adolescent can be easily led into an artificial relationship with literature. Year after year as freshmen come into college, one finds that even the most verbally proficient of

them, often those most intimately drawn to literature, have already acquired a hard veneer, a pseudo-professional approach. They are anxious to have the correct labels—the right period, the biographical background, the correct evaluation. They read literary histories and biographies, critical essays, and then, if they have the time, they read the work.[5]

As she suggests, the literature program devised to present information about literature deprives us of fundamental experience with literature, encouraging us to bypass a crucial step in reading. Rosenblatt's criticism is confirmed by the popularity in the schools of commercial study guides, short summaries of literary works with critical and historical commentary appended. Even for students who do not literally bypass the work, Rosenblatt's comment may be metaphorically accurate. If they read with no other purpose in mind than to find and recall information, we may legitimately wonder if they have had a more significant literary experience than that of the student who reads only a summary.

We are suggesting, then, that we look first at the actual reading. Interest in other approaches to literature will come, if it comes, from this first step; imposing the other studies on students without this step is likely to lead to the artificiality or pseudo-professionalism about which Rosenblatt warns us. Programs developed to teach a body of information about literature tend, unfortunately, to attempt to create literary historians and critics before they have created readers. Let us see, then, what sort of literature teaching may result from considering that neglected step, the actual reading of the work.

THE READING ACT

We suggested earlier that it was self-indulgence that drove readers to books, either lazy self-indulgence that seeks momentary release from work or worry, the destructive sort that seeks confirmation of biases and opinions, or the constructive sort that seeks a clearer understanding of the self and the world. The first sort does not concern us—idleness is only a venial sin—and the second is perhaps best confronted by close attention to the third. This third form of self-indulgence is introspective; it involves reflection on one's own values, beliefs, and ideas. It can be like a conversation between writer and reader, as the reader tests perceptions and insights against the writer's. The conversation is not easy; the writer's work is done, and the reader now bears the burden. To make sense of the work he must find connections with it. The reader cannot become the writer, seeing and thinking as the writer does. Instead, he gathers and refines his own impressions, and interprets, tentatively at first, then with more assurance, shaping the meaning and significance of the work. History, biography, and rhyme scheme are peripheral at this point—the focus of attention is the interchange between reader and text.

Let us explore the possibilities in reading one text. Consider yourself a student, read the poem that follows, and ask yourself what you have experienced.

As Best She Could

Old widow crazed with hunger, you came in crippled,
your backcountry eyes bright and furtive, your voice
careening between a whimper and wild thin laughter.

I saw you take the edge of the chair and cower
as the social worker cut through your explanations,
your patches of self-respect, with her curt queries.

Terrible your smile when asked about your holdings
in bonds, in bank accounts, in property,
your look when reminded of life insurance lapsed.

She wouldn't believe you lived as best you could
on the meager uncertain amount your daughters sent you
and paid no rent to an old and kindly landlord.

She took your naked terror of death for greed
and probable fraud, denied you, sent you off
for written proofs from daughters out of state.

Their misspelt notes came in some three weeks later,
your card for medical care went out, but soon
came back from Public Health a cancellation.

No blame attached, the regulations followed,
your death quite likely in any case, but still
I see you rise and quiver away, your stiff heart
pounding with baffled rage, with stifled pride.

—Donald Jones

Reflect for a moment. If nothing comes to mind, consider: What does the poem make you feel? If nothing, can you tell why? If something, then what, precisely? Does it remind you of anyone you know, anyone you have ever seen, or any experience you have had? Does it call to mind thoughts, ideas, or attitudes, even if they seem tangential? Is there any word in the text that you think captures the essence of the poem?

Responses vary, perhaps more widely than might be expected of what may seem at first a rather straightforward poem. One group of students reports feeling anger at the social worker. The old woman, they point out, is doing the best she can—she is uneducated, ill, inarticulate, and scared of a bureaucracy she does not understand. The social worker should have more compassion, they may insist, should be a bit more sympathetic, like the kindly landlord who has allowed the widow to live rent-free. After all, it is not her own money the social worker is dispensing; it does not hurt her to approve the widow's request.

Some students in this group begin to speak of the evils of big business and big government, which, they assert, have no feeling for individuals. Agencies like the one depicted here exist for the purpose of giving soft jobs to irresponsible people like the social worker, who want simply to collect their paychecks and go home. Some students may have had conflicts with institutions—insurance companies, the Department of Motor Vehicles, or perhaps the school—and may have stories of their own to tell, stories called to mind by reading the poem. Others may create stories to account for the events in the poem. One student speculated (though "speculate" is too weak a term, for the student insisted on the truth of her reading) that the social worker and the widow's daughters had conspired to obtain the widow's welfare money.

Let us not concern ourselves here with the accuracy or defensibility of each response, or even with its proximity to the text. Clearly, the student who compared the social worker with the generous landlord had made a statement more easily traced to the text than that of the student who invented a conspiracy to defraud the widow of her pittance. In the early stages of discussion the idea is to elicit, not to judge, the students' responses. It is not important to identify who is right; in fact, except on relatively simple and uninteresting points, it often is not possible to determine right and wrong in the reading of a poem. Rather, we are simply trying to find out what the responses are. We will then be able to look more closely at the readings to discover what we can about the readers, the text, and the reading process.

Although anger with the social worker and sympathy with the widow are the most frequent first responses to the poem, there are others. A second group, for instance, reports indifference to the widow's situation. She should have planned better, these students may say, and besides, she is not a very appealing character—she is crazy, her eyes are sneaky like a rat's eyes, her voice that of a witch, and her smile "terrible." No wonder the social worker distrusts her and demands that she obtain proof of her claims. Everyone cheats the welfare system, anyway, and someone should put a stop to it. The trouble with too many people, they may moralize, is that they want something for nothing.

Again, we may for the moment overlook the transformation of "crazed" into "crazy," and the acrobatic leap from the old widow to "everyone" and "too many people."

A third group of students may report a less partisan reading. They suggest that in a sense the social worker, as well as the old widow, did "as best she could." The ambiguity in the title suggests to them that neither of the two can really be blamed. The old widow may be trapped by her ignorance and her lack of bureaucratic sophistication, but the social worker is trapped also, by the regulations and procedures of the bureaucracy for which she works. These students say that the problem, larger than one welfare client or one social worker, is a problem with the whole system. Circumstances are at fault, not either of the two people. "No blame attached," they cite, and agree that no one is to be blamed, and that the widow's death *is* quite likely in any case. They point out that regulations do have to be followed, or we have anarchy. Even when regulations are followed, the welfare system, so the papers tell them, is rife with fraud and mismanagement.

Often the students in the last group cited seem more disturbed by the poem than do others. The students who respond with anger have a target for that emotion, and those who are indifferent to the widow have, they feel, justification for that lack of concern; but those who think that neither the widow nor the social worker can be held fully accountable are frustrated and annoyed by their inability to find someone to blame.

The three readings of the poem presented here are, of course, rough generalities; actual student responses will be as varied as the students themselves. But these serve to indicate the possible range of response to "As Best She Could." We might perceive a still broader range by imagining the widely varying audiences this poem might find in the schools across the country and predicting their responses (keeping in mind that such predictions are rash and unreliable). What, for instance, would be the likely response from students whose parents are on welfare; from students whose parents are unable to obtain welfare; from those whose parents are fraudulently obtaining welfare; from those who work after school and whose parents both hold two jobs to avoid having to take welfare; from those whose family income exceeds $100,000 a year; from those students who perform some sort of part-time social work; from those living in the largest cities; from those living in remote areas?

Consider also the variations that may arise from the special circumstances in which the poem is encountered. Might not a student's response on reading the poem in December, as Christmas approaches, differ somewhat from his response to the same poem in April, as income-tax deadlines begin to press upon his parents? It is at least conceivable that he may tend more toward generosity at one time, more toward stinginess at the other. Would responses perhaps be affected if the papers had recently featured stories in which welfare recipients had been cheated of much-needed money by dishonest government employees? Or if the story had been of recipients cheating the government and therefore the taxpayers?

Considering the infinite number of possible readers and circumstances in which they read, the responses described above may not seem to do justice to the variety of readings the poem will support. But the point is not to attempt to identify all possible reactions to the text. Rather, it is to suggest that variations are inevitable and legitimate. Coming from different backgrounds, with different attitudes, under varying circumstances, the students naturally have different readings.

Without speculating further about why students respond as they do, we can nonetheless see some justification or explanation for each of the above responses. The first response, for instance, in which the dominant feeling is anger toward the social worker, may be seen to reflect a natural sympathy for the victims of society. We may quarrel with the students' portrayal of the social worker and the vehemence of their condemnation, and we may doubt the efficacy of the action they say she should have taken, but probably we are able to accept the students' sympathy for the widow. In any event, if the text has awakened those feelings, they cannot be readily ignored—if the students themselves ignore them, they deny their own reading and replace it with someone else's, presumably the teacher's.

Similarly, there is some justification for the responses of those students whose immediate dislike of the widow or those who cheat the welfare system causes them to approve the social worker's cautious, professional handling of the situation. Again, we may quarrel with some aspects of their reading, possibly their insensitivity to suffering or their easy assumption that the widow is cheating the system, but we must admit that widow is not an attractive character, that some people do cheat the welfare system, and that a government employee is obligated to handle funds responsibly.

Those students who respond neither by blaming the widow nor by criticizing the social worker, but by rising to a higher level of abstraction and finding fault with "conditions," also have a point.

The title of the poem is ambiguous; we can see both the widow and the social worker as doing their best. Further, it is surely possible for bureaucracies to grow so large that they become unmanageable and ineffective, trapping their employees in unproductive routines. We may be critical of the students' shift of focus from this situation, these people, to the more abstract topic of "bureaucracies," and may judge it to be avoiding the issue raised by the poem; but the reading is nonetheless plausible.

We have, then, several different readings of the same text, each connected in some way to the words on the page, each linked to past experience or accumulated attitudes, and each containing imaginative leaps, or perhaps, errors. We suggested disregarding these for the moment in order to explore the basis of the responses, and we identified some foundation for each reading, either in the text itself or in the background of the reader. The poem could arouse anger in students inclined toward sympathy for society's defeated, leave indifferent those inclined to demand that their fellows accept the consequences of their own failure, and drive to higher levels of abstraction those able to see both sides of an issue or unwilling to commit themselves. In other words, the poem does support at least some aspects of each reading—some, but not all, for clearly several of the students' comments were dubious.

The New Critics would view this collection of responses as lying on a continuum at greater or lesser distance from a hypothetical perfect reading. That reading is most closely approached by the most perfect reader, presumably the one most experienced and best able to suppress his individuality in the interest of objective, uncontaminated reading. In this view, the students' readings are wrong, some more so than others. Those who adopt this New Critical perspective see the teaching of literature as a process of purging those elements that interfere with achieving a pure reading, usually the elements of personal perspective.

A clarified reading may be achieved, however, not by rejecting individuality, as the New Critic does, but by accepting it and using it as a point of entry into the literary work. We may, in other words, view these three different readings of "As Best She Could" not as misreadings to be corrected but as three different perceptions of one event, each perception having the potential to tell us about the event, the text, and the perceiver. The past experiences and acquired attitudes that shape these perceptions need not be seen as contaminants, but simply as the characteristics of the individual and therefore unique reader. If, in discussing the readings, we can identify demonstrable errors, then we may correct them. If, on the other hand, we discover that one reader's focus and interest are different from those of another, then we may wish to accept those differences and refrain from enforcing a conformity opposed to any serious intellectual tradition.

The poem gives each of us an opportunity to look at ourselves, putting our ideas and our attitudes into perspective. The poem is, in a sense, something that we create as we read. We bring to the text our understanding of the words, our expectations of the behavior of people, our ingrained biases and predilections, and from them create the experience that becomes for us the poem. Rosenblatt explains:

> The poem cannot be equated solely with *either* the text *or* the experience of the reader. . . . What each reader makes of the text is, indeed, *for him* the poem, in the sense that this is his only direct perception of it. No one else can read it for him. He may learn indirectly about others' experiences with the text; he may come to see that his own was confused or impoverished, and he may then be stimulated to attempt to call forth from the text a better poem. But this he must do himself, and only what he himself experiences in relation to the text is—again let us underline—*for him*, the work.[6]

To learn to read more perceptively and intelligently, we must reflect on our own perceptions of a work to see what they reveal both about us and about the text. Sympathetic readers of the Jones poem, for instance, may feel some satisfaction in observing that they care about the victimized widow, that they respond to this distress with sympathy. Or they could decide that their intense sympathy is too emotional and thoughtless, and that it would be more reasonable to recognize the constraints upon the social worker, taking a more sympathetic view of her. They may even come to think that their initial feelings of sympathy for the widow were false—that they responded in that way out of a sense of moral obligation dictated by the poem, but would not have felt anything at all, except perhaps revulsion or fear, if they had actually encountered such a person. The reading of a poem provides the opportunity to observe oneself reacting, reflect on those reactions, and thus learn about oneself.

Similarly, readers who felt no initial sympathy for the widow, and thought the social worker wise to act cautiously with her, have the opportunity to consider this reaction. It would be dangerous to try to analyze too closely why one response emerges rather than another; dangerous, at least, for anyone other than the readers themselves. But the teacher can note the response and invite reflection upon it. The students might confirm the original response, or they might decide that it was too hardhearted. Even though the social welfare system must be governed by rules, not whim or passion, they might still feel some sorrow for those whom the system cannot help. They may conclude that their first response derived from a childish distaste for people who seem different—deformed, aged, crippled, uneducated, or different in some other way—and that they must not indulge what seems now to be an immoral prejudice. Thus they may reverse their position and utterly change their understanding of the poem.

Let us not judge which of these possible outcomes of reflection on the poem would be best. Presumably, our own reading of the poem will predispose us to think of one as better than another. If we feel great sympathy for the widow, we are likely to think of those who do not as cold, unfeeling, overly rational people. In that case, we may see the reversal of our second hypothetical group as a desirable conversion, a literary experience that has yielded insight and an enrichment of the students' conceptions and attitudes. If, however, we favor a reading of the poem that keeps in mind the necessary and desirable constraints upon the social worker, we may see that reversal as weak-minded surrender to emotionalism. Our job is not shaping students to either viewpoint, but assisting them to read so they may shape themselves. To force them to make a stand they do not believe would be as immoral as to preach the virtues of Christianity over atheism, or of atheism over Buddhism—those are private decisions the teacher must not attempt to control. The task in teaching literature is to help students think, not to tell them what to think.

TWO PROBLEMS

Error Our discussion of Jones's "As Best She Could" has so far ignored two obvious problems: errors in reading and authorial intent. The first is the easier to deal with. It is clearly possible to make errors in reading a text. Our insistence upon beginning with a reader's response does not mean that the response is good or right, but simply that it is where one must begin. It is quite possible for a response to betray careless or thoughtless reading, with words misunderstood, sections of the work ignored, stock responses substituted for real ones, or personal associations and memories imputed to the text or the writer. A good reader learns to distinguish between what is in the text and what comes from associations with it, but young readers may not yet know the difference between the influence exerted by the words on the page and that of their own background and the context of the reading. Still, regardless of the influences upon students' readings, one must begin with their responses.

Discussion has the potential for refining responses either at the fairly sophisticated level of thought we have been examining or at a more primitive level. Consider two instances of error in the reading of the Jones poem. In the first, one young student responded to the poem with some disgust. "Her husband should take care of her; we shouldn't have to." Another student protested that she did not have a husband to take care of her, to which the young critic replied, "She has to have a husband—she has three daughters, doesn't she?" (presumably borrowing the "three" from the "three weeks" mentioned in the sixth stanza). When other students pointed out that she was a widow, he replied, "So what?" The problem was then obvious. He did not know the meaning of the word "widow," interpreting it as "old woman." The discovery that it meant something different compelled him to change his reading of the poem. The process of correcting the error was fairly natural and unthreatening. His response to the poem was not condemned; rather, the discussion revealed a misreading, which he then changed.

The conspiracy theory is also an example of an error in reading. The student who proposed that the social worker and the widow's daughters had conspired to steal the welfare money ultimately had to admit that there was no real evidence for that reading. She invented it and thought it would make a good story, but the words of the poem did not indicate that anything of the sort was happening. The reader had used the poem to stimulate her own imagination—a perfectly valid activity, but not quite the same thing as reading. Confronted with this student, a teacher would have to decide between two possible responses: either invite her to pursue the thoughts stimulated by the poem, however irrelevant to the text itself, or ask her to suspend those thoughts for the moment and try again to read the poem. As Rosenblatt has said, the poem is not solely either the text or the reader's response. The reader's experience falls somewhere on a continuum—at one extreme is a reading highly responsive to and closely controlled by the text, and at the other a reading triggered by the text but otherwise responsive to and controlled by the psyche of the reader. The conspiracy theory falls at the latter end of the continuum. There is nothing wrong with that sort of response —it may, in fact, lead to artistic creation by the reader—but if it is habitual with an individual, we may doubt that he is learning to exercise control in his reading. In any case, the student should be encouraged to observe the differences between close reading and free association and should not confuse the two.

When the investigation of responses leads to the discovery of errors in reading, the errors may be gently corrected and the discussion continued. Two extremes are to be avoided. The reading of literature must not become an exercise in avoiding errors, as is likely if comprehension questions dominate the discussions, if the teacher emphasizes some notion of "right" or "correct" reading, or if an error is considered an embarrassing blunder rather than a natural and desirable step in learning. Error-avoidance strategies will make students cautious, timid, and chronically unsure of their perceptions, damaging them as much here as they typically do in composition work. Nor, on the other hand, should errors be ignored, on the ridiculous premise that all is a matter of opinion, to which everyone is entitled, regardless of how foolish and unsubstantiated it is. Although words may be imprecise, they stand for a range of possibilities, calling to mind similar meanings, images, or relationships in all who know them. To disregard those shared understandings is to deny the possibility of communication at all.

We may see finding and correcting reading errors as part of the general process of refining one's perceptions of the text. In essence, there is little difference between discovering that a word means something other than we had thought and finding that our attitudes on an issue are slightly different from those we would have expected. In both cases linguistic control is improved. The child who discovers that the word "dog" refers not to any four-legged animal, but only to those with certain characteristics, and the adult who, reading *All Quiet on the Western Front*, refines his understanding of the emotions of war, are both going through the same intellectual process, though at different levels of sophistication. If students can be encouraged to think of the reading of literature as an opportunity to refine and clarify their ideas, rather than as a test of ability to read accurately and recall details, they may come to accept errors as a natural part of the process and become less inhibited and defensive about them.

Authorial Intent   The question of authorial intent often gives rise to discussion of error in literature classes. Presumably, much of the labor in reading literature is in trying to determine what the writer hopes to say, what effect he hopes to create in the reader. Those are, of course, perfectly legitimate questions. But should they dominate? We have suggested that the class deal first with student responses, trying to determine whether they derive from the text itself, from associations it calls to mind, or from somewhere else. The students, in discussing these issues, will be making statements about themselves: "I think. . . ," "I feel. . . ," "I believe. . . ." When the students begin to say, "The writer thinks . . . " or "The writer feels. . . ," they commit themselves to a different kind of discussion. They are no longer concerned with expressing themselves, but have assumed the task of marshalling evidence for their inferences. Both expressing the self and analyzing the writer's intent are important; neither should dominate, and neither should be neglected.

Consider "As Best She Could." It is quite possible to explain the reaction of the student who thinks the social worker justified in her skeptical and suspicious treatment of the widow. Is it equally possible to ascribe that attitude to the author? Can we say that Jones, too, feels that the social worker is doing her best, constrained by the regulations of the agency for which she works, and is therefore blameless? The poem offers little support for that contention. The social worker is described as "curt": she "cut through your explanations, your patches of self-respect": she disbelieves the widow, misinterpreting fear as greed and fraud; she "denied you, sent you off. . . ." There is little there to suggest that Jones, or to speak more accurately, the persona Jones adopts for this poem, approves of the behavior he has depicted. The evidence indicates that he sympathizes strongly with the widow.

It is important that students who sympathize with the social worker have enough perspective not to confuse response to the poem with interpretation of the writer's intention. That is not to say they should repress their response; they should simply not assume the writer shares it. Nor, if their response reveals a radical difference between their attitude and that of the writer, should they necessarily revise their opinions to conform to his. They should be encouraged to reconsider their attitude, but they need not feel obligated to submit to the writer's authority.

The move from response to interpretation involves, then, a shift in focus. In the beginning we are less concerned with the writer's intent than with the actual effect of the work. That is to say, the reader is first simply responding, without trying to impose a direction on that response. Whether it is visceral, emotional, or intellectual, it is as far as possible not manipulated, not "produced" to satisfy some self-imposed (or teacher-imposed) task, as it would be if the reader came to the text thinking, "I must devise some proposition about this work that I can then demonstrate," or "I must generate some feeling about this work, to show that I am a sensitive person." The reader is receptive at this stage, rather than aggressive. If any task or question governs this first encounter with the text, it is,

"What does this poem do to me—what does it make me feel or think?" Identifying the effect of the work leads naturally to the question, "What is the source of that effect?" As we have seen, the source lies partially in the text and partially in the reader's experience. Distinguishing between the two demands both introspection and analysis, resulting in the act of interpretation, which can be defined for now as drawing inferences about the meaning and significance of a work or about its intended effect.

Having abandoned the basic tenet of the New Critics—that there is an absolute and perfect reading of a work—we are left with a view of reading in which inferences about authorial intent are only one piece in a larger mosaic. We cannot be satisfied, then, with the submission of self in which, through suppressing or forgetting ourselves, we are assimilated into the world of the text—such a view shows too little regard for the reader. Nor can we accept the submission of text to self, for which the governing principle is "It's my opinion and I'm entitled to it." Such a view betrays indifference to the literary work. Teachers have too often found themselves in an unfortunate conflict, in which they held the former position and their students the latter. But the matter is not a simple either/or question, as Slatoff, discussing the critical literature on the topic of "belief," suggests:

> This discussion of "belief" has been valuable in many ways, but almost all of it focuses only on major conflicts or discrepancies between beliefs and implies that such conflicts are special cases or deviations from a norm of nearly complete harmony between author and reader. I would argue that such conflicts are merely extreme forms of a condition that obtains to one degree or another in all our literary experiences and that a complete correspondence of attitudes is not a norm but another extreme, one which may, in fact, interfere with a judicious or even adequate response as much as a violent opposition of values. . . . Our usual experience, it seems to me, involves a curiously complex set of adjustments and maladjustments between our own views and ways of feeling and those which inform the work, a set of adjustments much more like those in a successful marriage than in, say, a dream or brainwashing. As in any relation that is not completely harmonious, we will sometimes defer to the author, sometimes accept things for the sake of the argument, sometimes entertain notions indulgently and give the benefit of the doubt, sometimes suspend judgment temporarily, sometimes mutter or grumble or give a tolerant

smile, sometimes view with distaste, suspicion, alarm, or dismay, sometimes revise an impression eagerly, sometimes begrudgingly, sometimes rise fiercely up in arms, sometimes wonder anxiously where the author stands, and so on. The critical discussion of the matter so far seems to envision only two sorts of marriages—blissful and miserable.[7]

As Slatoff suggests, the interpreting process is neither one of submission nor one of tyranny—rather, it is an attempt to see clearly, giving both the author and the self their due. Interpretation, although it is an effort to say something about the meaning of the text, must keep the reader clearly in mind. There is always an "I" in the picture, speculating about the meaning of the words and the significance of their arrangement.

The question of author's intent is not negligible, then, nor is it the most important question. Rather, it is an issue that enables us to identify more clearly where we stand. Attention to the author's intent allows us to consider also the adjustments Slatoff spoke of that arise between reader and writer. As we see ourselves sometimes agreeing, sometimes tolerating, sometimes rising fiercely up in arms, we have the opportunity to watch aspects of our belief and thought manifest themselves. We have, in a sense, the opportunity to view ourselves as objects—not only to participate, but to observe, reflecting on our own minds and discovering how we feel about what we find there. The literary work represents another consciousness which, by its contrast with our own, enables us to refine ourselves, confirming, clarifying, modifying, or refuting perceptions, attitudes, and ideas.

SELF-DEFINITION

Thus, exchange with the text can become for the reader a process of self-creation. The entire process—responding, correcting errors, searching for the sources of the response, speculating about the author's intent, and weighing the author's values and ideas against one's own—culminates in a sharpened, heightened sense of self. Some part of the reader's conception of the world is either confirmed, modified, or refuted, and that changes the reader. If literature has the potential for contributing so much to the conceptual filter through which we receive the world, then we must teach it in such a way that the student, while retaining full authority for his moral and philosophical stance, nonetheless is given the opportunity to see the consequences of those attitudes. The student is changed by his responses to "As Best She Could" and to all the other poems, plays, and novels he reads. He needs the opportunity to see, judge, and reshape those responses, consulting his own heart and mind as he does so, since he is the one ultimately responsible for what he becomes.

AUTONOMY OF THE READER

The teaching that postulates one perfect reading toward which all must strive comes from an autocratic tradition viewing the student as shaped by the wisdom of the great authors, molded by the influence of teachers. It sees him as clay to be sculpted or as the *tabula rasa* on which author and teacher will write. This vision assigns too little authority to the student, who must, regardless of strengths or deficiencies, see things through his own eyes and construct his own image of the world, and too much responsibility and clarity of vision to the writer and the teacher, who are, after all, fallible.

Morse cautions readers about the dangers of submitting unthinkingly to representations of the world in the works of even the great writers. In an essay entitled "Prejudice and Literature" he offers examples of "vulgarities" in some of the most respected literature:

> Let us observe some cases, minor and major: the inadvertent offenders Valery Larbaud, James Joyce and Charles Lamb, the doubtful case of Charles Dickens, and the deliberate offenders T. S. Eliot, Ezra Pound and William Shakespeare. The result in each case is literary vulgarity.[8]

He explains each one's offense against reason—Joyce's prejudice against women, Eliot's racism and anti-Semitism, Pound's fascist sympathies, and Shakespeare's anti-Semitism, for instance—and then concludes:

> Let us not be overawed, even by Shakespeare, so far that we can't recognize vulgarity for what it is when it solicits our participation like a whore on a street corner.[9]

His point is that the reader is responsible: "Let *us* not be overawed. . . ." We, as readers, must be individually responsible for what we make of the literature. Absorbing the prejudices of great writers is little better than absorbing those of poorer writers—in both cases we are guilty of mindless submission to the text. What teachers should seek is not submission, but intelligent interaction. We should not, as Morse has said, be overawed by anyone, for to accept values, attitudes, and ideas without question is to decline responsibility for one's own mind, becoming at best the lucky disciple of someone wise, at worst the unfortunate pawn of a fool. Whether the unreflective reader falls under the sway of the wise man or the fool is, of course, a matter of sheerest luck, since, in his uncritically receptive state, he exercises no control over his thoughts and emotions, allowing himself to be shaped and molded.

The schools should not encourage such receptivity. Teachers do not necessarily know what students should think or feel or do, and should not be tempted to relieve them of the burden of their own intellectual decisions. Although they are older, more experienced in some ways, and probably more skillful, educated readers than their students, they must nonetheless exercise restraint. If they keep in mind that the poem they create as they read is one of many possibilities, shaped by their experiences and attitudes as well as by the words on the page, they will recognize that their readings have no special claim to authority. Students are different people, with different backgrounds and proclivities. They must not be molded in the teacher's image, but encouraged to grow along the lines natural to them, modified and shaped by reason and the necessity for compromise in a society.

ESSENTIAL POINTS

Our discussion of the reading act has made several points. The first and most basic is that the reader makes the poem as he reads. He does not seek an unalterable meaning that lies within the text for anyone with the wit and will to ferret out; instead, bringing to bear upon the text the perspective and knowledge he has accumulated over the years, he creates meaning from the confrontation. We have tried to forestall charges of permissiveness or anti-intellectualism by arguing that this view does not reduce reading to the simple task of reacting and emoting. Instead, it complicates it by requiring the reader to consider his personal investment in the experience and not make a pretense of suppressing his own perspective—an impossibility—to achieve objectivity and purity in interpretation. The value of clear, accurate, correct reading is not denied, but affirmed. Such reading is achieved, however, only through careful attention to both text and self, through conscientious reflection on the thoughts and emotions called forth by the work.

The second point is that the reader has the opportunity to see himself in his reading. Literature invites the reader to observe his own responses, to see himself as if in a photograph, some aspect of his emotional or intellectual self frozen and awaiting inspection;

thus, it rewards the reader with sharpened understanding of himself. For the moment, he can be both a participant, feeling and thinking, and an observer, watching himself feel and think.

Literature therefore enables the reader to remake himself—and that is the third point. Reading is an experience that shapes, perhaps confirming attitudes and ideas, perhaps modifying or refuting them. The student creates himself intellectually as he reads.

Thus, the reader must be active and responsible. He cannot be simply receptive, waiting to be provided with interpretations, to have significances pointed out and implications developed for him. To do so is to accept someone else's reading uncritically, adopting another's feelings and thoughts as one's own. Encouraging that docility makes for placid, malleable, lazy students, and places the English teacher in an untenable position, diminishing his role from that of teacher to that of spiritual leader, charged with the unethical task of molding his students.

We must qualify these four points about the reading of literature by acknowledging that we are speaking of its potential. We may seldom see this potential achieved in the classroom, may seldom achieve it in our own reading, but it remains, nonetheless, a goal. Let us turn our attention now to a practical question: What does the teacher do to encourage students to read in this way? Although the pattern is natural, it is also hard work, demanding thought, which is seldom easy. We have looked fairly closely at some of the possible readings of one poem. Let us briefly consider the conditions necessary in a classroom for obtaining those readings, and then speculate about the teaching of another poem to see what principles of instruction may emerge.

CONDITIONS FOR RESPONSE-BASED TEACHING

RECEPTIVITY

If the discussions are to invite the responses and perceptions of the students, it is necessary that these responses and perceptions be welcomed. The teacher must let the students know that their comments are solicited and will be given consideration. Pseudo-inductive plans, in which the teacher, under pretense of open discussion, leads the class to a preordained conclusion, will show students that their opinions are not seriously considered and that they are asked to speak only to contribute bits and pieces of an argument already formulated by the teacher.

A delicate balance is required. The teacher must establish an atmosphere in which students feel secure enough to respond openly, but must not deceive them into believing that initial responses are sufficient. Nor, on the other hand, should he make students think their responses are invited to provide the teacher and other students with clay pigeons to shoot. If responses are ridiculed, there will soon be few responses left to ridicule. This is not to say that response-based teaching demands the intimacy of a sensitivity session, that students will be required to lay bare their souls, but it does require reasonable freedom from fear of castigation or mockery, and from obsequious submission to the authority of the teacher or the author. The classroom must be cooperative, not combative, with students and teachers building on one another's ideas, using rather than disputing them.

TENTATIVENESS

Hence the second condition: students must be willing to be tentative, to express thoughts and feelings they are unsure of, to change their minds. Initial response, in other words, must be treated as a draft, as something to build upon, modify, or perhaps reject. A teacher who encourages the students' desire to be right—probably a desire that most of their previous schooling has carefully inculcated—is likely to find them holding back from the discussion, waiting for clues from the teacher or from stronger students, or resorting to commercial study guides for borrowed insights. Students should not be afraid to change their minds; revising one's opinions is a normal part of intellectual activity.

RIGOR

The third condition follows from the second: students must be willing to think. Unconsidered, unexamined response is simply the first step in reading. What must follow is rigorous analysis—searching for one's assumptions, drawing inferences about one's own attitudes and those expressed in the text, and considering other points of view offered by the teacher, other students, and sometimes critical works. Such study is more demanding than the comprehension and recall many reading programs require, or the memorization of information about literature. Further, it seldom reaches closure, at least for the group as a whole. The final step in this sort of reading is a personal statement: "I, because of who I am, conclude this about the work, myself, and the other students in the class. . . ."

Achieving such results is not simple. As Rosenblatt says:

A situation conducive to free exchange of ideas by no means represents a passive or negative attitude on the part of the teacher. To create an atmosphere of self-confident interchange he must be ready to draw out the more timid students and to keep the more aggressive from monopolizing the conversation. He must be on the alert to show pleased interest in comments that have possibilities and to help the students clarify or elaborate their ideas. He must keep the discussion moving along consistent lines by eliciting the points of contact between different students' opinions. His own flexible command of the text and understanding of the reading skills it requires will be called into play throughout.[10]

Rigor is demanded, then, of the teacher as well as the student. But rigorous scrutiny of the work and the responses should not obliterate the personal element of reading. It may change the reader's awareness of the personal or even sharpen it. Developing a tolerance for ambiguity and uncertainty, coming to accept the idea that meaning and understanding are private creations, not absolutes to be discovered, students may be weaned from the traditional demand: "Now that we've discussed this for an hour, tell us what it means." Unfortunately, the premise of much early schooling has probably been that there *are* right answers and it is important to find them. This is a false hope from which students should be freed.

COOPERATION

The fourth condition depends on the preceding three: the class must work reasonably well as a group. It must achieve a level of trust that will allow discussion of response, which is discussion of the self; it must accept tentative, groping statements and the necessarily uncertain progress of the talk; and it must respect both individuality and the constraints of logic and reason. Students must come to realize that others will often pursue lines of thought that they consider uninteresting or irrelevant, and they must learn to tolerate the occasional blind alleys into which they themselves stray. They must come to see that no discussion involving twenty or thirty people can be equally satisfying and interesting to all, and accept the responsibility for exerting some influence on the direction the class takes so that their own concerns are attended to. And they must learn to accept moments when the discussion takes another tack, pursuing a question that bores them, as opportunities to learn about classmates.

SUITABLE LITERATURE

The fifth condition, one that will occupy a chapter later in the book, is that the literature provide some substance—ideas, style, language, attitude, whatever—worthy of reflection. This condition is difficult to meet, because it involves matching student with text when there may be 150 students to consider, and either a limited collection of texts, in situations that restrict the teacher's choices, or an unmanageably large number, when the teacher is free to select almost any appropriate paperback. The matching involves careful analysis of the group, broad knowledge of the available literature, and luck. It can never be perfect, even when there is time to assign different works to individual students. Still, the pattern of instruction invites students to talk first about themselves and their responses, and thus even works that do not inspire instant love may nonetheless provoke sufficient reaction to start discussion.

None of these five conditions will ever be perfectly achieved in a classroom. They are not prerequisites to response-based teaching. In fact, class sessions dealing with literature should help cultivate the desired conditions. Still, however imperfectly realized, they represent the classroom atmosphere toward which the teacher might strive. Subsequent chapters will consider some of the techniques for achieving this tone in the class.

TEACHING A WORK

Let us consider now how we might teach the following poem to a class of high school students. Begin by distributing copies and reading it aloud.

A View of a Pig

1   The pig lay on a barrow dead.
    It weighed, they said, as much as three men.
    Its closed, pink, white eyelashes,
    Its trotters stuck straight out.

2   Such weight and thick pink bulk
    Set in death seemed not just dead.
    It was less than lifeless, further off.
    It was like a sack of wheat.

3   I thumped it without feeling remorse.
    One feels guilty insulting the dead,

> Walking on graves, but this pig
> Did not seem able to accuse.
>
> 4   It was too dead. Just so much
> A poundage of lard and pork.
> Its last dignity had entirely gone.
> It was not a figure of fun.
>
> 5   Too dead now to pity.
> To remember its life, din, stronghold
> Of earthly pleasure as it had been,
> Seemed a false effort, and off the point.
>
> 6   Too deadly factual. Its weight
> Oppressed me—how could it be moved?
> And the trouble of cutting it up!
> The gash in its throat was shocking, but not pathetic.
>
> 7   Once I ran at a fair in the noise
> To catch a greased piglet
> That was faster and nimbler than a cat.
> Its squeal was the rending of metal.
>
> 8   Pigs must have hot blood, they feel like ovens,
> Their bite is worse than a horse's—
> They chop a half-moon clean out,
> They eat cinders, dead cats.
>
> 9   Distinctions and admirations such
> As this one was long finished with.
> I stared at it a long time. They were going to scald it,
> Scald it and scour it like a doorstep.
>
> –Ted Hughes

After the reading ask the students for their reactions, urging them to say whatever comes to mind. The comments will typically vary:

"That's disgusting."

"I like the part about the greased piglet at the fair."

"What did he mean by 'distinctions and admirations'?"

"I've seen animals slaughtered on the farm—it's nothing to be upset about."

"Why would anyone write about something so unpleasant?"

"He doesn't seem to feel any sympathy at all—why does he bother to write on something he doesn't care about?"

"It's silly for someone to care so much about a dead pig."

The most common response of all is "Ycchh," or a similar expression of distaste. The poem is useful for experiments with response-based teaching primarily because it does elicit revulsion from so many students, giving the teacher the opportunity to smile in acceptance (and, if it happens to be true, to acknowledge sharing the feeling). The class is thus informed that it is not necessary to like everything the teacher offers, nor to disguise their reactions.

The students' comments may seem simple—a few questions, a few remarks about what they like and dislike or the feelings the poem has aroused. But despite their brevity, they provide an excellent starting point for the discussion. Even the semi-verbal expression of disgust is a place to begin.

Ask about the response, inviting the students to comment on both themselves and the text: "Why do you feel so disgusted by the poem?" They may reply with some comment about the text, perhaps citing a particularly repugnant image, or with an anecdote from their own experience, perhaps about seeing a dead animal or watching one die. Any of these responses is an opening into the poem and the students' readings of it.

If, for instance, a student expresses disgust at certain images in the text—let us say those of stanza eight—the teacher may ask if other students react the same way to the lines, or if they find different parts of the poem that disgust them. Or he may ask, if others report that stanza eight does not affect them in the same way, what effect it does have. The questions, although they still require personal statements rather than interpretation, begin to reveal differences in reading that may later lead into close analysis.

Consider another example. Perhaps a student has recalled coming upon a dead animal. In this case, a comment not about images in the text but about personal experience, the teacher may ask slightly different questions. "What details do you recall about the experience?" "What do you remember seeing, feeling, thinking?" "Did your experience seem similar to that of the speaker in the poem, or were there differences?" The responses, although again they are personal and anecdotal, nonetheless move the class further along toward a close and intelligent analysis of the text.

THREE RESPONSES

Suppose a student reports disgust at the images of the dead pig, and when asked which lines he finds most unpleasant, cites stanza eight.

The teacher, or preferably other students, may then point out that the images in stanza eight are of the living pig, not the dead pig, and ask if it is really the images of death that disgust him. The student is then driven back to the text, and may discover that his feelings derive from associations of his own—ideas or memories of death from other experiences—and that it is not actually the images of death in the poem that call forth his distaste. Or he may decide that, curiously, those images of the live pig disgust him, though he thought it was the idea of death. In either case he has the beginnings of an insight. He may see that the narrator in the poem seems not disgusted by the dead pig, but almost indifferent to it. In the first stanzas it is like an object: "less than lifeless, further off," and "Just so much a poundage of lard and pork." Those observations may yield further questions: Why does the speaker remain so indifferent to the dead animal, and yet stand there staring at it? Why does he present us with such an unpleasant picture of the living pig?

The last two questions move the discussion from the student's feelings to the text, but the student's perspective remains a central issue, for we have identified a contrast between his reaction to the images of death and that of the speaker. We have also identified two different possible sources for the student's disgust—his own past experience and the images of the living animal. But without pursuing those questions at the moment, let us look at another starting point and see where it takes us.

Many students are irritated at the speaker's indifference toward the dead creature. "How can he be so unfeeling and callous?" Or a similar question, revealing an inference about the author's purpose: "If the writer wanted us to feel sorry for an animal, why didn't he write about a horse or a dog? No one can feel sorry for a pig." The students either detect indifference on the part of the writer or find it in themselves and sense that it is inappropriate, suspecting that the writer would not want them to feel indifferent. These questions open a second pathway into the poem, especially if some other student objects that the speaker is not at all unfeeling, but instead cares more than any sensible person would.

If two or more students provide such disparate views of the speaker, the line of questioning is obvious. Pointing out the difference, the teacher may call for elaboration, asking, "What accounts for your view of the speaker's attitude?" Those who see him as callous may point out that he says as much: "I thumped it without feeling remorse"; the pig is "Too dead now to pity"; to remember its life is a "false effort and off the point." Those who think the speaker sensitive may point out that many terms suggesting feelings creep into his account. They may point to stanza three and note "remorse," "guilty," "insulting," and "accuse." True, he denies all the feelings those terms suggest, but if he did not either feel them or note their absence, would he mention them at all? Either he feels some remorse, the students may argue, or he thinks that he *should* feel it.

Once again, close attention to the text is called for. Both points of view are defensible: there is evidence that the speaker feels, and there is evidence that he does not. Neither student is clearly right or wrong, though their statements indicate that they have responded more to some aspects of the text than to others. Again, let us for the moment abandon this line of thought, and consider a third point of entry into the poem.

Our first path began with an expression of feeling, our second with an inference about the intent of the poem. The third will begin with what seems to be a digression. One student, after reading the poem, told the class about an experience it had called to mind. She had at one time been interested in medicine and had, in an anatomy class she arranged to attend, participated in dissecting a cadaver. She reported that the students had at first been very uncomfortable, laughing and joking awkwardly, but the uneasiness had gradually passed away, to be replaced, for her, by sorrow for the corpse that had recently been a living person. Those reflections passed too, as she settled down to the work at hand, but she could never completely suppress a tinge of sadness. She told of the incident briefly and simply, with apologies for the digression, and without understanding why she had thought of it.

This story, although not a statement about the text, nonetheless suggests some questions that return us to it. "Why do you think the poem called to mind that incident?" "Do you see any connections between that memory and the incident recounted in the poem?" Here again we are looking at the text and asking for close reading, but motivated by the desire to explore a response. We are brought, almost regardless of where we begin, back to the text. The first response, the expression of disgust, leads us to an examination of the speaker's attitude and the intent behind the images of the poem. The second response, an inference about the speaker's attitude, leads us to investigate how the poem presents that attitude. The third response, the anecdote, takes us into comparisons with the incident of the poem. As the comparisons are discussed, an interpretation of the poem begins to take shape.

Comparing the poem and the incident in the laboratory should focus attention on the attitudes of the student and the persona in the poem. In the poem, students may note a tension between sensitive and callous, introspective and objective. As they note the objectivity

in the beginning and near the end, and the sense of sorrow beginning in about the third stanza and culminating around the seventh
where the speaker wanders off into reverie, they may begin to see
that the poem moves between these two poles. They may suggest
that the poet begins coldly and objectively, then gradually comes to
feel accused by the corpse, remembers that it was once a living thing
with some dignity, and begins to feel something like sorrow, despite
asserting that such thoughts are off the point. A question might arise
about the strangely unpleasant imagery of the eighth stanza—the
"hot blood," the bite "worse than a horse's," the eating of "dead
cats." Asked to consider why the poet might turn to such repellent
images at that point, the students may come to see the stanza as an
effort to make the corpse disgusting, reducing it once again to a
lifeless object, so that the speaker may comfortably retreat from the
involvement he has begun to feel. One cannot, after all, sustain sorrow for something as insignificant and unpleasant as a slaughtered
pig; that would be silly sentimentality. Thus, the poet conjures the
distasteful images to justify ceasing to care—he reduces the pig to
nothing more than a doorstep, something less than lifeless and thus
not to be mourned.

The movement in the poem, then, is much like that of the student's anatomy class. There too we had a sense of diminishing distance as the student moved from indifference to sorrow for the lost
life, then a shift back to objectivity, though tinged with feeling, as
she began to work. The cadaver was less than lifeless; then its dignity was remembered; then it again became an object.

So, from the students' initial responses and the discussion they
stimulate, a reading of the poem emerges. This is an oversimplification, of course, for no reading is likely to be agreed upon by all
unless some suppress their own thoughts, or are too lazy to try to
discover what they are. The reading proposed here is simply one
possibility. It is a common ground that many readers have found in
the poem, to which they add much that is their own. For some, the
poem will be dominated by the associations it calls forth, as with the
student who remembered the anatomy class. For others, it confirms
the belief that emotions must be respected, but controlled. The
speaker, they think, is wise to pause and reflect on the dead pig, but
wiser still to assert his rationality at the end and prepare to pass on
to other matters. And others have a nagging sense that death has not
been adequately dealt with in the poem, where it is briefly moving
and then simply forgotten. Death, they believe, requires more explanation, or at least more ritual. They themselves would not want to be
so quickly forgotten.

Within such a discussion the teacher should allow students

their unique perspectives, yet also help them read more accurately, fostering awareness both of the text and of individual differences in viewpoint. What may result is keener understanding of both the work and the self, for neither is lost sight of during the discussion, and neither dominates for long. The teacher's questions should call for clarification and elaboration, always keeping in mind both self and text.

PREPARING FOR TEACHING

It is difficult to describe how to formulate appropriate questions, although our three approaches to the Hughes poem may suggest a style. Careful reading of the text will bring out some responses that may be encountered in the class. In "A View of a Pig," the tension between indifference and concern will alert you to some of the possibilities. The class may, of course, respond unpredictably and follow some unforeseen path. In that case you must react quickly, but your careful reading of the poem, if you are not too tightly bound to one interpretation, should enable you to follow the lead of the group.

Sometimes you might experiment with teaching a work that you have not carefully read in advance, perhaps inviting the students to submit works for the class to discuss. Lacking the insight that careful preparation would have given you, you are then forced to rely on the very process you are espousing for your students. Such an experiment gives you the opportunity to model some of the behavior you hope to elicit from them. Perhaps most important, it allows you to be wrong, to make mistakes, to be convinced by the sharper insights of someone else—in other words to engage in the natural activities associated with learning and thinking. It brings you into the class as a learner, not as one who has already learned and who means to dispense wisdom without acquiring any more in the process.

The discussion of the Hughes poem suggests several ways to begin and some questions that might lead the students to further reflection and analysis. Although no rigid pattern for teaching literature presents itself, several principles might be suggested.

PRINCIPLES OF RESPONSE-BASED TEACHING

Selection　First of all, the literature should be selected for its potential to interest the students. What that means will be discussed at greater length in later chapters, but for now we may say that selecting literature simply because it illustrates a genre, or exemplifies a period of history, or demonstrates certain literary techniques, is less likely to be successful than selecting it because it is appropriate to the students who will read it. It must not be too difficult or easy, either syntactically or conceptually, although that is hard to judge and much more complicated than applying readability formulas to several paragraphs of text. Nor, on the other hand, must it necessarily be relevant, as that term is commonly misconstrued. It need not deal specifically with the student's age group, his locale, or the personal problems that preoccupy him. *Beowulf* may be more relevant than some of the contemporary fiction directed to the adolescent reader (although much adolescent literature is excellent and useful).

Responses and Questions   Second, the discussion should concentrate, at least at first, on the students' responses. They should be encouraged to accept those responses, whatever form they take, and move from there to a closer analysis. The talk about response is, in essence, discussion of the poem, since it is about what the student has created from the text. As the discussion proceeds, of course, the teacher will want to help the student distinguish between what he has brought to the text and what he finds in it, so that he sees the difference between having feelings and inferring those of writer or character.

In general, the teacher should try not to shape responses with his questions, so as not to predispose the students to follow his own line of thought. The ambiguous, "Well?" or "Any thoughts or feelings?"—once students become familiar with the teacher's intention to open discussion with their responses—may be sufficient to start the talk.

Atmosphere   Third, the teacher must try to cultivate an atmosphere that is cooperative rather than competitive. Debate is an inappropriate model, since it assumes that someone is right and someone is wrong, that someone wins and someone loses. The discussions should build, one idea feeding the next, with participants gradually acquiring sharper insights, changing their minds, and adding the observations of others to their own, broadening their perspectives on the work. Students should see no merit in taking a position and holding to it stubbornly. Such intransigence is doctrinaire and authoritarian, and unsuitable in an academic environment.

Consequently, students should be encouraged to make tentative statements, aware that they are not bound to them, that they may later be withdrawn or revised. They should be encouraged not to wait until they are sure, or until they have divined the thoughts of the teacher and the rest of the class. To do this is to refuse an opportunity to see into themselves.

Relativity Fourth, there are no absolutes; the poem is made by each reader individually. Nonetheless, it is possible to have foolish or incorrect readings. The reader who insists that the word "proscribe" means what the word "prescribe" means is simply wrong. The child who thinks that "widow" means "old woman" is not entitled to that unique, individual point of view—again, it is wrong. The rejection of absolutes does not mean that everything is a matter of opinion. Individuals and society continually negotiate language—it is held in common and can be shaped by the individual only within limits, beyond which it is no longer language. Response-based teaching of literature is based on the idea that intelligent reflection upon one's responses leads to understanding, but it does not suggest that unconsidered response is all. A balance is necessary. The teacher, while respecting the individuality of his students and the difficulties of seeing clearly into their minds, and deprived of the clear and absolute standards that the New Criticism attempts to offer, must gently pull the students toward intelligent examination of their responses to the literature.

Forms of Response Fifth, the form of student responses will vary. Interpretation will not be the only, or even necessarily the best, culmination to the discussion. It is possible, for instance, for a student to be carried by a work into a line of thought far afield from the text itself. "A View of a Pig" might stimulate a student who had recently experienced the death of a friend or relative to reflect upon that death in a way that was not tied to the text, but might nonetheless be valuable for the student. He should not, of course, confuse reflecting upon other experience with reading, and the teacher might be suspicious if a student were invariably to find some digression crucial to the health of his psyche. Still, who is to say that the sincere digression, one that is not concocted to avoid the work of close reading, is less important than the text itself? Just as we may value a song because it reminds us of a distant friend, so a literary work may serve us by bringing some non-literary experience to mind.

The purpose of this first chapter has been to explore the nature of the literary experience. We have suggested that the act of reading is fairly complex, drawing in subtle and unpredictable ways on the experience and the attitude of the reader, and we have begun to establish some principles for instruction that will encourage the student to read more intelligently than he otherwise might. The next chapter will discuss in greater detail the work in the classroom.

NOTES

1. Walter J. Slatoff, *With Respect to Readers: Dimensions of Literary Response* (Ithaca, N.Y.: Cornell University Press, 1970), p. 23.

2. Louise M. Rosenblatt, *Literature as Exploration* (New York: Noble and Noble, 1968), p. 59.

3. Arthur N. Applebee, *Tradition and Reform in the Teaching of English: A History* (Urbana, Ill.: National Council of Teachers of English, 1974), p. 245.

4. Applebee, p. 246.

5. Louise M. Rosenblatt, "The Acid Test in Teaching Literature," *English Journal*, 45 (February 1956), 71.

6. Louise M. Rosenblatt, *The Reader, the Text, the Poem: The Transactional Theory of the Literary Work* (Carbondale: Southern Illinois University Press, 1978), p. 105.

7. Slatoff, pp. 69–70.

8. J. Mitchell Morse, *Prejudice and Literature* (Philadelphia: Temple University Press, 1976), p. 154.

9. Morse, p. 193.

10. Rosenblatt, *Literature as Exploration*, p. 71.

The Reader and Other Readers

2

Chapter One was about what happens when someone reads and reflects upon a literary work; it focused on the individual response to a text. Good reading, it was argued, is neither submission nor arrogance. That is to say, it is not simply a matter of absorbing the work, receiving it as one receives the comfort of a warm shower. Nor is it, on the other hand, an opportunity either to loose one's unconsidered opinions upon others or to indulge in quiet self-deception. Rather, it is a matter of responding to the text and of thinking carefully about both the response and the words on the page in order to understand both oneself and the work better. This notion of good reading recognizes limitations to any one person's knowledge and experience, and asserts that those limitations, that particular point of view, necessarily shape the understanding of the text.

In the discussion of the Jones poem, "As Best She Could," we examined how various readers' points of view might shape the readings of the poem, and how reading the poem might in turn shape the points of view. People will read the poem differently, and if they read carefully and thoughtfully, they will be slightly different people when they finish reading. The Hughes poem, "A View of a Pig," provided an illustration of the transition from response to analysis of the text, showing how the responses of students could raise questions that compel them to look closely at the words on the page for answers. So far, the discussion has concentrated upon the individual's private reading of the work, her transaction, as Rosenblatt calls it, with the text.

Once students are beyond the schools' reach, their reading is likely to be not only private, but also independent and solitary, unassisted by any other readers. They probably will not search out book-discussion groups or critical essays to help them think through their experiences with literature. While in school, however, they have the opportunity to invite others into the private exchange between work and self. Other readers can help tremendously by calling attention to different readings, alternatives that might not otherwise have been noticed. It is with this opportunity that Chapter Two will be concerned.

The opportunity to read in company with others is not without its drawbacks. Though the group provides a variety of insights and responses to work with, it demands tolerance of occasional digressions and ramblings; though it provides a forum for one's own thought, it demands that one share the platform with others; though it provides feedback for those who speak, it allows a retreat into anonymity for the timid ones; and though it may provide much stimulation for thought, it may also intrude disruptively into the private meditations that are part of the personal and solitary act of reading. Individual students may find themselves lost in the crowd, with little chance to express their thoughts, or perhaps even to think them. With other subjects the problem may not be so acute, but the teaching of literature must be grounded in the student's response to the text. The ideas taught in the literature classroom do not have identity and substance independent of the students; rather, they are produced by the students as they interact with the text. Unless students read and respond, there is no literature to teach—only texts and information about texts. The unresponsive student of algebra may grasp its basic principles, and the indifferent student of history may begin to comprehend the sequence and the rationale of events, but the student of literature who parrots the thinking of classmates, learns the critical judgments of scholars, or memorizes peripheral information about authors' lives and historical periods has not begun to learn the literature. Those parroted observations and memorized judgments reflect not less learning, but no learning whatsoever. They indicate that the student has failed to confront the literature and test herself against it. Insofar as the classroom permits students to avoid dealing with responses, it permits them to ignore the literature.

So the classroom may help or hurt, and the teacher's problem is to manage it in such a way that it helps more than it hurts. We may begin by considering how reading in a group differs from reading alone. What differences does it make to a reader to have twenty-five or thirty other readers around, all dealing with the same text? Perhaps the most significant difference is the group's pressure on the individual student to respond to the text aloud. Reading without anyone else to talk to, a student too easily puts a work aside without articulating her thoughts, and thus without fully digesting it. Without the talking or the writing that might follow reading, the student's reaction to the work remains undefined, unspecified. Henry describes the typical act of reading:

> We read at our own pace, finish with an inchoate lump of meaning unformed by language, and then go on to other reading or nonreading activity. Only when we try to communicate the ideas of the passage to ourselves or to others or to relate it to another work or passage do we determine what meaning is really ours. . . . In short, we must conceptualize it—join it to something. That is, we must synthesize it, which always entails bringing something of ourselves to it. The conclusion for teaching, it would seem, is that reading is inextricably tied up with both oral and written composition, with experience, with other concepts inside us, and with other reading.[1]

The group, because it consists of others whose inchoate lumps are different from mine, compels me to define my own more carefully, and thus see how I differ from those around me. Students who can be brought to sense their uniqueness can be encouraged to take interest in and explore it further. It is the group that gives one the sense of uniqueness—without others, the individual remains indistinguishable, an image without a contrasting background. The varying perspectives that may emerge in discussing a literary work with a class fill in that background for the individual, helping her to see more precisely where she herself stands; in other words, the group supplements her imagination by showing her alternatives that she might not have envisioned as she read the work. Recognizing those alternative readings assists and encourages her to clarify her own and thus to understand herself.

This testing of oneself against others may occur infrequently. Students are likely to resist it. Followers are, after all, more numerous than leaders; buying is easier than creating. Given the opportunity, students may simply accept, and even seek, someone else's reading. Teachers who try to encourage them to think independently, to reason out their own understanding of a text, soon come to hear in their dreams the constant refrain, "But tell us what it means." The students want something they can jot down in their notes, if they take notes, with assurance. The teacher, after all, is the one with answers—the answers that count, at least, on important things like tests. Raised on a diet of multiple choice questions, students come to view thinking as a process of choosing from among several statements, one of which is right and four of which are wrong. If occasionally intellection is complicated by an "E" that reads "all (or none) of the above," they suspect that someone has been careless, allowing ambiguity to creep in and muddy the processes of thought.

Such students, given the chance, will agree with the teacher's reading. If the teacher withholds her own interpretation, they will fall back on the second line of defense and accept the reading offered by that student whom they know to be most often right. Only when all else fails will they consider the desperate course of thinking for themselves. The pain that labor produces is likely to discourage them from attempting it again.

FINDING POSSIBILITIES

The testing of self against others is not natural or easy. Overcoming the inertia of the group and breaking down the students' resistance to the work of thinking requires some ingenuity on the part of the teacher. Her problem is solved in part by careful selection of works, an issue to be discussed more fully in later chapters. If a work touches upon matters in which students have a vital interest, and if the students can read it with enough ease to be able to grasp the fundamental issues, then they may react strongly enough to the text to need to speak.

Yet it is also surprising how often works that seem to have little relevance to the students will nonetheless sustain a long and energetic discussion. The energy for these discussions often seems to come not so much from the work itself as from the lucky appearance of a difference in the readings of several students. It is as though the literary work has served as the catalyst to an examination of oneself and one's friends in the classroom.

Those moments are hard to predict and harder still to arrange, but the teacher who seeks them can do several things to increase their frequency. First of all, she can demonstrate that they are welcome, which she may do by inviting and accepting personal response and by encouraging attention to the statements made by students in the class. Using them simply as building blocks in an argument of her own, as steps to a predetermined reading to which she will lead the class regardless of its inclinations, tells the class that their insights and questions are valuable only insofar as they contribute to her labors. On the other hand, listening to them and dealing with them indicates that the teacher considers them significant and worth investigating. In such an atmosphere the students are more likely to make statements interesting enough to stimulate thought and talk.

RESPONSE STATEMENTS

Further, the teacher can find ways to put mild pressure on the students to think and to formulate their reactions to what they have read. For instance, she may deprive the students of the opportunity to seize upon someone else's reading by asking them, immediately after they have finished reading a work, to take five or ten minutes to note their first responses to it. Without dictating a form for the notes, she may suggest that they could be questions, observations about the worth of the piece, memories it called to mind, speculations about the writer, or confirmation or rejection of the ideas presented. Required to verbalize, however briefly, in solitude, students will be forced at least to begin to make sense of their impressions of the text. No one else will have said anything with which they can simply agree; they will have to begin, by themselves, the labor of conceptualizing. Having begun it, they may feel some commitment to develop it or explore it, since it is their own.

Thus, those brief notes may yield the substance of the discussion. The teacher may ask for several students to volunteer to read or paraphrase their notes, or else collect the papers from the class and, looking through them, read out several that she thinks may be provocative, preserving the anonymity of the writer if that seems desirable.

Depending on the group, the instructor may want to allow discussion to begin informally, when one of the short statements read aloud elicits a reaction from students, or may wish to use the first several minutes of talk to select from among the statements several that will then be arranged as an agenda for the session. These may be listed on the board and discussed one at a time.

An active, alert, outspoken group might be content to listen, as the responses are read, for the ones that arouse interest. On the other hand, if the students are too outspoken, too eager, submitting them to the discipline of working by an agenda, to ensure that all of the worthy statements are considered, may be more effective. A more reticent group, happy to let the teacher read all the remarks without commenting at all, may need more than a casual invitation to comment on whatever statement appears interesting. For that group, the formality of an established agenda may be more productive.

The complexity of the work under consideration may also influence the teacher's choice of method. A work complex enough to elicit a wide range of response, touching several different themes, might be better handled in the more orderly fashion, again, to ensure that the various issues raised by the students are all given time.

Regardless of the technique, the teacher should keep in mind that the brief writing period is intended to force the students into solitary, unassisted thought about the work read and to obtain that thought from them so it can be discussed by the group. The justification for this method is that the students' responses will more likely be their own and that the collection of responses will be more varied and wide-ranging. Thus the teacher needs to demonstrate her respect for that variety by refraining from criticism of the statements and by managing the discussion with some discretion. If she too blatantly selects statements she likes or disagrees with, or those of particular students, either good or bad, it will soon become clear to the students that the statements are not used to begin a discussion of their responses and concerns, but are simply vehicles for the teacher's own views.

That is not to say that the teacher should completely avoid guiding the discussion—the excesses of the overly humane teacher who confuses freedom and anarchy do the student little good. There is nothing wrong, for instance, with suggesting that the class pursue certain questions before it undertakes the discussion of others. For instance, a poem might elicit the following two hypothetical responses from two students in the class:

"I like the character in this poem. She seems to me to be a bit confused, but good-natured and kind."

"This poem represents everything that is wrong with twentieth-century poetry. It is the worst of Dylan Thomas and Bob Dylan wrapped up in one."

The teacher would, of course, have to take the class into consideration, but if the class is typical, beginning discussion with the first response rather than the second may yield more lively talk. The first response focuses on something fairly specific—the character—and comments on it in a personal, subjective manner. The remark could easily lead to further talk about what the student, and other students, find appealing or unappealing in people, and to observations about the specifics in the poem that develop an impression of the character. The second response, on the other hand, tends toward the abstract, the formal, and the scholarly, and it makes broad statements that would be difficult for most high school groups to handle very well. What, for instance, does the speaker mean by "twentieth-century poetry"? And to what characteristics of Thomas and Dylan is she referring?

This second response, if dealt with early on, seems likely to impede the discussion. First, it will probably intimidate or annoy those students who feel uncomfortable with the vast concepts to which the speaker has so casually referred. A high school student who can easily sum up all twentieth-century poetry and test this particular poem against that summation either has an imposing intellect or is a pompous fraud. Even if such a response does not antagonize the rest of the class, it is likely to lead to vague talk that, by avoiding specifics, manages to sound impressive without saying much at all. A discussion of twentieth-century poetry presumes a knowledge of twentieth-century poetry, and most students probably do not have the background to handle such a large and slippery concept.

The first response will draw more students into the conversation. It does not pretend to great scholarship, breadth of reading, or depth of insight; it simply comments on the person created by the poem. More students are likely to feel capable of discussing such a mundane, human issue. The talk is also more likely to lead to specifics—who is the character? how is she represented to the reader? what is the source of her confusion? why does she seem kind? All of these questions redirect attention to the poem, calling upon the students to refer to and draw inferences from the text.

The first response may also lead to reflection upon one's own perceptions or values—what characteristics do you consider desirable or attractive in people? What features do you share with the character in the poem? These reflections, too, might lead back to the poem: does this character actually have those virtues you have said are desirable, and if so, how are they shown? Such discussion is concrete, built on specific observations and inferences that can be traced to the text. It demands actual thought, not simply the facile manipulation of phrases which is likely to be encouraged by too hasty an effort to discuss "twentieth-century poetry."

After the sort of concrete discussion the first response might promote, the class may be ready to deal with the more abstract second response. Students may be reminded of other poems as they talk, and thus may recall specific examples of "twentieth-century poetry" to compare with the poem before them. By replacing the generalization with examples, they can retain some of the concreteness of the earlier discussion. They may even arrive at a statement about twentieth-century poetry in general. Questions may also arise about the characteristics of Dylan and Thomas, and samples of their work may be presented for examination by the group. The second response is not, in other words, a useless statement to be discreetly avoided by the teacher. But it is more difficult to deal with effectively, and therefore not a good place to begin.

After discussing the first statement about the poem, the class may sense the vagueness and ambiguity in their efforts to deal with the second. They may see that the second response brings up issues they are not yet ready to handle comfortably. That student who offered the second response may be gently led to qualify or perhaps even retract it. She may be compelled to reflect on the possibility that the response was not really a response to the poem, but an effort to impress the teacher and the class with insight and knowledge she did not possess. That, however, is a judgment for the student herself to make. Although the teacher may suspect such a possibility, she should not voice her suspicions too openly, for fear students will hesitate to contribute in the future. The purpose of these response statements, after all, is to initiate discussion. They are not to be treated as the products of thorough, painstaking thought, but as guesses or suggestions to be explored. If the exploration leads nowhere, nothing is lost but a little time, and the class may turn its attention to other possibilities, one of which may lead to insight.

The teacher may assist in finding the most productive route for the discussion to take, but should not deceive the students about the nature of thought by suggesting that it is all orderly, cumulative, and successful. Students must learn, largely by experience, that some beginnings are more likely to lead to productive discussions than others, and they must also learn to tolerate uncertainties and failures. A class that moves logically, almost inexorably, from beginning to end may give the teacher a satisfying sense of craftsmanship, but it does not accurately reflect the process of thinking any more than a research report accurately reflects the process of scientific experimentation. The classroom should, as often as possible, demonstrate the process of thinking as well as its results.

PATTERNS OF DISCUSSION

Brief responses, jotted down in the five or ten minutes after reading, may serve as the basis for a variety of patterns of discussion. As we have noted, they may be read aloud by the teacher, with pauses for discussion when one of them provokes a reaction; the teacher may call upon volunteers to present their statements to the class; or the statements may be listed on the board and rearranged into a formal agenda for the class session. There are other possibilities as well. For instance, the teacher may wish to pair students initially, asking them to read one another's statements and react to them. The pairing for this activity could be purposeful; two students whose views are radically different might be placed together, so that under the teacher's watchful eye they could learn to listen more attentively and tactfully to opposing viewpoints. The teacher might even prescribe that students must first find something in their partner's statement to agree with or commend, if only the neatness of the handwriting.

After discussing in pairs, the class might combine pairs into groups of four, and perhaps later into still larger groups. Discussion in these small groups will be easier for students to handle than discussion with the full class. The talk will be less likely to jump from one issue to another, but may instead be progressive, allowing the students to build upon and come to understand one another's ideas. After the groups have reached a certain size, perhaps four or eight, the entire class may come together again to hear the ideas developed in the smaller groups.

Discussion first in pairs and then in slightly larger groups serves a purpose like that of the brief writing period following the reading—it allows ideas to germinate and grow vigorous enough that they cannot be ignored. In the full class, the ideas of the more vocal students are likely to command attention while the equally valuable ideas of more timid students may wither away unnoticed. If, however, those fragile thoughts grow for a few minutes in the more comfortable setting of small groups, they may root firmly enough that students will be willing to present them to the class. As the short writing period discourages students from simply waiting for someone else's ideas about the reading, so the small group discussions attempt to nurture ideas until they can stand on their own before the full class.

The talk will wander far from the original statements, and when discussion has concluded, those statements may again become useful. Students may be asked to look at their first notes, reflect upon them, and again write briefly. Have their original ideas changed? Have they seen the poem from other perspectives? Have their first responses been confirmed? Has anything been revealed to them about their classmates or themselves? The original statements may serve the students as a journal might, to remind them of how they felt and what they thought. Reviewing those notes may help to show them what they have learned in the discussion. They may even grow less eager for the teacher's explanations of works and less dependent on the narcotic of grades for their sense of accomplishment.

These notes will also give the instructor an excellent way to judge the effectiveness of discussion and the appropriateness of the literature. If the notes show that the students have been thinking and listening to others respectfully but not submissively, then they are likely to be enjoying the work. If the responses remain arid and detached, and if the notes written after discussion indicate that little or nothing has happened, then the teacher should reconsider the material or her conduct of the class.

FOCUSED WRITING

The teacher can also vary the pattern by placing constraints on the written responses. She may ask the students to respond to a certain aspect of the work: the motivation of a character, the influence of the setting on the mood, the nature of the conflict between two characters, the values implicit in the choices characters make, or the values and beliefs of the writer as shown in the work. Or the teacher may suggest that they respond from a particular perspective. If, for instance, she wishes the students to compare the works of two authors, one of whom the class has recently read, she may have them read the first work of the new writer and respond as though they were the writer they have already studied. Such an assignment is, of course, more complicated and demanding, and the teacher must judge the group carefully before making it.

Further, the teacher must keep in mind that any restriction on student response sacrifices something. The virtue of the free response is that it identifies the student's most vivid connection with the text. It may be a memory, an interpretation, an image, or even a digression that seems entirely unrelated, but it is the immediate consequence of the encounter of reader and text, and is thus material from which meaning might be made. Constraints on the response diminish the chances that it will be so intimate a part of the reader. The constrained response is the result of the encounter of three forces—the reader, the text, and the assignment; that third variable might interfere with the interaction of the first two. Presumably, compensation lies in stretching students to new perceptions they might have missed, or in increased efficiency in teaching some element of literary art. The teacher may judge that it is worth the sacrifice, but she must not let the assignment dominate the literature itself. If students' responses are too frequently or severely constrained, the students may come to see the literature only as a basis for prescribed exercises, and may find themselves taking the pseudo-professional approach to their reading that Rosenblatt decried. The essential feature of response-based literature teaching is that it makes every effort to ensure that students discover their own routes into the literature.

LONGER RESPONSE PAPERS

Instruction may be further varied by expanding the brief writing period. Students may be asked to write a long response, perhaps several pages, identifying and elaborating on their reactions to a work and tracing them as far back into their own history and as deeply into the text as they can. A longer response statement is, of course, more than an effort to identify starting points for discussion; it demands that students sustain their thinking alone, without the support and questioning of other students or the teacher. In a sense, it asks them to discuss the work with themselves, to reduce the dialogue of the classroom to an internal monologue. More difficult than the ten-minute response, it nonetheless has the virtue of allowing students the opportunity for uninterrupted reflection, at length, on their own perceptions. They need not suspend their thoughts to consider those of their classmates, or compete for the time to voice opinions; they can follow their own thoughts wherever they lead.

Like the shorter writing assignments, long response statements may be constrained in some way by the teacher if it seems desirable. Constraint may be of more value to the students than with the shorter statement, in fact, since it helps sustain and focus their thoughts. Responses longer than a page or two, however, may be difficult for students not yet used to the technique and aware of what to expect. The self-reliance demanded by a longer paper will quickly drain those unpracticed in pursuing their own responses, so it may be wise for the teacher to begin with very brief writing assignments and then gradually ask for more extensive statements.

Response papers can be assigned so that only limited direction is given. Adler proposes a technique that he calls "answering the unanswered question." Observing that "For too long we have tended to ask students questions, bypassing their questions," Adler suggests inviting students to identify the unanswered questions in a work of literature and propose answers to them. He points out:

> As readers, all of us have found gaps in stories wherein we wish the author had supplied us with more information. For example, if we read in a story that a character did something after discussing a situation with a friend, we wonder what the dialogue between them might have included, or how the two persons conducted that dialogue.[2]

The student seeking the question or questions that remain, for her, unanswered, or at least not explicitly answered, is looking closely at the text and at herself. The assignment does not neglect the student or declare her to be irrelevant, but forces her to ask herself, "What is it that *I* do not understand, in this work?" The question is general enough to allow the student's individuality to surface, and yet may inspire a bit more confidence and sense of direction than the instruction simply to respond.

Assignments like Adler's may help make longer response papers more palatable to the class. Bleich, in *Readings and Feelings,* offers several more strategies for eliciting responses from students. He proposes a sequence that "begins by asking for the most important word in the work, then the most important passage, and then the most important feature, whatever it may turn out to be."[3] As one might predict, "It is immediately clear that each person has a different sense of what 'importance' means. . . ."[4]

Those different senses of importance indicate unique readings of the work. The statements made are often specific enough to discuss intelligently, and the very presence of the word "importance" seems to compel people to offer reasons. "This word is the most important because. . . ." What follows the "because" is the substance of the discussion.

One or more class sessions might be planned around Bleich's sequence. The discussion might, for instance, be divided into three sections. First, students would be asked to read the work and answer the question, "What is the most important word in the poem and why?" After giving them several minutes to reflect on the question and jot down brief notes, the teacher could call on several students for their comments, and use them to begin a discussion. If the resulting talk seems energetic and productive, it can be pursued. It might be exhaustive enough that no further impetus is necessary. On the other hand, if talk begins to fade, it may be revived by means of the next question, "What is the most important passage in the work, and why?" Again, several minutes of reflection and writing might precede the discussion, which may in turn be interrupted for the third question, asking for the most important feature of the work.

The technique, like Adler's, provides a task, thus giving direction and purpose to the students' thinking, but the questions are sufficiently open to allow students their own responses. The shifts in focus, although minor, may be enough to refresh a discussion and reawaken the flow of ideas. The technique is a compromise between freedom and control, directing the students, but directing them to look inside themselves.

Like the brief written response, Bleich's teaching pattern may be varied in several ways. For instance, the teacher may vary the length of time for reflection. At one extreme, she may wish to raise the question as soon as reading is completed and encourage the students to respond with their first thoughts. The spur-of-the-moment choice of most important word might be different from the choices they would make if given a leisurely period for contemplation. That rash choice may lead them to a surprising discovery. Or students may reject it after they have had several minutes to think, and thus learn something about the difference between instinct and thought.

At the other extreme, students may be asked to prepare three- to five-page papers to answer one of the three questions. These longer papers, explaining the student's choice of most important word, passage, or aspect, ask the student to look at both the text and herself and examine the transaction that has taken place between the two. The assignment allows the student a fair amount of latitude. Her choice may spring from her own concern with a particular issue, conceivably one of minor importance to the author, or it may be an exercise in close textual analysis, an effort to identify a key to the writer's intentions. Ideally, a student will encounter a diverse enough collection of literary works that her papers will fall at both ends of the spectrum, some dominated by an interest in self-understanding and some by a fascination for the workings of the writer's mind. The virtue of teaching literature with attention to student responses is that it allows this latitude; the challenge for the teacher lies in the difficult judgments such teaching demands, for she must look for patterns in the students' responses and encourage them to try new things, not clinging to one proven method or the other.

DEALING WITH LONGER RESPONSE PAPERS

Both the spontaneous, unconsidered choice and the fully developed paper can promote the exchange of ideas within the classroom. Discussion after long written response, however, may be somewhat more difficult to manage than that following brief periods of writing. Those hastier responses are fragments or kernels of thought, and are fairly easy to handle. The longer statements, on the other hand, are likely to be not fragments of ideas, but full logical chains. They are more difficult to discuss because they are more complicated, because they are themselves "works," literary essays. The teacher might respond to them in several ways.

One way, of course, is to reply in private, either in conference or through notes returned with the papers. Both are time-consuming. Notes, because they are easily ignored, are of questionable value, although they are traditional and students may feel neglected if nothing is written on their papers. A brief note is probably a good idea, if only to reassure students that their efforts have been given a serious reading.

Too often, however, students come to view papers as exercises in avoiding errors or predicting the teacher's views, perhaps as a result of too many futile lessons on grammar and usage or too many comprehension questions in basal readers. When comments on papers consist of little more than approbation or correction, students come to see them not as part of a dialogue about their writing progress, but as a final, authoritative judgment of their work. This misapprehension is reinforced by the absurdity of grading; comments written on papers, regardless of their content or motivation, are likely to be taken as judgments or corrections. The teacher who wishes to participate with students in thinking about the literature may have to shake them loose from some of their preconceptions about her role, and that may be easier in short private conferences than in lengthy notes on the students' essays.

Conferences   Conferences allow the teacher to speculate with the student, to make remarks that in writing would require careful phrasing too time-consuming to undertake regularly. The teacher might, for instance, consider that a student's response is facile and evasive, skirting a difficult issue in the literature. To explain this might require a lengthy analysis of the student's paper, carefully worded to avoid accusation. Such a comment might more easily be made orally, where the teacher's tone and bearing can demonstrate that she hopes to understand, not accuse—to help the student think, not tell her what to think. In conference, the teacher can observe the effect of her remarks on the student and can adjust and correct.

In these conferences the teacher might strive for several goals. The first is a sense of shared purpose with the student, as people working together for a better understanding of the literature and of themselves. The teacher should neither represent herself as absolute authority on the literature nor deny the sharpened insight that broader experience and fuller knowledge will have given her. On the other hand, students too have a rich background of experience that provides the context for their reading and shapes their response. In a conference, the teacher must demonstrate respect for both the perceptions of the student and the words of the text. She must convey somehow that she is not the source of the meaning; meaning is created through the subtle process of reasoning about one's own responses to the words. The conference is a cooperative venture in which student and teacher reason together. The student contributes what she knows of herself and her responses, while the teacher contributes what she knows of the work, the process of reading, and the student. Again, as with all aspects of instruction in literature, a delicate balance is required.

A second goal for the conferences, and one that might be made explicit, is to model in miniature the kinds of exchanges hoped for in the full class. First of all, the talk is cooperative, rather than competitive; the point is to understand, not to win arguments. Students should learn to suspend their own thoughts momentarily for the purpose of listening to another's. They should maintain respect for differing points of view, but also for reason, logic, and evidence. And they should consider both the reader and the text. These criteria are more easily met in discussions with two or three than in a group of thirty. If they can be modeled, even occasionally, in the smaller groups, then they are more likely to be met in the large group.

A third goal is to evaluate the student's work. The seriousness of her efforts to understand the literature and deal rationally with her responses to it may be more readily judged in a private conference than in the aftermath of full class sessions. Furthermore, the student herself will be involved in the evaluation. She is, after all, the only one who can know with any assurance whether she is thinking conscientiously about her work. Others, including the teacher, are too easily fooled. The final judgments upon her work are the student's; if she is to continue to learn from her reading in the years after school, she must begin to assume responsibility for those evaluations, rather than leave them in the hands of others. In private conferences the teacher may be frank, asking more penetrating questions, encouraging the student to take responsibility for self-examination.

Group Discussion Dealing with long written responses in groups and in the full class, although it will be made easier by conferences, remains a difficult task. Patterns similar to those used with the very brief writing periods are possible, but the work is complicated by the greater length of the papers. One alternative is to provide an outline for the discussions, divide the class into the appropriate size groups, and ask them to follow it. For instance, students may be paired and given a set of instructions like the following:

1. Read your partner's paper, taking careful notes on:
   —any questions you have about her ideas,
   —any points you think need to be explained more completely,
   —any disagreement you have with her interpretation of the text.
2. Discuss your notes with the author of the paper, encouraging her to elaborate and explain as much as she wishes. Keep in mind that your purpose is to help her think, not to change her mind. If you disagree with points she has made, you might express those disagreements, but only to show her another perspective or another reading, not to persuade her to accept it. After talking about one paper, reverse the roles.
3. When both papers have been discussed, add a paragraph or

two of postscript to your own paper in which you record any additions, clarifications, or changes in your thinking that have resulted from the conference.

Groups may need either more or less guidance than this brief outline would provide. They may need time limits for each step. The purpose of the outline is simply to provide security and direction for students who may not feel comfortable finding their own way through a discussion of one another's papers. Ideally, the time will come when such outlines can be discarded and students given the freedom of the open request, "Discuss each other's papers." That time may not come quickly, however, and shallow, perfunctory efforts to discuss one another's works may be discouraging in the meantime.

Variations   Other patterns for discussing the longer responses are worth experimenting with. In groups of three, for example, two students may be asked to discuss the third student's paper. While they talk, the writer remains silent, taking notes on the conversation. After a specified time, the writer is invited into the discussion to reply to points made and questions raised. In larger groups, of perhaps four or five, students might be asked to read the papers written by members of the group, identify one major issue, question, or idea that the group seems either to share or to disagree on, and then discuss that issue. The group might then summarize its talk for the entire class so that the class can discuss it.

Even if the students' papers are not discussed directly, they can serve as a source of ideas for discussion. The teacher can abstract interesting issues from the papers; having written them, the students are likely to have opinions they want to express. It is also possible for the papers to suggest by their neglect of an issue that it might be appropriate for the discussion. For example, if all the students have commented on the events of a story, but have failed to consider the motivations of the characters, the teacher may want to give time to that issue. That is not to say that the response statements should be ignored, but neither should they be allowed to dictate the topics treated in the classroom. Having given thought to the papers, the students may be expected to discuss more intelligently whatever arises in class, whether it is drawn directly from those papers or not.

Of course, sessions may be devoted to analysis of the students' writing problems and accomplishments, as well as to exploring the literature. Our concern in this chapter has been with promoting interactions among the students, and so we have concentrated on the usefulness of the response statements in stimulating thought and discussion. They may also serve in other ways. For instance, the teacher may display them, if that seems a desirable way to reward performance or make the students' thoughts available to one another (and if, of course, the writers are willing). Or she might compile them into a journal to be distributed within the class, perhaps near the end of a unit, as a sampling of the students' reflections on the material. They might also serve as the basis for long papers of other kinds. If, for example, a student's response to a work speculates about the author, the teacher might encourage the student to undertake a research paper on that writer. Or if the response suggests other possible outcomes of a story, or reminisces about characters the student has either encountered or envisioned, the teacher might be able to persuade her to try writing fiction of her own. If the student speculates about the intentions of the author, she might work on a critical essay, binding herself to careful analysis of the text, and perhaps undertake the study of other critical statements about the work.

At the very least, response papers will serve as a source of some insight into the students themselves. That insight might be the discouraging revelation that a student is barely comprehending, or that she is comprehending but remains unmoved by the literature; but even that may help the teacher to reconsider her selections, her teaching, or both. At best, the responses afford a privileged glance into the mind, allowing the teacher to understand aspects of the student's thought and personality that might surface in no other way. Revealing or not, the response papers should indicate clearly to the students that their feelings and thoughts are important in the classroom.

THE TEACHER'S ROLE

It may seem that this emphasis on the responses of the students, whether they are visceral and ill-considered or carefully reasoned, diminishes the authority and stature of the teacher. In a sense it does, for by choosing to view reading as an act of creation rather than a search for one true meaning, the teacher relinquishes the traditional authority of the pedagogue. The abdication is not complete, however, for she must assume a new responsibility: to counsel her students through the difficult act of thinking. The attention to students' first reactions is not meant to substitute for thought, but to precede and prepare for it. As Bleich says, "feeling precede[s] knowledge"[5]; a student must desire to know before she will undertake the labor that results in knowing. The literature teacher encourages students to feel and then to think about what they feel in hopes that the thinking will then matter and the students will give more to it. If this succeeds, and the students begin to discover that the literature does raise questions that matter to them, it might become easier to encourage and demand careful thought. In so doing, the teacher may find herself talking about her own responses, lecturing about the work or the writer, or arguing with the students about their interpretations. But that may not be out of place in a style that emphasizes student participation. If a class begins to work well, the students may accept the teacher as a participant in the same processes of responding and thinking, able to contribute as another learner. The teacher who has achieved this stature with her class may find that she slides easily back and forth between the roles of teacher and student. At one moment she may be managing the class, assuming all the responsibility and authority that implies, and at another moment she may be seated in discussion, joining the group as an equal, shown no more and no less deference than any one else.

AUTHORITY

A teacher who achieves that relationship with her students has a rare opportunity to influence their thinking. Having abandoned the authority of might—the threat of grades and tests—she may retain the authority of reason. Rather than present the result of her thought, she joins in the process of thinking, giving the class the opportunity both to challenge her and to observe her. In other words, the demand that the teacher respect student responses is not a demand that she ignore her own. She should refrain from imposing her perceptions on the students, but if the class has matured enough to accept her views without holding them sacred, it may be useful to present them. They may broaden the discussion, showing the class how an older person, with more experience of the world and of books, reacts to the work. The students should receive her opinions as she would receive those of a published critic—not as the final word, but as the reflections of an experienced reader. In an untrained class that expects a great deal of telling and explaining, the teacher must move cautiously, withholding her own thoughts to give the students room for theirs. But when the class comes to understand the process of responding and building on responses, and sees that differences in readings are not only expected but desired, the teacher may state opinions with less fear that they will be taken as law.

In such circumstances, the teacher's responses and thoughts may even serve as models for the class—not because they are right or correct or best, but because they may demonstrate interesting lines of inquiry that the class has not discovered for itself. In one class, for instance, many students had recently watched a film entitled *Deathwish*, the story of a man whose family is killed by housebreakers. The courts fail to convict the killers, and the hero decides to seek justice by setting himself up as a potential victim for the sort of spontaneous crime that took his family, and then, when assaulted, summarily executing his attacker. He becomes a vigilante wandering the streets, apparently vulnerable to anyone looking for an easy victim.

The students, almost without exception, heartily approved. They agreed that crimes against the defenseless were inexcusable, that the courts and the police were inefficient, that punishment for violent crime was too mild, and that the efficiency and finality of the hero's method were laudable. He was, in their eyes, a modern-day Robin Hood, a little soiled by his surroundings—his city was grimier than Sherwood Forest—and by the brutality of his method, but nonetheless a hero, defending the weak against predators.

The teacher, on the other hand, although he shared the students' vicarious satisfaction with the rapid and well-deserved executions of the criminals, was not so pleased with the movie, and said so. He told the class he thought the film had exploited his natural anger at stupid and violent crimes, moving him to applaud a form of justice he really did not condone. He suggested that leaving justice in the hands of either victims or vigilantes was likely to lead to some terrifying abuses. The hero had made no mistakes, but would all who modeled themselves on him be so lucky? Might they not shoot someone running from the scene of a crime and then discover that she was a frightened bystander rather than the criminal? Further, the crimes the hero dealt with were all clear-cut cases of violent aggression, many of which could be stopped by violence. But if vigilante justice were approved and accepted, it might be exercised in situations of less clear and obvious crime, perhaps when someone felt deceived in a business arrangement that was not quite illegal, but not completely upright. In short, the teacher disliked the film because it seemed to him to promote a dangerous conception of justice by playing upon natural feelings of rage and impotence and using incidents carefully conceived to support its principles.

The discussion of the film was a digression from other class work, and the teacher was not attempting to lead an analytical attack on the movie. He was simply expressing an opinion, and intended to return quickly to the work at hand. His observations, however, suggested a line of thought the students had not recognized. They had been caught up in the emotional satisfaction of vicarious revenge, but he had modeled for them a more complicated response to the film that involved reflecting on the implications of its notion of justice. The students accepted his thoughts not as the voice of authority, but as an interesting alternative to their view. Some were annoyed, apparently because his reservations about the film diminished the pleasure they could take from it, and some seemed almost chastened, perhaps by the discovery that they had neglected to consider the implications of what they felt. In any event, the teacher's reflections contributed to the students' thinking about the film, even though he had presented them directly, perhaps even didactically, without making any subtle effort to raise doubts or elicit further thought.

In other words, he was not trying to teach, in the sense that teaching is leading students in their own thinking, but by simply telling he did teach. He had for the moment been accepted as one of the class members—his opinions were neither noted down to be returned to him on the next test, nor disregarded as the irrelevancies of an academic. It was a lucky happenstance, of course; both students and teacher had seen the same film and wanted to talk about it, interested in the film and in each other's responses. The incident may serve as a model of the sort of relationship between student and teacher toward which the procedures outlined in this chapter strive. When such a relationship is achieved, when students talk for the sake of the literature and themselves and not for the teacher or the grade, then the teacher may feel more comfortable joining in the discussion.

RANGE OF RESPONSE

We have suggested several techniques for encouraging students to respond and work with their responses. It might be appropriate now to consider what kinds of responses the literature and discussions might provoke and how these will influence the course of the talk. The range of response is, of course, infinite; each reader is unique, and will react differently from day to day depending upon the circumstances. Still, the responses seem to fall into rough categories, which are useful as a crude checklist for observing what takes place in the classroom and judging how best to intervene.

Personal Some responses are comments about oneself. They may express feelings produced by the work read or describe incidents or individuals it called to mind. These responses may draw heavily upon the text, but they are more likely to depart from it or abandon it completely, as the reader explores memories awakened by the work. Although such responses may seem to offer little potential for teaching, the teacher might use them in several ways. She might simply encourage the student to follow her own thoughts and see where they lead. If the reading has generated enough enthusiasm and energy, this process may be very satisfying, even if it does not reflect the goals traditionally associated with literature instruction.

If the student is unable to elaborate on her thoughts without assistance, the teacher might suggest exploring their connection with the work. What, she may ask, are the similarities and the differences between the incident you recall and that presented in the story? Or, how does the person you remember differ from the character in the play who called her to mind? Such questions provide the student with a small task that may help her to think further. The questions may be appropriately dealt with either in class or in writing; in the classroom, however, the teacher must keep in mind her obligation to the group. Other students may or may not be interested in the comparison between a story and the memory it brings to one student. The teacher might remind the class that discussion will not do justice to all possible issues, and that they should make a note of questions that interest them so that they can either consider them in private, use them as topics for future papers or journal entries, raise them again later in the class session, or talk them over in private conference with the teacher or with friends. In class, it may often be necessary to move the discussion on to other matters.

Personal responses are unquestionably desirable in the literature class, but the teacher might be alert for three possible problems. One is the possibility that students will use personal digressions as a way of avoiding serious thought about the work. Responding with opinions and feelings is not the sum total of reading. Students also need to learn to analyze, to interpret, and to seek evidence for their conclusions.

The second possible problem is that the classroom may become for some students an orgy of self-expression and for others an exercise in voyeurism. There are occasional students who cannot resist the temptation to bare their souls, and who are likely, when invited to respond to a literary work, to embarrass the class, the teacher, and perhaps themselves with vehement outbursts or intimate revelations. The instructor needs to defend both the class and such students themselves from that sort of behavior. That is perhaps best done by gently guiding the discussion into other paths or by encouraging others to speak, but it may also be necessary to speak privately with a student who is too outspoken, both to find out why she is and to recommend greater discretion or restraint in the future.

The third possible danger, the most subtle, is the tendency of personal comments to invite amateur psychoanalysis. Neither the class nor the teacher is qualified to analyze a student's psyche on the basis of her response to a literary work. To do so is to become badly distracted from the task at hand, which is to deal with a literary work and the responses to it. The student's *response* may be examined and analyzed, but the student should not be, except insofar as she wishes to do so herself.

Topical   Some responses are *topical*, focusing on the issue raised by the literary work. A book like *Go Ask Alice* may encourage some students to talk about their own encounters with drugs, or about friends who have run into difficulties like those Alice faced, but it may also elicit more general discussion of the issue of drugs or of parent-child relationships. Responses in which the issue is the most prominent concern may also digress widely from the text. In the discussion of *Alice*, some students may bring up the hypocrisy of a generation that can devote time at a smoke-filled cocktail party to condemning marijuana, or they may lament the ineptness of the police and the courts in enforcing the drug laws. They may, in other words, have a backlog of thought on the issue that they can call forth at will, with little or no regard for the text.

The teacher's charge in that case is to direct the energy of the students to the work at hand. If students are interested in the issues raised by the text, then they may be led to take an interest in the attitudes it expresses toward those issues. The teacher might encourage them to compare their opinions with those offered by characters in the story or by the author. When the responses focus on issues, the teacher is likely to have little problem getting the students to speak out—her difficulty may instead lie in persuading them to pause long enough to hear what the writer has to say.

Interpretive   The third form the response may take is *interpretive*, an effort to judge the significance of the literary work. Here the reader focuses mainly on the text, intrigued by what it says and does. Thus students may respond to *Go Ask Alice* by wondering, "Is that really what it is like to be addicted to drugs and run away from home?" They may be reminded of no similar person or incident, and may not previously have considered the larger issue of the availability of drugs, but the work may still capture them and make them want to understand it. Of course, students need not be indifferent to the subject to want to interpret. Those with strong opinions may seek both the opportunity to express them and the chance to hear someone else's views. They, too, may wish to understand, as accurately and thoroughly as possible, what the writer has said. Many of those students who responded so strongly to *Deathwish*, although they were at first satisfied with their vicarious revenge, quickly became interested in interpreting the movie, in determining the implications of acting as the hero did and the significance of the narrow range of incidents the writer had selected for his story.

Skill in interpretation has been a prominent goal of most literature instruction, and although our concern with response may reduce the emphasis on this skill, interpretation remains crucially important. The responses of the reader establish a basis upon which interpretive statements may be made and judged. An interpretation is, after all, the statement of one person, and thus, although bound to the text, it is still idiosyncratic. But students should recognize that there is a difference between stating a feeling or an opinion and stating an inference. In the first, the student is restrained only by the demands of honesty—her feelings are her own, and do not need proof or defense. An interpretation, however, is an inference about someone else's statements, the author's or a character's, and inferences do require demonstration. Thus, when a student says, "The author means . . . ," she obligates herself to a clause beginning with "because" and containing evidence for her conclusion. Marshalling such evidence is an extremely important skill that deserves a significant place in the literature classroom.

Formal   A fourth possible topic for the response is *form*. Young children take great pleasure in the repetition and rhythm of nursery rhymes and other children's poems. They seem to feel no void when the meaning remains obscure or simple, as it frequently is in children's verse. Their pleasure derives from the formal elements—the sound, the rhythm, and perhaps the images evoked. Although adolescents seem less patient with works that lack a strong narrative line, they too respond to formal elements, whether consciously or not, when they read. The reader who speaks of the suspense in a mystery or the buildup of fear in a novel of the occult is noting effects created by careful manipulations of form. Interested students should be encouraged to discuss those elements and even analyze them if the question, "How did the writer accomplish this effect?" arises. Such analysis should not be overemphasized. If it is, the students may see the text as something to work on, rather than an experience to live through, and reading will no longer be an aesthetic experience. Rosenblatt cautions against the tendency to

> hurry the student away from any personal aesthetic experience, in order to satisfy the efferent purposes of

categorizing the genre, paraphrasing the 'objective' meaning or analyzing the techniques represented by the text.[6]

Rushed into the scientist's role, students are likely to bypass the literary experience:

> The great problem, as I see it, in many school and college literature classrooms today is that the picture—the aesthetic experience, the work—is missing, yet students are being called upon to build an analytic or critical frame for it.[7]

So the talk about form should not be purely analytical. There are, of course, works that call conscious attention to their form, and almost demand that it be analyzed. Reed's "Naming of Parts," with two voices, the drill sergeant's and the bored recruit's, sliding back and forth into one another, seems to compel the reader to look at technique. So does a work like Cormier's *I Am the Cheese,* an adolescent novel sufficiently complex and disturbing to capture the interest of the most sophisticated adult reader. Cormier's book tells about a terrifying event in the words of a child whose mind has been disturbed by it. The story itself is intriguing, but more intriguing is the author's skillful management of form. Readers will want to examine what he has revealed, what he has concealed, and how he manages to do both. The analysis of form in such instances can be very productive and satisfying; it comes as a natural part of the reading, answering questions that the reading inspires. But when it is imposed as an exercise, not to answer questions raised by the text, it can supplant the aesthetic literary experience rather than support it.

Broader Literary Concerns   Finally, the reader may address *broader literary concerns.* These include interest in biography, literary periods, the working habits of the writer, and the history of the times portrayed. Mary Renault's novels may inspire an interest in early Greece and Rome, Poe's short stories may stimulate curiosity about his unhappy life, *The Night Thoreau Spent in Jail* may lead some students to read *Walden* and perhaps Emerson's essays, the movie *One Flew over the Cuckoo's Nest* may be compared with the book, and *2001* may arouse an interest in computers and artificial intelligence. Such interests are to be encouraged; they are the lucky events of teaching. A teacher with several good bibliographies (like *Books for You* and *Your Reading*—see the end of Chapter Five) or a helpful librarian can entice a student into a great deal of independent and valuable reading when she discovers that a literary work has awakened curiosity.

USING THE CATALOG OF RESPONSES

This list of responses, with its five crudely drawn and overlapping forms, has proved useful for some teachers in observing class discussions. They have found it helpful to note, for instance, those classes in which one form of response predominates. Some classes make little effort to do anything but interpret the works read. Raised on comprehension and interpretation questions, they seem to have allowed their capacity for emotional response or personal involvement to atrophy. In such cases the teacher may wish to encourage a more personal interchange with the text using the techniques discussed in this chapter.

The catalog is more likely to be of help, however, in judging the performance of individual students. Students tend to stick with the response modes they are used to, fearing to venture into new territory, and the teacher should adjust her instruction accordingly, encouraging the patterns each student neglects. The range of responses is broad, and students are better off learning a whole scale than restricting themselves to one note.

VARIATIONS

One problem that may have become apparent as this chapter progressed is that many of the techniques presented here are extremely demanding, both for teacher and students. Response papers demand concentration and careful reading, and analyzing and discussing the responses may be even more rigorous. To teach in these patterns every day, five periods a day, may well be too exhausting. Teachers will find that when things go well in the classroom—when students do respond enthusiastically to the text, and the discussion is active, with most participants enjoying it and learning from it—the lessons may generate energy rather than drain it. Nonetheless, there will be days when it seems desirable to plan something simpler.

Strategies will suggest themselves in the course of other lessons. If, for instance, students develop an interest in the life and times of the writer they are studying, a session or two on that topic would be appropriate. We have discouraged substituting such information for direct experience with the literary text, but if the direct experience sparks historical or biographical interest, there is no reason not to satisfy it. The teacher might either lecture herself or ask students to prepare lectures or short papers to deliver to the class. Both experiences can be valuable, retaining the focus on the literature but providing some respite from the more severe demands of response-based discussion.

Class sessions devoted simply to quiet reading may also be

beneficial. They are first of all pleasant, allowing students a small island of solitude in the middle of a day filled with other voices. They may also be used, if further justification is necessary, for private conferences, conducted quietly off to one side so as to distract as little as possible. The good results of sustained-silent-reading programs, in which everyone in the school suspends other work for a certain time each day to read, provide evidence for the virtues of this simple activity.

The strategies of creative drama might also be applied in literature teaching. It may take time for the class to grow comfortable with pantomime, improvisation, and role-playing, depending on previous experience and how comfortable the students are with one another; but once used to the techniques, the students may find they provide insights into the literature that are inaccessible through other approaches.

For instance, students asked to read and analyze literature may become cold-blooded in their judgments, showing no empathy for the characters portrayed. Acting out a scene from the work may help these students sense the feelings of the characters more clearly than they otherwise would. For instance, pairs of students might act out the confrontation between the old woman and the social worker in "As Best She Could." One student would imagine the thoughts and emotions of the old woman. She could be asked, in that role, to think about such questions as: "How do you feel about asking for welfare? What do you know about the welfare system? Do the conditions of your life make you confident or pessimistic? How do you feel about your daughters and about the social worker?" The other student could imagine herself as the social worker: "How many clients have you seen today? How have they treated you? Are you well paid for what you do? Are you compassionate and eager to help, or are you tired and bored? How often have you been deceived by welfare clients?" Then the students could play out the scene.

After the improvisation they would be asked what they felt and thought as they acted out the scene. Many students report feeling emotions they had not anticipated, or feeling expected emotions more strongly than they had anticipated. The social worker, for instance, may report real anger toward the client. Simulating the experience produces some of the emotions and insights the actual experience might have yielded, giving students a perspective they could not attain through the more intellectual and distant process of analysis. It is one thing to say, "Well, she might be angry at having to deal with someone without the necessary forms who seems to want all the rules bent just for her," and quite another to say, "I was furious!"

Students may also find through improvisation that things need not have worked out as the author arranged them. The student playing the old woman may grow so angry with the social worker that instead of stalking away, she erupts in an angry tirade. Or the social worker may sympathize with the old woman and decide to bend the rules for her. If improvisations vary from the text, so much the better, for this demonstrates that the poem is the result of the author's choices, and that other choices could have been made, revealing different values and ideas and resulting in different poems. Just as varying response statements yield discussion by showing alternative readings of a poem, so might varying improvisations reveal the alternatives from which the writer has selected.

The premise of the first chapter was that students should be encouraged to experience the literary work, allowing it to stimulate images, feelings, associations, and thoughts, so that reading might be personally significant. The premise of Chapter Two has been that group discussion will yield insight into varied readings and perspectives, and will both deepen the capacity to respond to literature and sharpen the powers of analysis. Toward that end, students should be encouraged to speak with one another about their readings and analyze them together. Chapter Three will introduce the third element—other texts—and attempt to show how a collection of literary works can be compiled and taught so as to further broaden response and sharpen analysis.

NOTES

1. George Henry, *Teaching Reading as Concept Development: Emphasis on Affective Thinking* (Newark, Del.: International Reading Association, 1974), p. 17.
2. Richard Adler, "Answering the Unanswered Question," in *Re-Vision: Classroom Practices in Teaching English, 1974–1975*, ed. Allen Berger and Blanche Hope Smith (Urbana, Ill.: National Council of Teachers of English, 1974), pp. 74–75.
3. David Bleich, *Readings and Feelings: An Introduction to Subjective Criticism* (Urbana, Ill.: National Council of Teachers of English, 1975), p. 50.
4. Bleich, p. 50.
5. Bleich, p. 3.
6. Louise M. Rosenblatt, "What Facts Does This Poem Teach You?" *Language Arts*, 57, No. 4 (April 1980), 391–92.
7. Rosenblatt, pp. 393–94.

The Text and Other Texts 3

We approach books with preconceptions, memories, biases, beliefs, and attitudes; and, if we read well and have been lucky enough to find a book with substance, we encounter other conceptions, beliefs, and attitudes. While we read, we think, looking for new perceptions, or perhaps for the similar, the old, the usual, made more noticeable by the text. We may begin to reshape our thoughts, finding some confirmed, some refuted, and some modified. We change as we read, perhaps in subtle ways, finishing the book slightly different than we were before.

We then talk about our reading, bringing with us perceptions of ourselves, the book, and the world, and finding in others still different perceptions and attitudes. Again, if we are intelligent and lucky, the confrontation allows us to grow and learn by reshaping our thoughts. Similarly, we may read other books and find there further variations in thoughts and attitudes that may lead us to still another reconsideration, helping us to understand not only ourselves and others but the first text as well.

In the interchange between reader and work, some say the text predominates. We are expected to be accurate and thorough in our reading, to do justice to the text. We are, in a sense, expected to submit to it and be guided by it. This notion of literature and of the reader's experience is expressed by Wellek and Warren:

> . . . the real poem must be conceived as a structure of
> norms, realized only partially in the actual experience of
> its readers. Every single experience (reading, reciting, and
> so forth) is only an attempt—more or less successful and
> complete—to grasp this set of norms or standards.[1]

Somewhere in the text lies meaning, pure and clean, waiting to be grasped by the perfect reader. There is, of course, no perfect reader, but he is approximated by the preeminent critic, whose reading becomes the norm. We read well insofar as we approach his reading, poorly when we depart from it, and thus our individual points of view are sources only of confusion. The accuracy of our reading depends on our ability to suppress or ignore our unique experiences and perceptions.

In this view, the students' readings are inevitably imperfect, and the teacher's goal is to help them move toward the approved interpretation. To achieve that perfect reading, unblemished by the subjectivity of the individual, the teacher naturally encourages, with each new work, a total concentration that isolates the work. Each time, the perfect reading of the single text, always beyond reach, is the goal. Since the students can never read one work adequately, what point is there, one may argue, in trying to comprehend groups of works?

Our conception of reading is slightly different. As the first two chapters state, we view the reader not as submissive, bending to the author's will, but as creative, making meaning rather than finding it. Thus, the text is not all-important. The reader's task is to build meaning out of the confrontation of past and present experience, and each work read should be seen as part of this process: not only a valuable experience in itself, but a contribution to something larger.

What that something larger is depends primarily upon the students themselves. It may involve the refinement of a particular concept. Students who read and reflect upon "A View of a Pig" may find their notion of death has changed slightly as a result. They may find it easier to accept their own detachment about the deaths they hear of, concluding that some distance is necessary, as it was for the speaker in the poem. Or they may find themselves thinking more frequently and painfully about the disasters of others. If the poem affects them at all, it is likely to contribute in some degree to a reshaping of their views.

In broader terms, literature contributes to who they are. As students' ideas shift and their experience broadens, each one of them evolves and changes. Literary works contribute important material to this evolution. The literature class should help the students make connections between the books and their experience, continually revising their conception of the world and their place in it.

This view of both the reader and the process of reading suggests a more aggressive, self-affirming approach to the text. Rather than submit to the work, seeking only to find its "structure of norms," the reader instead forces the work to submit to him. That is to say, he uses it, incorporating it into himself. He tests its perceptions against his own, not to bend to the vision it offers, but rather to take what he can from that vision in clarifying or enlarging his own. He approaches the text not as a disciple looking for answers, but as a thinker looking for possibilities. The individual work, then, is not an end in itself, but part of a longer process of building one's own picture of the world, a process that involves many books and many other experiences.

Unfortunately, too few people steadily revise their notions about the world. Our tendency to remain with the political party of our parents, to continue in the religions imposed upon us as children, and to retain our prejudices despite evidence that might accumulate against them suggests a willingness to settle comfortably into patterns of thoughts and behavior. Albert Ellis points out that

> ... man achieves so-called free will almost in direct inverse ratio to his becoming a socialized human being. The mere fact that one has, and early in one's life is raised by, duly conditioned and biased parents reduces one's possible free will to meagre amount; the fact that one, additionally, is raised among hundreds of other human beings, and among humans who have a long history and an intrenched culture, further reduces one's potential free will to near-zero proportions.[2]

Culturally established norms become so deeply ingrained in consciousness that they come to seem as substantial and immutable as physical reality itself.

The creative and thoughtful person tries to assimilate and comprehend his culture without being trapped by it to the point where he can no longer see in other ways. He reflects and questions, attempting to see through to his assumptions and reconsider them, to absorb new information and insight even when it contradicts the notions he holds at the moment, and to modify his conceptions to accommodate the new experience. He is, in other words, unwilling to grow too complacent with the way he sees the world at the moment —it's the best he can do now, but he is unwilling to presume himself infallible, knowing that he might, sometime in the future, see more clearly and understand more completely.

He is also unwilling to presume that anyone else can have perfect and complete understanding. As a result, he is less likely to labor endlessly in pursuit of the one perfect reading that some critical schools assume to lie beneath the surface of the literary work. A critic's reading may matter, not as a norm or standard for his own, but as another perspective to consider. Likewise, the author's vision of the world may be important to the thinking reader, but again not simply as an end in itself. It matters insofar as it contributes to his pleasure and understanding, that is to say, to his own vision. He himself, rather than the author, is of primary importance in his reading. He reads not to satisfy an obligation to the writer, but to satisfy an obligation to himself.

Good readers revise their perceptions on their own. They are researchers; unwilling to be led by one source, they weigh one item against another, comparing, balancing, seeking their own formulations. For such readers, the concept of power in *Macbeth* may be fascinating and worthy of lengthy contemplation, but it is not complete. Their own concept of power will be a thoughtful distillation of power as seen in *Macbeth*, in *All the King's Men*, and in their encounters with teachers, police, employers, and others in authority. They will agree with Newton that we see further than our predecessors by standing on their shoulders, neither rejecting them casually nor accepting them uncritically. For such readers, the text is not more important than the self. They do not submit to the authority of the printed word—not, at least, until they have thought about it long enough to make its ideas their own. Unwilling to be indoctrinated, they prefer to reflect—they seek the insights of others not as answers to their questions but as the raw material from which to construct their own answers.

The comparison between literature and research may seem strange. Researchers start with a problem or question and look for information and ideas to help them solve it, but reading is not quite so purposeful. Usually people pick up a novel not to help with a specific problem but to pass the time, to entertain themselves, to relax after the worries of the day. Researchers are organized and methodical, selecting the materials they find most useful and studying them in an efficient pattern, but readers of literature, unless they are professional scholars, are likely to select their reading somewhat more haphazardly. They may know that they prefer mysteries, or romances, or stories by a particular writer, and those preferences will impose a casual organization on their reading—they are unlikely to plan more thoroughly.

Still, there are some similarities between ordinary reading and scholarly research. Both scholars and readers formulate ideas based on the material they have read. Both methods lead to the same sort of cumulative product—a vision created by words. Our cultural vision itself, with its infinite personal variations, is essentially a creation, pieced together over centuries of reflecting, observing, reading, and talking. Part of the experience that yields such visions, a greater or lesser part depending on the individual, is reading. We may imagine an intelligent reader engrossed in a story of political intrigue, wondering if people really do behave that way, pausing occasionally to compare the characters with those of other works on a political theme, perhaps again *Macbeth* or *Advise and Consent,* or reflecting on what he learned from the Watergate episode or what he remembers from political science courses. If he makes such connections between previous experience and the current experience of the story, the thought stimulated will have contributed in some way to his vision of the world. Not research, exactly, but similar in the kind of thinking involved.

But what of less skillful or intelligent readers? Not quite so alert to the pleasures of reflecting, they will probably find the story less rewarding. They may read uncritically, as if the story were a factual report from a trustworthy source, or they may be surprised by some unexpected event and reject the entire work as unrealistic. But they are less likely to make a conscious effort to assimilate it, to fit it into their own scheme of things. Unaware that reality is less a concrete world of things and events than a conception of that world, they are not likely to be interested in the prospect of reshaping their ideas. They may not realize that it can be done, and must be done, if they are to remain intellectually alive. Instead, a work may lie undigested in their minds, unconnected with anything else in their experience, read but unread, touching them momentarily if at all.

Such readers as these—and we may assume that many readers in the secondary school classroom will be of this sort—require some help in seeing the possibilities in their reading. If they are ever to approximate the behavior of thinking readers, who seek connections between the text before them and other works, they must be helped to see those connections. Their reading must be organized for them, at least in part, to show how one work may affect the reading of another and to provide a variety of points of view. If works are selected in this way and students are encouraged to test the works against one another, they may come to expect and seek out lines of thought that bind single texts together into a cultural fabric.

PAIRING TEXTS

Selecting works to be paired, and then to be joined together in still larger groups, requires compromise. If the teacher chooses as haphazardly and casually as the typical reader might choose his books, he may have to struggle to find connections between them. On the other hand, choosing works that fit together, either because they deal with similar situations or because they reveal similar or contrasting attitudes, is likely to predispose the teacher toward a certain line of inquiry. For instance, he may choose two works that seem to him to deal with the issue of responsibility. Perhaps, however, the students see in the first work reflections on the idea of freedom and autonomy and have little if anything to say about the notion of responsibility. How, then, does the teacher make the connection between the two works? If he is committed to pursuing the responses of the students, he will discuss the notion of freedom with them. He may then have trouble finding a link between that first work and the second. If he forces the discussion to the issue of responsibility, regardless of the students' concerns, he may be able to make the connection, but it will be with *his* reading of the work, not with theirs.

And so he compromises. He must predict possible student reactions to the works, and choose texts that seem related in some way. But he must also remain flexible and responsive to the group, taking care not to neglect their responses in trying to direct the talk down the paths he has mapped.

Consider the possibilities in two simple poems, suitable for a junior high school class. The first, Longfellow's "The Children's Hour," may lead to discussion about the relations between parent and child.

The Children's Hour

1   Between the dark and the daylight,
      When the night is beginning to lower,
    Comes a pause in the day's occupations,
      That is known as the Children's Hour.

2   I hear in the chamber above me
      The patter of little feet,
    The sound of a door that is opened,
      And voices soft and sweet.

3   From my study I see in the lamplight,
      Descending the broad hall stair,
    Grave Alice, and laughing Allegra,
      And Edith with golden hair.

4   A whisper, and then a silence:
      Yet I know by their merry eyes
    They are plotting and planning together
      To take me by surprise.

5   A sudden rush from the stairway,
          A sudden raid from the hall!
       By three doors left unguarded
          They enter my castle wall!

6   They climb up into my turret
          O'er the arms and back of my chair;
       If I try to escape, they surround me;
          They seem to be everywhere.

7   They almost devour me with kisses,
          Their arms about me entwine,
       Till I think of the Bishop of Bingen
          In his Mouse-Tower on the Rhine!

8   Do you think, O blue-eyed banditti,
          Because you have scaled the wall,
       Such an old mustache as I am
          Is not a match for you all!

9   I have you fast in my fortress,
          And will not let you depart,
       But put you down into the dungeon
          In the round-tower of my heart.

10   And there will I keep you forever,
          Yes, forever and a day,
       Till the walls shall crumble to ruin,
          And moulder in dust away!

                              –Henry Wadsworth Longfellow

The homey, comfortable picture may strike some students as archaic and funny, and the comparison between the rush of the three little girls and the assault of bandits on a castle may seem forced and unnatural. But students may also have a stronger reaction, a hostile reaction, to the father's possessiveness, especially if they themselves are at a stage where they want more freedom than their parents are willing to allow them. Students may feel that they should not be considered possessions to be locked up in the round-tower, but should be turned loose to make their own decisions. The attitude they may see in the father is that of the parent who owns, and therefore controls, his child. He is kindly, but superior nonetheless—he presumes to see and understand what the children cannot:

> Do you think, O blue-eyed banditti,
>   Because you have scaled the wall,
> Such an old mustache as I am
>   Is not a match for you all!

I am more than a match for you, he asserts, though you don't see it. He claims further to be their captor:

> I have you fast in my fortress,
>   And will not let you depart.

The tone is good-natured and light, but the imagery is that of prisons, prisoners and captors, and the relationship between the powerful and the weak. The students, identifying with the children in the poem, may resent their captivity, despite the affection the lines clearly display. If they are chafing under the restrictions of parents, loving or otherwise, they may well be annoyed by Longfellow's portrayal of the children as pleasant, simple baubles, owned by their father.

Thus, in discussing the poem, the class may want to talk first about the relationship between parent and child, focusing on associations called to mind by the reading rather than on the text itself. The students may want to tell about times in their own lives when their desire for independence conflicted with their parents' wish for control. Although the poem is written from the point of view of the father, it may not lead the students to adopt that view, and may in fact bring into sharper focus their own struggle for independence.

The second poem in this pair offers another angle on the issue. Gibran's "On Children," from *The Prophet*, begins with a mother asking a question of the prophet:

On Children

And a woman who held a babe against her bosom said, speak to us of children.

And he said:

Your children are not your children.

They are the sons and daughters of Life's longing for itself.

They come through you but not from you, And though they are with you yet they belong not to you.

You may give them your love but not your thoughts,

You may house their bodies but not their souls,

For their souls dwell in the house of tomorrow, which you
cannot visit, not even in your dreams.

You may strive to be like them, but seek not to make them
like you

For life goes not backward nor tarries with yesterday.

You are the bows from which your children as living arrows
are sent forth.

The archer sees the mark upon the path of the infinite, and
He bends you with His might that His arrows may go swift and
far.

Let your bending in the archer's hand be for gladness;

For even as He loves the arrow that flies, so He loves also the
bow that is stable.

—Kahlil Gibran

Although the speaker is not a child, the poem represents the
child's viewpoint in some ways. Most interesting, perhaps, is that it
puts the parent in the child's position. The mother is being instructed by the prophet just as children are often instructed by their parents. She is not the authority, the figure of power, the source of
guidance or rules; instead, she is submitting to the wisdom of someone else. In "The Children's Hour" the adult knows all that he needs
to know—here the adult is asking for guidance.

"On Children" invites a more sympathetic view of the parent.
Portraying the mother as the questioner, and suggesting, through
the prophet's advice, some of her doubts and unhappiness, Gibran
invites the reader to understand the dilemma of the parent. She naturally feels possessive toward her children, but she must allow them
their own thoughts and lives. They will live in the future, which is
beyond her reach, and she must accept this, even though it is painful
to let them go.

So the two poems present different views of parents, inviting
the students to modify their own notions about that role in life. The
first poem may encourage talk about the domination of parents,
about their unwillingness to undo the bonds and recognize their
children as individuals with their own thoughts and feelings. The
second, the Gibran poem, may suggest that this domination and
control could arise from worthy motives—love, the desire to protect,
or perhaps the wish to preserve a relationship to which the parents
have given much time and energy. It suggests also, of course, that
the child must ultimately be released. The two poems, by providing

two perspectives, should lead students to clarify their own views, and may help them put their ideas into words.

One student proposed that parents can both hold and free their children. They free them by allowing them to grow, releasing them as the archer releases the arrow, and at the same time they hold them by capturing them in memory, as the man in the Longfellow poem did. That student saw no conflict between the two poems; they offered, he thought, complementary visions of the parent-child relationship. This interpretation raises an important point. The poems are not chosen to represent a "right" and a "wrong" view, although of course individual readers may see them in that light. The goal is not that the students adopt one perspective or the other, but that they use both to clarify their own ideas. The teacher would not want to convince his students that all parents try to control their children because they love them—numerous cases of child abuse suggest that other factors may be involved. Similarly, students should not be encouraged to believe that only by freeing children completely can a parent demonstrate love. Students should not be catechized; they should be invited to reflect and judge for themselves. The poems may help them do that reflecting and judging, but the ultimate responsibility is theirs. They must assimilate the poems into their experience with their parents, using them to derive their own notions about parents and children, rather than simply accept the vision offered by Longfellow or Gibran.

Teachers naturally find it hard to keep from expressing their judgments about the comparative worth of two works. One story may seem profound, the other trivial, one character realistic and the other stereotypic, one poem lyrical and the other clumsy, one essay moral and intelligent and the other unethical and stupid. It will seem negligent to allow students to persist in unenlightened readings when it would be so easy to inform and direct them.

In the ideal class, one that accepted the teacher as another reader, the teacher would feel comfortable participating fully, expressing his opinions, arguing his points, passing his judgment on the works. In classes less than ideal, however, a teacher who is free with his opinions may encourage students to depend on him for "right" answers, lazily waiting for him to explain. Students will come to see the literary work not as an experience to think about but as a puzzle to be solved by someone who knows more than they do. When that happens, they are not learning to read literature, but to follow blindly and unthinkingly.

Thus, the teacher's decision about how much to say will be a compromise. On the one hand, his job is to teach—to help students think and reason—and that help calls upon his strongest resources. If he thinks one essay is well-reasoned and another is foolish, then in teaching his students to read critically he will try to help them see the reason in one and the foolishness in the other. On the other hand, he must not encourage dependence, and he must be alert for legitimate but unexpected readings that reflect a perspective different from his own. The uniqueness of each student must be recognized, and the demands of logic and reason must also be admitted, though sometimes the two create an awkward conflict for the teacher.

Neither the Longfellow nor the Gibran poem is especially difficult. Perhaps neither is a great poem. Still, because they treat similar subjects from different points of view, each can stimulate thought and help the reader clarify his attitudes about parent-child relationships. That clarification might take the form of agreement with the stance of one poet or the other, reconciliation of the two poems, or rejection of both in favor of some other view.

We have discussed the two poems to demonstrate how they might illuminate one another and contribute to the readers' thinking. The lines of thought that connect the two poems might clearly be extended to other works. Let us consider a few possibilities to show that the teaching of literature can be organic, evolving in response to both texts and students.

ROUTES THROUGH THE LITERATURE

After reading the Longfellow and Gibran poems, the class might become interested in particular aspects of the discussion. One student might like to read more of Longfellow's poetry; another might want to read and talk further about parent-child relations. Some students' readings might take them outside the realm of literature into psychological or sociological works. They may want to read about the increase in adolescent suicide and speculate about its connection with the rising divorce rate or about the evolution of the family as a basic social unit. Others, thinking about their own family experiences, may be stimulated to try producing literary work of their own —a short play, perhaps, with an autobiographical basis. The teacher might encourage all of those students to pursue their interests, allowing time in class for some of the work. If he is fortunate, the interests will fall into groups, making it simpler to organize the students and evaluate their work.

Perhaps a large enough group of students to justify including the entire class will express an interest in Gibran, or more specifically in *The Prophet*, the text from which the Gibran poem was taken. A brief explanation of the format of the book—a wise man being questioned about roughly twenty-five issues—might awaken curiosity about the ideas expressed. The teacher could read aloud the table of contents, stopping when students seem interested, or identify some promising sections and prepare them for distribution the next day. Several might provoke curiosity: "On Love," "On Work," "On Joy and Sorrow," "On Good and Evil," and "On Death" are good choices.

Let us assume that students want to read Gibran's brief essay "On Love." Since they have recently read his "On Children," the teacher might ask them to speculate about "On Love" before they read it. What might Gibran have to say about love? This question requires students to make a bridge from the preceding poem to this one, not from the theme, as they did with the Longfellow and the first Gibran poem, but from inferences about the author. The poem "On Children," now part of their background, is used to prepare them for "On Love."

It may be objected that raising preliminary questions confines the students' responses, channels their thoughts, and we grant that it does not leave them as free as simply placing the poem before them. On the other hand, readers come to literary works in various ways—they stumble on some, have others recommended by friends, see films made from others, read reviews of them, or are assigned them in classes—and the source is likely to have an influence, however subtle, on the reading. Students need to be aware of that influence and learn to use it. Coming to a text without premeditation can be valuable, but so can coming to it with expectations and predictions in mind, as long as those expectations do not prevent one from seeing the text itself. In this situation, moving from one Gibran poem to the next, the students have simply been asked to form their own ideas. They have not been offered a judgment of the poem to agree with, nor have they been forced to deal with issues in which they have no interest. Rather, the teacher has responded to their curiosity about Gibran and has posed questions that any good reader might ask himself to assist them in approaching the second poem. All teaching requires compromise.

After speculating about the poem aloud or on paper, the students would read it.

On Love

Then said Almitra, Speak to us of Love.

And he raised his head and looked upon the people, and there fell a stillness upon them. And with a great voice he said:

When love beckons to you, follow him,

Though his ways are hard and steep.

And when his wings enfold you yield to him,

Though the sword hidden among his pinions may wound you.

And when he speaks to you believe in him,

Though his voice may shatter your dreams as the north wind lays waste the garden.

For even as love crowns you so shall he crucify you. Even as he is for your growth so is he for your pruning.

Even as he ascends to your height and caresses your tenderest branches that quiver in the sun,

So shall he descend to your roots and shake them in their clinging to the earth.

Like sheaves of corn he gathers you unto himself.

He threshes you to make you naked.

He sifts you to free you from your husks.

He grinds you to whiteness.

He kneads you until you are pliant;

And then he assigns you to his sacred fire, that you may become sacred bread for God's sacred feast.

All these things shall love do unto you that you may know the secrets of your heart and in that knowledge become a fragment of Life's heart.

But if in your fear you would seek only love's peace and love's pleasure,

Then it is better for you that you cover your nakedness and pass out of love's threshing-floor,

Into the seasonless world where you shall laugh, but not all of your laughter, and weep, but not all of your tears.

Love gives naught but itself and takes naught but from itself.

Love possesses not nor would it be possessed;

For love is sufficient unto love.

When you love you should not say, "God is in my heart," but rather, "I am in the heart of God."

And think not you can direct the course of love, for love, if it finds you worthy, directs your course.

Love has no other desire but to fulfill itself.

But if you love and must needs have desires, let these be your desires:

To melt and be like a running brook that sings its melody to the night.

To know the pain of too much tenderness.

To be wounded by your own understanding of love;

And to bleed willingly and joyfully.

To wake at dawn with a winged heart and give thanks for another day of loving;

To rest at the noon hour and meditate love's ecstasy;

To return home at eventide with gratitude;

And then to sleep with a prayer for the beloved in your heart and a song of praise upon your lips.

—Kahlil Gibran

The students might be invited to discuss their responses to the poem, the accuracy of their predictions, the correspondences they find between "On Love" and "On Children," and their judgments of Gibran's notion of love. Do they agree, for instance, that love is something to submit to? Does it give both pleasure and pain? Do you have to expect both, or can the pain be avoided? Is the pain in the failure of love, rather than in love itself? Gibran portrays love as a force, almost a being, external to man—is that view helpful, or is love better seen as something that man develops than as something outside him to which he submits? Such questions as these, selected and worded to fit the class, might provide a transition from the poems read earlier and help the students to investigate this one.

Where to from here? Perhaps to other selections from *The Prophet*, if the class is so inclined; perhaps to other poems, stories, or plays about love; perhaps even to non-fiction. Gould and Iorio's *Love, Sex and Identity* contains, along with imaginative literature on the topic, a collection of essays on love. The first, by Albert Ellis, argues that our culture's notion of romantic love, which he describes in terms somewhat similar to those in the Gibran poem, is inadequate and even dangerous. Ellis suggests that by thinking of love as something we submit to, rather than something we build and cultivate, we become less able to control our lives.[3] In a class sophisticated enough to handle it, such an essay might expand the discussion, providing a viewpoint that contrasts with Gibran's and thus inviting thought. Confronted with one idea, it is easy to shrug and submit. If it is well-expressed and seems reasonable, we tend to accept it rather than undertake the labor of thought. But confronted with two different ideas, we have to choose—or, in the process of deciding, create instead a third idea more palatable than either of the first two.

The routes through the literature may develop naturally—that is, you might watch carefully as the students discuss works, to see what concepts, writers, and genres seem to capture their imagination, and follow the leads you find. Or the routes can be gently managed, keeping in mind the need to respect students' responses. Few teachers will have the luxury of teaching a literature course without some sort of syllabus. They may have some freedom of choice, but they will usually have to teach certain specified works. Composition teachers may find themselves in a better position for teaching literature. Since their task is to teach writing, they can select literature to support the composition work—literature that offers ideas the students wish to write about. With no obligation to cover the Romantic poets or twentieth-century American playwrights, or whatever, the teacher can select works to which his students will respond, so he may find himself teaching, along with the composition, a very interesting literature course.

The teacher in an established literature curriculum, however, has less freedom, and his transitions from one work to the next may not be quite as smooth. Let us suppose, for instance, that the teacher who presented "The Children's Hour" and "On Children" to his class was beginning a unit on "The Family," a topic that might conceivably appear at some point in the junior high school English program. The digression to Gibran's "On Love," although it focuses on romantic love, might provide a path back into the prescribed content, even to such an unusual story as "The Stone Boy." In this story, one question raised is, "How does one behave if one loves another person?" The young boy, who accidentally shoots and kills his brother, is outwardly unemotional. Shocked almost into immobility, he acts as though untouched by the accident, and his inability to show grief or remorse angers and frightens those around him.

There may be few obvious connections between "On Love" and "The Stone Boy," but the larger context established by the two poems on children might enable the students to explore not only the ties between parent and child or between man and woman, but also between brothers or friends. The teacher might ask the class whether or not siblings typically feel love for one another. Is love the appropriate term? Is it too broad, applied to too many different sorts of relationships? Does love motivate predictable behavior—that is, can we observe someone's behavior and confidently say that it does or does not indicate love? Questions like these might lead the class relatively smoothly into "The Stone Boy."

Of course, the teacher also has the option of not making a transition. He may prefer simply to begin the new work, allowing the students to respond to it without the channeling that comes from transitional questions. Each method has its virtues and its defects. When a transition is made, students are more likely to see a direction in the work and feel that they are making progress. On the other hand, the transition limits responses. In the example of "The Stone Boy," the questions raised may predispose the class to think of the story as a statement about love. When transitions are not made, new lines of discussion may open up. But the students may also feel that their work is fragmented, jumping at random from one thing to another. Perhaps the best answer is first to discuss one work, then leave it to deal as openly as possible with another, then recall the first work and compare it with the second. Thus the students have the benefit of undirected response to each of the works as well as the intellectual challenge of bringing the two together.

THEMATIC TEACHING

Clearly, we are moving toward larger collections of related works. Whether they are all by the same author, from the same period, on the same theme, or in the same genre, a relationship can be developed among them, and out of that relationship may come a sharpened understanding of literature or life. Works carefully selected for their diverse points of view can lead to sustained thinking about a topic.

As we have seen, though, arranging works into related groups can narrow the possibilities of response. George Henry, whose book, *Teaching Reading as Concept Development*, is the most thorough explanation of the rationale and procedures for teaching groups of literary works, discusses this problem:

> Some reading tests prefabricate the structure and lead the pupil through it by the hand, so to speak, still calling it discovery and invention. But the teacher using such texts has taken the relations and the structure from the text or its workbook. There is little discovery or invention for the pupil in such a case or when the relations and structures are relayed from a borrowed unit or perhaps a set of questions from an anthology. This process is not concept de-

velopment because the pupil does not himself seek a relation or himself build a structure of relations.[4]

The danger is that the teacher's attempts to relate the various works
will inhibit honest response to the text. Students may try to predict
the teacher's thoughts, to follow his reasoning rather than develop
their own.

This danger simply has to be admitted. The teacher cannot afford complete freedom in the literature class; to follow the interests
and inclinations of the students all the time would be inefficient and
exhausting. The teacher would never know for certain what he
might be reading and teaching in two days. He would have very
little time to find and prepare material for the class—books could not
even be purchased in advance, because the discussion might lead
into unforeseen areas. For some issues the teacher might not know
of appropriate works and would have to do hasty and tiring research
to follow the students' leads.

Thus, some freedom must be traded for control and organization. But throughout his teaching the instructor must keep in mind
the obligation to let students react to the work and test themselves
against it. The goal is to involve students in building ideas as they
read and talk, becoming thinkers, not followers. The intelligent reader negotiates with the text. He comes to it hoping to sharpen his
insight or understanding, reflects on what is there, and finds his
visions confirmed, modified, or refuted by that reflection. He neither
changes his views easily and casually nor holds stubbornly to them
despite new information. If his vision of the world is confirmed, he
has the satisfaction of finding his position strengthened; if it is modified, he can see progress toward a clearer view; and if refuted, then
he has the pleasure of new discovery.

EXPANDED CIRCLES

We began Part One by considering the relationship between reader
and text, emphasizing the overwhelming importance of the reader
and suggesting that what he brings to the work be respected in the
literature class. We then discussed the relationship between the
reader and other readers, pointing out that one can broaden one's
views through encountering the views of others. In this last chapter
of Part One we have examined the possibility of juxtaposing texts,
suggesting that concepts and perceptions can be expanded still further by comparing works that have some elements in common. The

three relationships might be seen as sets of ripples on a pond, affecting each other as they meet.

These ripples can expand to encompass more and more. The other readers, for instance, could well include critics. Instead of giving them the authority the New Critics claim, the students could view them as other students and thus consider what they have to offer, allowing it to shape their own perceptions as reason and instinct dictate. Similarly, the other texts could include almost anything. Students who become interested in the author may wish to look into biographies, and that may lead to an interest in the history of the period in which the work was produced. Those who become intrigued by cultural differences might look into the imaginative literature of other groups or into sociological or anthropological studies. Bright and mature students may wander far afield from the poem or play with which they began, and they should be encouraged to do that exploring. Other students may not have the intellectual energy or interest to travel the same paths, but they, too, should be helped to pursue their ideas. A teacher sensitive to his class and willing to allow time for the work can elicit a great deal of reading and writing from some of his students. He must, of course, be flexible—he must not hope to keep all students moving at the same speed through the same material. But it is possible, if he respects both individuality and reason, for his teaching of literature to be personally significant and intellectually rigorous.

NOTES

1. René Wellek and Austin Warren, *Theory of Literature* (New York: Harcourt, Brace and World, 1942), pp. 138–39.
2. Albert Ellis, *The American Sexual Tragedy* (New York: Twayne Publishers, 1954), p. 98.
3. James A. Gould and John J. Iorio, eds., *Love, Sex, and Identity* (San Francisco: Boyd and Fraser, 1972).
4. George Henry, *Teaching Reading as Concept Development: Emphasis on Affective Thinking* (Newark, Del.: International Reading Association, 1974), p. 14.

PART II
The Literature

The Nature of the Genres

4

The emphasis on response in our discussions so far should not suggest that knowledge about literature is unnecessary. We have noted the dangers of artificial approaches to teaching that substitute information for actual reading. To avoid such approaches, we have focused on the essential experience with literature, the process of noting our reactions to the text, evaluating them, and creating meaning from the exchange. Still, we have not rejected as irrelevant the vast bodies of information about writer, genre, history, and criticism. We have simply relocated them, and perhaps reduced their significance. We have suggested that they are not the primary reasons for teaching literature—not, at least, in the elementary and secondary schools, which have broader goals than the production of literary scholars.

EXPECTATIONS

Nonetheless, information about literature can be both interesting and important, even though examining responses comes first. As we have shown in our discussion of "A View of a Pig," student responses can lead to questions about history, literary technique, cultural patterns, or the life of the author. Response-based teaching can, in other words, arouse an interest in things outside the literary work and the reader's psyche. Further, information that students may not seek out can nonetheless help them read more intelligently and with greater pleasure. A discussion of the various genres, for instance, may help them avoid the frustration of coming to a work with false ideas of what to expect.

The genres do differ significantly in their aims and methods. Students who, from a composition class that demands clear, precise, fully documented essays, come to the complex poetry of Gerard

Manley Hopkins, may feel they have been deceived. If good writing is clear and unambiguous, then why must they suffer through an obscure and confusing poem like "God's Grandeur?" If the poem and essay had similar goals and could be judged by similar standards, this objection would be well taken, but of course the two forms work differently. The essayist is arguing a point, hoping to convince her readers. She does not want to lose them in ambiguous references or convoluted logic. The poet, on the other hand, is not usually so direct; she may work through suggestion, intentional ambiguity, to invite readers into the poem, allowing them to shape their reading in unique ways. The poet may try to evoke moods, capture scenes, arouse emotions, but she is unlikely to attempt extended argument. The poetic mode is less suited to complicated reasoning than the essay, and students should learn to expect that difference between the two genres.

Similarly, there are differences between, say, historical novels and biography. In a historical novel the author can play with the facts, rearranging some, drawing bold inferences from others, and inventing still others to fill gaps in the historical record. The biographer is denied this freedom and held more strictly accountable for the accuracy of her work. Readers who come to a historical novel expecting an accurate account of historical events will be either disappointed or deceived. Likewise, readers who come to biography expecting the completeness and narrative flow characteristic of a novel are likely to be unhappy with the author's inability to fill in where details are not available. Each genre has its own requirements.

Information about the purposes and methods of the various genres will help students know what to expect, reducing the chances of frustration and disappointment. Let us consider the genres most often encountered in secondary schools and see what each demands of the reader and offers in return. Several categories are reserved for later chapters. Adolescent literature, because it is a sprawling and important body of literature in almost all genres, will have a chapter of its own. The visual media—theater, television, and film—because they are watched and heard rather than read, will also be treated separately. The genres that traditionally dominate in the secondary school we will discuss here, beginning with poetry.

THE POEM

Poetry is many different things, of course. It ranges from Frost's two-line "The Secret" to Spenser's book-length *The Faerie Queene*, from Jarrell's simple and direct "Death of the Ball Turret Gunner" to

Milton's complicated and allusive *Paradise Lost*. It contains both the private meditations of Keats's "On First Looking into Chapman's Homer" and the public satire of Pope's "The Dunciad." Poetry is at times sensual, and at other times lofty, at times dramatic, even violent, and at other times peaceful. It may be presumptuous to try to discuss any topic so large and varied as "the poem" or "poetry." Some theorists, Richard Lanham in particular, say that poetry differs not in kind but in degree from other modes of writing. The distinction between poetry and prose, he suggests, is not so simple as the textbooks would have us believe. Rather, prose and poetry are ranges along a spectrum. Poetry, he says, is language that calls attention to itself, inviting the reader to take pleasure in the words, rhythms, and sounds as well as in the statements made. Prose, on the other hand, tends to be more transparent, directing the reader to elements of the world, the things outside that the words call to mind. But, he points out, good prose is also enjoyed for its sounds and rhythms, its poetic elements, and good poetry is seldom completely without referential meaning. The two, prose and poetry, run together, transcending simplistic distinctions about the layout of lines on the page.[1]

COMPRESSION

Nonetheless, there are observations we may make about "the poem," granting that we may often find our generalities refuted by particular poems. Perhaps the most important feature of poetry, the one likely to give young readers greatest difficulty, is its compression. Poems are typically compact, each word carrying a heavy burden. They rarely introduce and summarize in great detail, and often fail to tell the whole story. They are not explicit in the same way that we urge student writers to be explicit. Few poems begin by spelling out their purpose or delineating the ground to be covered, and few lay out their conclusions and implications, striving for clarity and completeness. They present rather than explain. They sketch a picture, recount an episode, portray a character, suggest a mood, and then stop. The following poem by Randall Jarrell is an example:

Death of the Ball Turret Gunner

From my mother's sleep I fell into the State,
And I hunched in its belly till my wet fur froze.
Six miles from earth, loosed from its dream of life,
I woke to black flak and the nightmare fighters.
When I died they washed me out of the turret with a hose.

As an essay, this is lacking. Who is the "I?" Where and when does all this take place? The writer has failed to give us details that even a freshman journalism major would know to include. And what's the point? The writer does not tell us why this death is significant, what conclusions we should draw from it. What he is saying, what this means, is all left unclear.

But expecting that sort of clarity from a poem is unfair. Jarrell is not trying to write a news account or a philosophical essay on the ethics of modern warfare. Rather, he is presenting a set of images, inviting the reader to observe them and react to them. The poem encourages speculation about both the writer's notions and the reader's.

We might, for instance, speculate about the images of the speaker we find here. He falls into the state, which then becomes a bomber, hunches in its belly, finally wakes, dies, and is washed away. He does not seem very powerful or important; he seems always to be controlled from above, apparently by the state. Is Jarrell complaining about the power of the state? Possibly. Is he objecting to war in general, because it can reduce people to bloody messes to be cleaned up with a hose? Again, possibly, perhaps even probably. But the poem is not an elaborate commentary on the powerlessness of the individual in the state, nor is it a treatise on war—it may invite commentaries and treatises, but it is neither. It is, rather, a collection of images working together to create an effect, suggesting lines of thought but not outlining a detailed argument.

The image of the last line is especially powerful. That the human body can be reduced to a mess that can only be washed away, not picked up and carried off, is shocking, perhaps largely because the idea is stated in such simple, direct language. The reader is tempted to draw conclusions from this imagined scene, condemning war for its casual destruction of human lives and lamenting how easily we can be obliterated. But those would be the reader's conclusions—Jarrell has stopped short of making them for us. He has stopped with the image, the particular; the inferences you and I draw, the generalizations we make, are our own responsibility, though he has set us on the path.

One of the pleasures of poetry is that it allows us that freedom. But the reader must expect it; she must know that poetry works by suggesting and directing, and often stops short, leaving the reader with raw material from which to create meaning. In that sense, a poem is like any other of life's experiences—none of them come with explanatory footnotes or critical commentary. They happen, and we make sense of them as best we can. So it is—almost—with the poem. It happens, and we make of it what we can.

It isn't that simple, of course. The poem doesn't just happen; rather, it is written. Its patterns are a product of the poet's imagination and planning. A poem has shape and design. It is not, however, always designed to show things directly; but it leaves much for readers to infer and conclude. It gives us an experience, compressed, carried in few words, sustained by several images, but never fully disclosed.

So the teacher needs to help students adjust their expectations of the poem. She may do that, in part, by direct explanation. She may suggest that students pause when confused and look for suggestions of meaning through unusual comparisons, abrupt changes, and unexpected images. If, for example, students falter over the rapid transition in the first two lines of Jarrell's poem, they need to look closely at the source of confusion, aware that the poet has compressed his meaning into compact images. The speaker falls into the state, hunches in its belly. Then suddenly the belly is that of an airplane—"Six miles from earth. . . ." The change is abrupt, unannounced, and probably confusing. The state has become the bomber. Students should be encouraged to ask themselves why the poet would make this sudden change. Their speculations will help them to understand the comparison between state and plane, a comparison that Jarrell has created but left his reader to elaborate.

The poem is like a field to be played in, rather than a path to be followed. It doesn't fully control and direct its readers. Instead, it sets us free to feel and think—not completely free, for its patterns and themes must be recognized if we are to say that we have read the poem, but free within the bounds it marks off for us.

EVOCATION

Evocative, image-laden poems like Coleridge's "Kubla Khan" invite a different sort of appreciation. If Jarrell's poem leads almost inevitably into the realm of ideas, Coleridge's poem leads us into the realm of visions. Jarrell's poem is discussable, suggesting issues to consider; Coleridge's is less so. Its meaning has to be approached in a different way. It is not easy to ask students to draw inferences from "Kubla Khan," as one might with Jarrell's "Death of the Ball Turret Gunner." What can they make of the images in "Kubla Khan?"

To make anything of them, students must first enjoy them as a performance. They must let the words conjure pictures for them, and then be willing to look at the pictures and allow their minds to wander in the scene. In "Kubla Khan" the scene is a fascinating mix: bright, sunny hillsides are contrasted with deep, sunless caverns, cold and lifeless; the river erupts violently from the earth, spewing boulders about as though they were light as hail-stones, and then wanders quietly through an idyllic landscape and finally disappears down into the earth. Where do these visions take us? What do they mean? Jarrell's poem is easily—perhaps too easily—taken as a condemnation of war; it leads us to discuss war as an issue. Coleridge's does not do that. It presents us with images, with a picture, but not, apparently, with an idea. How, then, do we have students work with the poem?

We might first make the point that not all poetry is philosophical or ethical in its intent, and we need not assume that the poem has a message. We might instead compare it to a picture, which we enjoy or fail to enjoy for its shape and color, not for a meaning we abstract from it. "Kubla Khan" is a poem that might be enjoyed in the quiet mood that permeates a good museum. Looking at paintings, we notice whether or not they please us; only before certain ones do we stop to ask what they mean. We may listen to Beethoven's symphonies and enjoy them immensely without trying to explain them. "Kubla Khan," too, may be read or listened to without concern for interpretation and enjoyed for the simple pleasure of its sounds and imagery.

Students who insist on explanation (and who may be more interested in the teacher's than in their own) may become less adamant if you ask them to bring in a favorite poster or record. Some of these, at least, will defy interpretation. They may be photographs of movie stars or instrumental pieces that are beautiful but do not mean anything. Asked to explain them, the students will have to admit that it cannot be done. A portrait of an actor doesn't mean—it just is. Similarly, a poem might not mean—it might just be.

To help students temporarily stop trying to interpret, you might have them listen to "Kubla Khan" with eyes closed and visualize the scene Coleridge paints. Ask them to listen as though it were music and to observe how it affects them. Read the poem aloud once or twice, and then ask the students to consider the dominant impressions they have of it. These need not be interpretations—just impressions or feelings. Some students may focus on the sunny gardens and be cheered; others may imagine the ominous caverns, the tumult, the prophecies of war, and find their mood darkened; some may notice the presence of both elements and be curious about the contrast. All of these responses can be discussed.

The discussion need not be prolonged, but if it begins to touch on memories and associations, so much the better. The poem will have provoked responses and feelings in much the same way as a painting reminds us of a person or a song recalls a scene. Students may find that they have made something significant out of the poem, that they have not found but created meaning for it. For one student, "Kubla Khan" might come to represent the range of experience possible in the world, from the peace and beauty of the gardens to the violence and fearfulness of the caverns and lifeless ocean. Light and dark, sun and ice, peace and war—she would like a taste of them all, and the poem, when she finds herself too lazy to seek them, may remind her that she does not want to pass through the world without touching it. This may not be what Coleridge had in mind, but it is one reader's playing out of the poem, her performance. It can be valuable and satisfying even if it departs from Coleridge's intent. Songs that remind us of old friends and other places were not intended by their writers to do that, but we are content to let them work that way. If students have similar experiences with poems—and not all of them will with "Kubla Khan," of course— then they may return to poetry with pleasure and perhaps with sharper perceptions.

This kind of reading requires close attention to the words of the poem. Although the students may not be analyzing each line, they are asked to visualize and imagine. These skills are as important in every sort of reading as the skills of analysis. If students cannot imagine the "twice five miles of fertile ground" and the "gardens bright with sinuous rills," they cannot read the poem. The teacher can do little to help except invite and encourage, freeing students now and then from having to interpret the work and gather evidence for their statements. But if students will accept the idea that poetic imagery might work as the sounds of music do, it may free their imagination and their thoughts so that they can read creatively.

Which approach to reading one chooses will depend on what the poem is like. If it works with ideas and seems to make a point, then students might profit from an intellectual approach. If, on the other hand, it seems to paint a picture or sing a song, they might do well to wander in the imaginary gardens or listen to the melody. They should learn to be open to the poem's potential, paying careful attention to the words and their own responses. They must listen and participate; the poem won't give them everything, even if it is a poem with a point. They must play the game it offers, but they must understand that reading is a creative act, much more than a simple matter of receiving something given.

In a sense, readers of poetry must balance between passivity and activity. They must allow themselves to be led, but they must not follow mindlessly. They have to let Coleridge show them the gardens and the caverns, or they have missed his poem. But what those gardens and caverns come to represent may be something other than what Coleridge had in mind. If they are nothing more than his landscape, the poem will be soon forgotten, but if the reader finds personal significance in them, her work will be rewarded. Readers can choose how much to be led by a poem. If, like Lowes, they are fascinated by the imagery and want to understand Coleridge better, they may follow the critical path that led Lowes to *The Road to Xanadu*. If the poem brings up personal associations, then they may prefer to use the imagery to stimulate their own thoughts. They may follow, or lead, or do both. Students should know that they have that choice, that a poem need not be an exercise in interpretation.

SYMBOLISM

We have said that the language of poetry is compressed, with each word carrying a heavy burden of meaning, and that poets often work by suggesting rather than stating. More traditional language would have served us as well—we might have spoken of "metaphor" and "symbol" instead of "compression" and "suggestion." But "metaphor" and "symbol" too often become technicalities for students to trip over, rather than statements about how the poem works. It is much more important that students understand the nature of metaphor than that they be able to distinguish between a metaphor and a simile. That distinction is among the most useless in the lexicon of literary criticism, but the general idea of both terms—linking two images so that one sheds light on the other—is crucial. Students who fail to grasp it will remain bewildered by most poetry. "The road was a ribbon of moonlight" can only be nonsense or a ridiculous lie to them. But if they understand that the poet tries to suggest qualities and feelings by such comparisons and that those qualities and feelings demand active participation, then the poem can begin to work.

Similarly, if students come to see that a symbol is not just a substitution of one thing for another but an association that invests an image with new meaning, they will be more inclined to play with the symbol. Rather than dutifully search for and define it, reducing it to a simple-minded equation, they are more likely to toy with it, explore it, and wonder about its ambiguities. Students who can say, "The flag is the symbol of our country" have memorized a simplified definition of symbol and managed to apply it in one instance. It is near useless knowledge, but harmless enough, as long as they know that symbol and thing symbolized are not the same. But other students can play with the symbol, asking questions about it: Does the flag represent the country as envisioned by the writers of the Constitution, or as it has become? Does it represent the place, the people, a system of government, or a set of values? Such students comprehend that the symbol is not a neat equation, a closed system of meaning, but instead suggestive, open-ended, challenging them to explore the possibilities it presents. If they understand that about the poetic symbol, they will be able to think creatively about the poetry they read.

PROBLEMS

Inverted Word Order Poems do pose problems. Although not unique to poetry, these problems occur often enough in poems to be discussed here. One is inverted word order:

> One morn before me were three figures seen.

> —Keats, "Ode on Indolence"

> Whan that April with his showres soote
> The droughte of March hath perced to the roote,
> And bathed every veine in swich licour,
> Of which vertu engendred is the flowr. . . .

> —Chaucer, "Prologue," *Canterbury Tales*

Students who have played sentence-combining games in composition or language study may have a sharp enough sense of the flexibility of English to face these uncommon constructions calmly. They might be asked to rephrase the lines in more familiar patterns and then consider the difference in style or effect. How, for instance, does "I saw three figures in front of me one morning" differ from Keats's phrasing? This sort of analysis is imprecise, and students should not get the impression that the poet has magically found the only way to state the thought. But different wordings do change the emphasis, rhythm, and tone, and thus alter the meaning slightly, yielding different impressions of the writer and evoking different responses from readers. Students should begin to consider the effects that can be achieved, even if they do so in vague and impressionistic terms.

For students unable to handle the peculiarities of the sentence structure, a technique suggested by Bernstein might be useful. He recommends offering the students a paraphrase before they confront the work.[2] Although his purpose is not to help students understand confusing word order but to emphasize the nuances of the phrasing, giving the students the gist of the passage would no doubt help them to work more easily through the original.

Paraphrasing, by students if they can do it or by the teacher if they cannot, could also help with dialect, or, as in the example from Chaucer, archaic language. A teacher who has spent some time with her students may be able to judge how much help they will need. If not, she might test their comprehension by offering them several lines from the poem they are to read as a trial run. Eight or twelve lines from the Chaucer, for instance, given to the class with a request to try to translate them into modern English, would be enough to suggest how much help the students will need without being so frustrating that they come to dislike the work. If no one comes close to translating the test lines, the group will need assistance. The Middle English is beyond them. If most of the group does well with the trial run, then it might be appropriate to challenge them with much or all of the poem in the original.

The same issue is faced with a poet like Burns:

To a Mouse

Wee, sleekit, cow'rin', tim'rous beastie,
O, what a panic's in thy breastie!
Thou need na start awa sae hasty,
    Wi' bickering brattle!
I wad be laith to rin an' chase thee
    Wi' murd'ring pattle!

—Robert Burns

This stanza would be impossible for some groups and reasonably easy for others. Some students would even be able to approximate the sense of "brattle" and "pattle," though they might not deduce their exact meaning. Some contemporary dialects may also pose a problem, though they are probably not so difficult as Middle English or Scottish dialect.

Allusions Poems full of allusions will also be hard for students unfamiliar with the source of the allusions. It would be foolish to teach Yeats's "Leda and the Swan" without some explanation of the myth it draws on. That explanation can come before or after the reading, depending on what the teacher hopes to do with the poem. Contemporary poetry is almost as likely to contain unfamiliar allusions as that of the Neo-Classicists. The middle stanzas from Frank Horne's "Nigger" would be lost on someone who had not heard of Hannibal, Othello, and Crispus Attucks:

Nigger

Hannibal . . . Hannibal
Bangin' thru the Alps
Licked the proud Roman,
Ran home with their scalps—
"Nigger . . . nigger . . . nigger . . ."

Othello . . . black man
Mighty in war
Listened to Iago
Called his wife a whore—
"Nigger . . . nigger . . . nigger . . ."

Crispus . . . Attucks
Bullets in his chest
Red blood of freedom
Runnin' down his vest
"Nigger . . . nigger . . . nigger . . ."

—Frank Horne

A reasonably bright class would deduce from the pattern of the poem that the three were black men and heroes, so a long introduction might not be necessary. Slower groups might be told very briefly who the three men were, to help them understand the poem.

Voices The problems of specific poems are not insurmountable for a teacher who is sensitive to both the language and the students. Brief analysis will often suggest a teaching method. Reed's "Lessons of War," for instance, has two voices, the drill sergeant's and the recruit's. It does not, however, have the usual signals to indicate who speaks which lines. The voices flow into and out of one another, and the reader must determine who is speaking from what is said.

A discussion of responses to the poem may lead students to discover the pattern, but some groups, again, will require more help than others. The help may take the form of questions: "Where do you find the poem confusing?" "What do you hear in the poem?"

"Can you place the images in two groups?" "Can you find two lines that sound as if they were spoken by the same person?" The teacher could help more directly by reading the poem aloud, slightly emphasizing the change in voice. Or she might have students read the poem, assigning the sergeant's lines to one reader and the remaining lines to another.

Each strategy offers the students slightly more help than the one before—the trick is to help enough but not too much. If the students can understand the poem without much assistance, so much the better. Their success will be sufficient reward for the labor required. If the teacher finds herself doing all the work, leading the students through the thinking step by step, she may suspect that either the poem is too difficult or the class is being lazy.

BAD POETRY

Bad poetry can be almost as enjoyable as good poetry, though in a slightly different way. The contorted, contrived, and trite can give a satisfying sense of superiority. True, it is a little bloodthirsty to enjoy someone's weakness in this way, but it is pleasant nonetheless. Contemporary popular magazines are rich with doggerel in praise of god, country, motherhood, fidelity, family life, the democratic way, and assorted other vacuities. Perrine's *Sound and Sense* contains a chapter entitled "Bad Poetry and Good" that provides some examples. Perrine suggests pairing a good poem with a bad one in order to help students see the sentimentality and the bombast. Clough's "Say Not the Struggle Nought Availeth," for instance, is joined to "The Man Who Thinks He Can" ("If you think you are beaten, you are;/If you think you dare not, you don't . . . ," and so on).[3]

Such pairings help the students learn to evaluate and judge. Each poem serves as a base against which the other may be tested: the pretension of one reveals the sincerity of the other, and clichés and borrowed thoughts will seem dimmer and drabber when contrasted with originality and freshness. The distinctions, however, will not always be obvious, especially to inexperienced readers. Some will feel an honest liking for what strikes the teacher as a very poor poem. The purpose of these comparisons is not to homogenize the tastes of the students, making them agree with the teacher, but to give them an opportunity to compare the merits of different works. Although glaringly bad poems invite ridicule, it must be engaged in cautiously, so that students will not feel that the disparaging remarks apply to them as well. Intimidated by the severity of the teacher's judgments, they may grow less and less willing to risk their own, and this attitude will isolate them from the poem, preventing them from reading. Perrine warns:

> A final caution to students. In making judgments on literature, always be honest. Do not pretend to like what you really do not like. Do not be afraid to admit a liking for what you do like. A genuine enthusiasm for the second-rate is much better than false enthusiasm or no enthusiasm at all. Be neither hasty nor timorous in making your judgments. When you have attentively read a poem and thoroughly considered it, decide what you think. Do not hedge, equivocate, or try to find out others' opinions before forming your own. Having formed an opinion and expressed it, do not allow it to petrify. Compare your opinion *then* with the opinions of others; allow yourself to change it when convinced of its errors: in this way you learn. Honesty, courage, and humility are the necessary moral foundations for all genuine literary judgment.[4]

That caution might be extended to the teacher. Do not, by extravagant praise or severe condemnation, lead your students to accept judgments they do not feel. To do so is to encourage intellectual dishonesty, and thus to discourage learning. Instead, share your judgments with them in a way that encourages them to form reasoned judgments of their own.

THE SHORT STORY

One advantage of the poem is that it is usually short and compact. The class can cover it in one fifty-minute period: examine its diction and structure, explore the personal associations it evokes, and conclude with a sense of having finished something. Novels, on the other hand, are long. To examine one as if it were a poem, paying close attention to nearly every word, would be impossible—neither time nor the patience of students would allow it. The short story lies somewhere in between. It repays close analysis, because it must be tightly constructed to be successful, but it is more leisurely than a poem. Not quite so compressed and dense as poetry, the language of the short story often seems more relaxed and comfortable. Reading it is like listening to a friend's account of an interesting event. The short story seems less like a formal performance than the poem. At the same time, it is less complete than a novel. We can live in a novel, with its detailed characters and scenes. But we can't live in a short story—it goes by too quickly, always concentrating on the event or idea that sustains it.

PLOT

The short story shares the compression of the poem, but it is less the linguistic compression of rich, dense lines than a compression resulting from focus on one event or idea. Compare, for instance, the poem "The Man He Killed," by Hardy, and the short story "The Sniper," by O'Flaherty. They are both about the same idea—the strange irrationality of killing in warfare—and they are both brief, even for their respective genres. "The Man He Killed" is only twenty lines long, and "The Sniper" would fill no more than four or five pages. But they achieve their effects in different ways.

Hardy contrasts a possibility with a fact. The speaker and his victim might, had they met under other circumstances, have sat down together for a drink or two; instead, they met on the battlefield and the speaker killed his enemy. The first two stanzas present the alternatives, and in the third the speaker tries to explain why it should have worked out as it did. His first answer—"Because he was my foe"—fails to satisfy him. He tries to undergird it with expressions of assurance—"Just so; my foe of course he was;/That's clear enough; although"—but in that "although" and in the hesitation of the semicolons, his doubt shows itself. His foe was a man like the speaker himself, perhaps caught up in the war for reasons as insubstantial as his own—out of work, little else to do, and so off to war. It is a strange reason for killing a man, but the speaker has no other. In the end he says that war is "quaint and curious," and leaves it at that, trying to resolve his confusion with a label. But the label is inadequate justification for the killing.

How has the poem worked on us? It has given us a likeable fellow, serving for the moment as a soldier, and through him it has given us contrasting images, one of two men chatting amicably over a drink in a cheerful tavern and the other of those same two men trying to kill one another in battle. The first is the speaker's fantasy, and the second his account of what actually happened. The images are brief and compact. The battlefield is not there in gruesome detail, nor are the personalities of the men fully presented. We are neither revolted by the gore of warfare nor distressed by the death of a character we have come to like. Instead, there is a simple contrast between the possibility of friendship and the actuality of killing.

Much lies in the hesitation: "I shot him dead because—." The speaker pauses at that dash, as if uncertain of what is to follow. At the end of the stanza, "although" asks us to pause again and doubt the reason offered. Then, having been asked to doubt, we are given no explanations. The killing is dismissed in vacuous terms, "quaint and curious," and we are left to realize that behind this pleasant but empty-headed speaker there is another presence, one suggesting that the killings are senseless and ridiculous.

Thus, a few carefully balanced images set the scene for us. A dash, a conjunction, and "although" suggest an attitude underlying that of the speaker, and expressions like "foe" and "quaint and curious" confirm the presence of that attitude. A very few words have carried us to the perceptions of the last lines.

What about O'Flaherty's short story? It, too, is short. Is it compressed in the same way? Do individual phrases carry as much of the burden as does "quaint and curious" in Hardy's poem? Briefly, the scene for "The Sniper" is Dublin during the Irish civil war. The sniper from whose perspective the story is told discovers another sniper on a nearby rooftop and, after an exchange of fire, kills him, the body falling into the streets below. The victor then descends to the street, curious about the man he has killed, and discovers that it is his brother.

The story buys its effect cheaply, depending as it does on the coincidental relationship between the two men, and one might argue that the word "brother" carries as much weight as the phrase "quaint and curious." Certainly changing the last line, "Then the sniper turned over the dead body and looked into his brother's face," so that it ended with, "and looked into the man's face" would drain the story of much of its impact. But the shock of brother finding brother is prepared for not by one carefully balanced inner conversation but by a detailed account of the events leading up to the final scene. We see the sniper first lying on a rooftop, impatient, eager, so restless that he lights a cigarette despite the risk of exposing his location. He is then fired on, and finds and kills two targets of his own. Then he is wounded and has to bind up his wound and plan his escape. Event follows event; details of the setting accumulate along with information about the character. We stay with the man through much of the night, watching the armored car move into position beneath him, watching him kill the soldier and the woman who reveals his hiding place. In Hardy's poem the war is described only briefly: "ranged as infantry,/And staring face to face, I shot at him as he at me." The short story gives us much more detail:

> Cautiously he raised himself and peered over the parapet.
> There was a flash and a bullet whizzed over his head. He
> dropped immediately. He had seen the flash. It came from
> the opposite side of the street.[5]

The shooting here is described, not merely mentioned as it is in the poem. We see the movements, hear the bullets, see the flash.

The rhythms of the language follow the events. When events move quickly, the sentences move quickly—the machine gunner looks out of the car and is killed, the woman runs, the sniper fires again, and the woman falls, all in one short paragraph. But when he is wounded and falls back to the roof, six slow paragraphs creep by as he suffers the pain, binds the wound, and reflects on his situation. It is almost as though the writer is not organizing events for us but simply presenting them, allowing us to live through them as though we had been there on the roof. Of course, that's much too simple. The short story writer organizes, as does the poet, but somehow his presence is felt less strongly. Lacking the steadier rhythms of poetry, the prose of the short story seems more colloquial, more like the language of a friend simply telling.

Still, the story is compressed. We know only certain things about the man, the time, and the place; we see the events from only one perspective. And we see only one short episode—the sniper's activities the night he kills his brother. Although the language is not as condensed as that of the poem, the focus of the story results in a similar compression. In the story the eagerness of the sniper and the violence of the shootings are juxtaposed suddenly with the reminder that men have brothers, that families are torn apart by war. On the one hand are the excitement and savagery of war, on the other the concept of brotherhood and all that it connotes. The story implies a criticism of war much like that of Hardy's poem. People who could be friends (in the poem) or who are brothers (in the story) find themselves killing each other for the vaguest and least satisfying reasons. But while Hardy compresses his condemnation of war and killing into a set of contrasting images, O'Flaherty develops his idea in a carefully selected sequence of events.

The difference, of course, is plot, the core of the short story. Plot is action and movement. If a story is successful, it will be a carefully planned sequence, not a haphazard collection of events. The author's vision will govern what the reader sees. There are, of course, stories in which plot seems nonexistent, but we will ignore these for the moment. In the O'Flaherty story the plot is simple. It focuses on the excitement and pain of the fighting itself until the last sentence, when the sniper's unexpected discovery suddenly reminds us of another realm of experience. It is the contrast between that last event and those preceding it that raises the questions. It forces us to imagine for ourselves the thoughts and feelings that fill the mind of the sniper as he looks down at his brother.

The compression of the short story lies, then, in the selection and arrangement of events. The author chooses what to include, what to leave out, and what to gloss over based on what she wants the story to say. Students should recognize that these are choices and learn to consider the purpose of each. Such reflection will help them to understand both the craft and the vision of the writer.

CONFLICT

Plot depends on conflict, which in turn depends on character. The elements of fiction are intertwined. The plot of a story is often most easily discussed in terms of the conflict that arises—the imbalance, the opposition in motives or desires, that gives the story its tension and movement. It can be a simple physical conflict, such as one person attempting to rob another, who resists. Or it can be an intellectual or moral struggle—a banker plans a complex embezzlement scheme (the intellectual challenge) and at the same time wrestles with a conscience that condemns the theft (the ethical conflict). But without some sort of conflict, there is no story. Perfect harmony may be pleasant, but it is unlikely to be interesting—nothing moves, nothing happens, and there are no surprises. Such a story would find few readers.

In "The Sniper" we witness a gradual change in the nature of the conflict. The conflict moves, as if by steps, more deeply within the character. The struggle is first external, the physical conflict of men fighting. When the sniper is wounded, the struggle becomes internal as he tries to control the pain and continue fighting. Toward the end the conflict shifts from his body to his mind as he struggles with fear and disgust at having killed his enemy. O'Flaherty does not describe the conflict at the very end—he leaves us to imagine the thoughts and feelings that would accompany the killing of a brother —but the gradual shift from external to internal suggests that the final conflict is deep within the psyche. The killing of a brother must touch some deep, fundamental chord.

Simple classification of the nature of the conflict is an insufficient analysis of the events of a story. To categorize the conflict as man against man, man against nature, man against society, or man against himself is to take only the first halting step toward comprehending it. The reader must further consider what the nature of the conflict reveals about the vision of the writer. Does O'Flaherty see the drama and excitement of war as a screen obscuring much more significant issues? Or could it be that he intends no general condemnation of war, and makes no judgment about the rightness of the Irish civil war, but is simply dramatizing the sort of tragedy that may occur in such a battle? Such questions as these, based on the conflicts within the story, lead us to the crucial issues. The concept of conflict is simply a tool that may help us discuss our responses to the work.

CHARACTER

The investigation of conflict leads logically to the question of character. Conflict does not exist without character. A storm at sea may be fierce and tumultuous, but there is no conflict in the scene until we place characters in a boat on the waves and challenge them to survive. "The Sniper," with which we began, may not serve well to illustrate characterization in the short story. Its protagonist, the nameless soldier, is sketchily portrayed. We know only that he looks like a student, that he has a fanatical glint in his eye, that he shoots well, and that he is Republican rather than Free Stater. Still, we glimpse his feelings as the story proceeds, and so we may examine the interaction of character and plot.

In fact, the vagueness of the character seems to be consistent with the design of the story. We noted the absence of comments about the war—neither side is depicted as morally superior, and no purpose is given either for the war in general or for the sniper in particular. We don't know what he is fighting for, only that he is fighting. Further, he is essentially indistinguishable from his enemy; both are simply snipers. The lack of detail about both the war and the character suggests that they are not the central issues for the writer. He is apparently not concerned with the particulars of this war, nor does he seem to be interested in the details of this man's life. Instead, perhaps, he wants to represent all wars and all soldiers. Further detail about the character might make him too unique, too unlike you and me, allowing us to set his experience aside from our own. By leaving him largely undefined, O'Flaherty invites us to see him as everyman, perhaps to imagine ourselves in his role.

Students may notice that O'Flaherty doesn't name either his protagonist or the dead brother. What is the effect of not naming them? One consequence, of course, is to lessen the distinction between them. They are somehow alike. That observation suggests the further question, "Are there any significant distinctions between them?" The only apparent distinction between the two is that they are on different sides in the war, but no importance is attached to that. Neither side is identified as right, or superior, or virtuous—the men are simply enemies. The absence of a distinction between the two men, and the omission of any references to the causes or principles of the war, tends to make the war seem pointless, a meaningless exchange of lives. In that context, not naming the men suggests that the event portrayed here, although it is one specific encounter in a long war, can be generalized to other men. The two snipers, trying to kill one another, may be seen to represent all soldiers who fight, enthusiastically, but without awareness of the tragedies they inflict on others and on themselves. We cannot say, of course, that the writer purposely decided not to name his characters, but we can say that the absence of names enhances the effect of the story by suggesting that all men at war are in one sense killing their brothers.

Thus, even in a story where character seems thin, the characterization may help to indicate the significance of the events. In other stories, characterization may be the reader's dominant concern from the beginning. "The Stone Boy" by Berriault is a good example. A boy, Arnold, shoots and kills his brother in a careless hunting accident. The story focuses on Arnold's strange reaction to the event —he appears cold and unmoved by it—and the effect of this reaction on his parents and other people in the community. Clearly the major concern in the story is character. What accounts for the boy's behavior? Is it natural or unnatural? Are parents and other adults sufficiently understanding? Is the problem one of communication—that is, does Arnold simply find his emotion beyond his ability to express? Is it one of comprehension—does he not understand what has happened? Or is it that he just doesn't care?

"The Sniper" and "The Stone Boy" make an interesting pair, since in both stories one brother kills another. How, we might ask the students, do the two killings differ? How do the reactions of the surviving brothers differ? True, we do not see the reactions of the sniper, but we can imagine. How would we expect him to react? How do we think O'Flaherty would expect him to react? What clues do we have?

We might also ask students to explore the writers' characterization techniques. Which character do we come to know more fully? Most students will feel somewhat more knowledgeable about Arnold than about the sniper, even if his reactions to the death remain mysterious. How, then, do we come to know him better—how are we shown what he is like? The students may observe that Arnold is carefully described, and his feelings, even those he does not articulate, are presented to us in some spots ("To dispel emphatically his uneasy advantage over his sleeping brother, he threw himself on the hump of Eugie's body"). Moreover, he is represented in his own dialogue and in the speech and actions of other characters. Balanced against the sparse characterization in "The Sniper" these techniques add up to a fairly complete description of Arnold.

A reminder—the techniques of characterization are not important by themselves, and they should not be taught in a way that distracts students from the stories. But if knowledge of these techniques, as of other technical elements of literature, is acquired during the exploration of responses, it may add to the exploration. As students react to Arnold and the people surrounding him, they will seek evidence for their reactions in the text. It is important that they know how to evaluate the evidence they find there.

For instance, a student may conclude that Arnold doesn't care about his brother's death and may point to several remarks that seem to substantiate the observation: " 'Not a tear in his eye,' said Andy," and " 'He don't give a hoot, is that how it goes?' asked Sullivan." That student needs to realize that the comments of characters in the story are not necessarily accurate and complete. Their points of view should be weighed in the balance with information from other sources in the story. Portraying one character through the observations of others is a powerful technique, but in most cases the judgment of others will not be final or conclusive—it is simply one bit of data to keep in mind.

Berriault gives us no answers about Arnold, but she does carry us through a sequence of events and conversations which offer some insight into his feelings and thoughts. Clearly the most interesting material for drawing inferences about him is in the last lines. Arnold has come to his mother's door in the middle of the night, presumably to tell her how he feels about killing his brother, and has been sent away with an angry remark. At the story's conclusion his mother asks him what he wanted.

"I didn't want nothing," he said flatly.

Then he went out the door and down the back steps, his legs trembling from the fright his answer gave him.[6]

Why does that simple answer frighten him? What does it imply for his future relations with his family? The answer lies not in one line of the story but in the knowledge of Arnold that accumulates throughout. Our understanding of his character depends on observations and information gathered from every scene.

We began our discussion of the short story with a tentative effort to distinguish it from the poem. It is not, finally, distinguishable from either the poem on one side or the novel on the other. All of them are ranges on one spectrum. We could probably find twenty literary works that could be arranged at equal intervals on a scale, with the lyric poem at one end, the short story somewhere in the middle, and the novel at the other end. The lyric might be represented by one of Shakespeare's sonnets, or perhaps by Wordsworth's

"My Heart Leaps Up." As we move toward narrative, we would find "The Highwayman" and "The Rime of the Ancient Mariner," poems that tell stories. Somewhere along the line might be Poe's "Fall of the House of Usher," with its sonorous, poetic opening lines, and then less poetic stories like Hemingway's "The Killers." Beyond this short piece we would find stories spanning several episodes, like Chekhov's "The Lady with the Pet Dog." By degrees the stories would lengthen, approaching the complexity of the novel. Henry James's "The Beast in the Jungle" is either a long short story or a short novel. Tolstoy's *The Death of Ivan Illich* is longer still. Ultimately we would arrive at *War and Peace*.

Thus the genres blend together to some degree, sharing techniques and subject matter. As we move off in other directions, too, the transitions are smooth and gradual. Some stories contain mostly dialogue, so that they approach the form of the play. Some novels are so full of historical fact or autobiographical detail that they seem to blend history and fiction, or autobiography and fiction, as in the realm of television the "docu-drama" blends documentary and drama.

As we move from the short story to the novel, the blending of genres is obvious. Both are narratives; they seem to differ only in length and scope. But despite their similarities and their common strategies, there are some significant differences between them.

THE NOVEL

In our brief glance at the short story we mentioned plot, the events that form the foundation of the story; character, the imitation of person through dialogue; description; action; and conflict, the energy and purpose in the interaction of character and plot. Much that was said of plot, character, and conflict in the short story applies to the novel. Like the short story, the novel is narrative. Length alone, however, is a significant difference, and affects all of these elements.

Plot provides an example. Short stories tend to emphasize one event, issue, or idea. "The Stone Boy" is about an accidental killing and its aftermath. The later scenes all develop the consequences of the killing. Had the story grown into a novel, we might have followed Arnold through adolescence into maturity, perhaps into old age. Even if the killing remained the most important event in the tale, it is unlikely that it would have occupied our attention throughout the story. A novel is too long to be devoted entirely to one incident, though the writer might often return to the crucial episode, tracing its influence on Arnold's life. The novel has a wider scope than the short story. It usually covers more time, more events, and more characters.

That breadth has several consequences. One is that novels typically convey the impression of reality more effectively than short stories or poems. A poem is clearly a performance, an art form, and a short story is an episode, a short segment cut out of a larger tapestry. But a novel, especially once we are deeply involved in it, is as rich and full and detailed as life. We learn the characters' habits and their tastes in food, music, and entertainment; we rush through their busy moments and grow bored along with them in the dull moments between; we see their friends and family. We are immersed in detail, just as we are in our own lives. The short story gives us selected detail, just enough to carry the incident narrated. The novel gives us selected detail, too, but it doesn't seem to. It seems to give us everything and thus leaves us with the impression that we are living in the world it creates.

Many readers report a sense of dissociation after finishing a novel that has captivated them. It is, they say, like coming out of one world into another. The room in which they sit seems, for an instant, less real than the imaginary world they have just left. That may be part of the reason for the popularity of series books and sequels—readers may wish to re-enter a world they have come to enjoy. The sense of reality in the novel carries with it a penalty, though, for unsophisticated readers. They may lose track of the patterns and themes in the novel that give it meaning, just as they may lose track of the patterns and themes in their own lives. A poem is clearly and unmistakably a vision of a writer, but many novels just seem to happen.

However, it is important to maintain a sense of the author's intent if one is to learn from a work. Unsophisticated readers, forgetting that the novel is a constructed work of art, may submit it to crude tests, or worse, not question it all all. They may, for example, judge it against their own notion of reality, a perfectly valid way to begin. Finding that they don't know people like the characters portrayed, they may dismiss the work either as idle fantasy or as something irrelevant to their own experience. Or they may accept without adequate reflection the picture the work presents. They may fail to question the heroism or villainy of characters identified as heroes or villains, accepting superficial stereotypes in place of real characters. They may neglect to explore the codes of ethics implicit in a work. They may, in other words, fail to think about the novel as a vision, a literary work that might be worth examining. Treated thus, the novel may entertain them, but it loses its power to enrich their thought.

One of the teacher's goals must be to encourage reflection on the novel as an art form so that students come to realize that it is a vision of reality and not reality itself. That is perhaps best done by encouraging them to test their own visions against that of the work. They will quite likely respond to questions about the logic of events and the nature of the characters. Do people behave as these characters behave? Would you, in similar circumstances, act that way? Do events really follow one another as these do? Are these events coincidental, or are there cause-and-effect relationships among them? Are they exaggerated or diminished by the telling? Such questions, phrased appropriately for the book and the class, lead almost inevitably to discussion of the form of the novel.

PLOT

Questions about the logic of events, for instance, are questions about plot. That is perhaps most easily demonstrated in mystery or adventure novels—Conrad's *The Secret Sharer*, for example, or Collins's *The Moonstone*, or a contemporary novel such as Bennett's *The Dangling Witness*, Ludlum's *The Bourne Identity*, or Forsyth's *The Day of the Jackal*. In these books, the dominant issue is often, "What happens next?" or perhaps "Why did these events happen?" This easily leads to questions not about the events themselves, but about the guiding vision from which they grow. "What has the writer told us, and what has she failed to tell us, perhaps intentionally?" "What scenes or episodes has she emphasized, by giving them a great deal of attention?" And finally, "How might they be connected to one another? Do they reveal a pattern?"

Much of the reading of a novel is a search for patterns in the mass of detail. If no patterns exist, the reader is likely to be very unhappy with the work. It will be a shapeless, pointless collection of episodes, and although that may be much like real life, it is not satisfying in fiction. Sometimes, however, an apparent lack of pattern is itself a pattern. A novel like Remarque's *All Quiet on the Western Front* may leave some readers dissatisfied for this reason. *All Quiet on the Western Front* is a war story, but it is not a story of adventure, triumph, or even survival. Raised on television war movies, students may expect to read about the excitement of battle or the nobility of fighting for one's country. Instead, they find a series of events that seem loosely strung together. There is a battle here, a gas attack there, an advance that seems to go nowhere, and a retreat. Several events may make a strong and lasting impression, especially the encounter between Paul, the novel's main character, and the French soldier. But the events seem related only because they happen to

Paul and his friends—there is no sense of progress in the book. There is simply the constant filth, hunger, and dying.

Finally Paul is killed, on a quiet day with little action anywhere, pointlessly, uselessly, and almost completely unnoticed. Where, the students may ask, has the book taken us? The answers to that question lie in patterns that the students may have observed without realizing their significance. Events in the book do not seem to build on each other as we might expect them to. The battle does not move. We see no strategy, no contest of opposing minds, no brilliance leading to victory or blundering leading to defeat. But there is nonetheless a pattern.

Part of it is in the absence of the perspective that would allow us to see the larger design. We see the war through the eyes of a front-line infantryman; his perceptions fill the book. And what he sees is endless killing without any apparent point, continual suffering, gradual decay of the spirit, and finally his own gloomy death that seems to matter to no one, least of all himself. That pattern, although it does not build to a grand climax in which mysteries are solved, wrongs are righted, or justice is satisfied, nevertheless does make a point. It suggests that war, for the foot-soldier, is not that kind of noble, exciting, patriotic adventure. The purposes, causes, and ultimate results of the war recede into relative insignificance for him in the face of other matters. He is reduced by war to the point at which death seems a relief.

We are not trying to provide a comprehensive interpretation of *All Quiet on the Western Front*. The point here is simply that identifying the patterns of events and characters in a novel may help us understand the author's intended message.

THEME

The meaning growing out of these relationships among the events and characters in a work is the theme. Theme registers first as a set of impressions, feelings, or thoughts left by the work. As those feelings and thoughts are articulated and clarified, they become a statement of the theme.

The concept of theme poses at least two problems. Students may try to simplify it to one word or a short phrase—in the case of *All Quiet on the Western Front*, "war," or perhaps "War is hell." These may be true enough, but they are not complex enough to do justice to the work. Students may also extend them much further than the work justifies, or credit them with more authority than the work merits. Teachers, on the other hand, sometimes divorce the concept of theme from questions of personal significance, asking students to accept a statement bleached of relevance to their own thoughts and lives. An interpretation, whether it owes more to the words on the page or the personal experience that informs the thought, must recognize both the mind that creates it and the text that constrains it.

Oversimplification The problem of the oversimplified statement can be frustrating for a teacher. Seeing subtleties that the students miss, aware of implications they have neglected, the teacher may grow impatient with their willingness to accept crude generalizations. She may help them awaken to other possibilities in several ways. One simple technique is to have them compare the statements they have offered. Suppose, for instance, that a reading of *All Quiet on the Western Front* has produced comments like the following:

- War is hell.
- War is disgusting.
- War is unjustifiable.
- War is not very exciting.
- War hurts the young men, not the politicians responsible.
- War is degrading.

Asked to identify the similarities and differences among these brief statements, students may discover ideas they did not express at first. For instance, the two statements, "War is disgusting" and "War is degrading," are obviously similar. However, the student who finds war disgusting may point out the mud, the bad food, the lack of sanitation, the inability to sleep comfortably. The student who finds it degrading may point out the reduction of men to the status of tools, the loss of self-determination, and the obligation to kill other men. The elaboration reveals the differences in the two students' ideas. We could debate which insights are more significant, but it might be more useful to combine the observations of each student into a more complicated statement of the theme. Reducing the meaning of the work to one word obscures what the text has to offer, but drawing contrasts among such statements may encourage the students to look for details that will flesh out their interpretations.

Students could, of course, be asked directly to supply such details: "Why do you say that the theme of *All Quiet on the Western Front* is 'War is hell'?" By contrasting the different statements of theme that arise in a group, however, we make use of the students' natural desire to understand each other and explain themselves as well as their wish to comprehend the text.

Stating the theme trades specificity for control. We must give up a certain amount of detail for the sake of a manageable summary. Still, students must recognize that the thematic statement is not an end in itself but a tool useful in thinking about the mass of material the book offers. Its purpose is not to dismiss detail but to organize it. If it is too simplistic to contribute anything to the discussion, then the effort is wasted.

Overextending the theme is a danger related, perhaps, to the tendency to oversimplify. *All Quiet on the Western Front* clearly does not glorify war; it depicts it as dirty, degrading, demoralizing work. But would it be fair to Remarque to assert that he condemns all warfare? He has depicted one war, or rather, part of one war, from the perspective of a foot-soldier, but that is hardly a basis for asserting that he would consider all wars unjustifiable. He has not commented on the purposes of the war—they are beyond the scope of his novel—and though readers may have opinions about the morality of war, and might use *All Quiet on the Western Front* to initiate discussion of those opinions, it would not be legitimate to attribute to Remarque ideas that he did not express. Students must learn to push inferences only as far as the work will carry them.

Individual Response and Theme   The second problem—that of the relevance of personal experience to the discussion of theme—arises naturally from the teacher's desire to train students to read accurately. For this purpose she may insist that they be faithful to the text in forming interpretations. That faithfulness, however, does not require abandoning their own perceptions or ignoring their feelings or associations. Rather, it means defining the relationship between these associations and the text. Statements of theme will thus vary, and the sophisticated reader is likely to accept the validity of many of the variations.

Let us return to "The Stone Boy" to illustrate the point. We might read this as the story of someone unable to cope with his situation. Arnold cannot understand or react to his brother's death; it is as though the event is so far beyond his comprehension that it does not register upon his emotions at all. Because he does not demonstrate the emotional response those around him expect to see, they reject him. This view might lead us to a thematic statement like "You must respond to an event in a socially approved manner, regardless of your real feelings, or you are likely to be ostracized."

That is a reasonable interpretation of the story, although it neglects several particulars. Consider, however, how the thematic impact of the story might differ for someone in circumstances like those of one of the characters. A parent, for instance, might note the importance of the moment Arnold goes to his mother's door and is sent away. He is apparently beginning to react to the killing at that moment, but his mother's rebuff destroys the opportunity, silencing him and isolating him from her. This may lead our reader to include in her thematic summary some reference to the fragility of human relations and the possible catastrophic consequences of even a small gesture of irritation such as the mother commits in her anger and sorrow. That interpretation might borrow strength from the similarities between the mother's lapse and Arnold's. Dragging the rifle through the fence is a small carelessness, resulting, perhaps, from haste or impatience. But its consequences, too, are disastrous. The pattern suggests that very little things, insignificant remarks, moments of slight inattention, might yield horrible fruit. It is a theme that a parent would be interested in; it respects both her unique viewpoint and the content of the story. And it may give the story personal significance by helping her shape her own perceptions and behavior. Good literature ought to do as much for the reader.

Another reader, a teacher, might tend to emphasize the inarticulateness of the characters. Arnold cannot speak of the killing, even to say that he does not understand his own feelings. His parents are unable to help him; their inadequacy is vividly represented by the father's final, feeble remark to the sheriff: " 'The gun ain't his no more.' " The sheriff can only say that Arnold is either a moron or reasonable beyond his comprehension, crudely oversimplifying the possible reasons for Arnold's strange behavior. The teacher, aware of the power of language to ferret out information, to express feeling, to shape reasons, to comfort, to strengthen bonds between people, could not help noticing that the characters in this story seem totally incapable of using language for any of these purposes. She might see the failure to communicate as one theme of the story.

Theme is not purely in the work, on the page. It resides in the interaction of the reader and the text. Thus, different readers may see different themes in a work or state the same theme differently. If both teacher and students recognize this, theme can be a useful tool in discussing a work of fiction.

OTHER GENRES

Discussion of genre is exceptionally difficult. The distinctions are subtle and elusive, and a full treatment of them is far beyond the scope of this text. This chapter has described the characteristics and demands of a few genres, as well as some of the concepts useful in discussing them. Teachers who plan to teach works from other genres—drama, epic, essay, or the like—might explain briefly to the class the important features of each. If they keep in mind that their purpose is not to teach the technicalities of genre analysis but to bring student and text together in intellectually and emotionally productive ways, then worries about the technicalities will diminish. They will be able to encourage students to observe the techniques of the writers as they raise and examine questions about human behavior. Knowledge of the genres will develop from and support the search for meaning.

NOTES

1. Richard Lanham, *Style: An Anti-Textbook* (New Haven, Conn.: Yale University Press, 1974).
2. Abraham Bernstein, *Teaching English In High School* (New York: Random House, 1961).
3. Laurence Perrine, *Sound and Sense* (New York: Harcourt, Brace and World, 1956), pp. 214–30.
4. Perrine, pp. 218–19.
5. Liam O'Flaherty, "The Sniper," in *Types of Literature*, ed. Robert A. Bennett, Verda Evans, and Edward J. Gordon (Lexington, Mass.: Ginn and Company, 1979), pp. 2–4.
6. Gina Berriault, "The Stone Boy," in *Man in the Fictional Mode, Book 3*, ed. Hannah Beate Haupt (Evanston, Ill.: McDougal, Littell & Co., 1970).

Adolescent Literature 5

In the last chapter we argued that a class focusing on responses to the literature might logically be led to investigate the technical elements of literary art. We discussed genres to illustrate how such issues could fit in naturally with response-based teaching. Other topics could arise as well—meter, rhyme, historical influences, and the like. But it is not our purpose to set forth that information in detail; others have already done so. The teacher will notice when such background is needed and supply it, always in the context of students' responses to a work.

Our topic here is the literature itself. In the last chapter we discussed the three genres most often taught in high school literature classes. We also mentioned that two categories—adolescent fiction and viewed literature—would be considered apart from the question of genre. Though often overlooked, these categories have special relevance to response-based teaching, since they are the types of literature that tend to attract students outside of class. They are broad enough to require extended treatment, and we will devote a chapter to each.

IMPORTANCE OF ADOLESCENT LITERATURE

If we are to begin our teaching with students' responses, we need literary works that provoke responses, stimulating students to think, feel, and talk. Without such works, awakening interest in discussion and writing can be very difficult. The teacher is forced to trick students into temporary interest in something that doesn't really appeal to them. Planning becomes a search for games and gimmicks to hold the attention if not engage the mind and heart. Given a text inappropriate for his students, there is little else a teacher can do.

A quick glance at typical secondary school English curricula will suggest that the literature has not been chosen primarily for its appeal to the students. Senior high school programs, for instance, are often organized historically. British literature is taught in the twelfth grade, beginning with *Beowulf* and "The Seafarer" and continuing as far into the present as time allows. American literature, often in the eleventh grade, begins with sinners dangling above Jonathan Edwards' fiery pit and works its way forward until June or the censor's fiery pit stops it.

This is not to say that the literature found in historically arranged courses is necessarily uninteresting—simply that it was selected for its historical suitability rather than its interest for the students. Historical significance, however, does not guarantee personal significance. Secondary school students may not have the knowledge or interest to appreciate the progress of literary art, and they may not share the interests and concerns of the writers who have found their way into the standard anthologies. Students who are brought too early to writers they might later appreciate often report their unhappiness. Milton simply may not reward the efforts of young students, and even such an adventure story as "The Rime of the Ancient Mariner," taught too soon, may leave them cold and indifferent.

Many readers can recall responding differently to a work at different times in their lives. Young people read *Gulliver's Travels* as an exciting fantasy, a strange adventure in an imaginary world. When these same readers have grown and matured, Gulliver is a vastly different character and his adventures assume another meaning. Maturity accounts for the differences in the readings. If younger readers were expected to analyze the satire of the work, to read it as a commentary on the social mores of the time, they might respond less sympathetically. *Gulliver's Travels,* however, is one of those rich works that appeal in various ways—it is both an adventure story and a social commentary. Few works are quite as flexible, and I mention *Gulliver's Travels* not because it is typical but because it is atypical. The difference in our readings of *Gulliver's Travels* as young children and as adults indicates the gulf between childhood and maturity and suggests the importance of considering that gulf in planning literature instruction.

There is, fortunately, a growing body of literature well suited for adolescent readers. It has not always been considered respectable, and by many it still is not, but literature written for adolescents has, in the past several decades, attracted the attention of many librarians and teachers as well as the students themselves. Writers who did not originally think of themselves as writers for young adults have been drawn into the field by the responsiveness of adolescent readers and the encouragement of publishers, who have found a profitable market in readers of junior high and high school age. Schools are beginning to include works of adolescent literature in the English program, sometimes as books to be discussed in classes, but more often as supplemental or independent reading.

In spite of the debate over adolescent fiction, some works have been so well received that they have been recast as movies, perhaps the ultimate compliment for a literary work in this era. Sheila Schwartz's *Like Mother, Like Me*, Bette Greene's *Summer of My German Soldier*, and S. E. Hinton's *The Outsiders* are three such works. Literature for adolescents has also begun to attract the attention of scholars —Schwartz's *Teaching Adolescent Literature* was published in 1979, and Donelson and Nilsen's comprehensive and readable *Literature for Today's Young Adults* in 1980. Literature for adolescents is, in other words, now a significant body of works that merits the attention of English teachers.

Doing them justice in one chapter presents a complicated problem. A historical treatment would require us to include books that might not be as useful to teachers as more recent works, and since our concern in this text is teaching literature, we'll refer those interested in the history to Donelson and Nilsen's scholarly work. A comprehensive survey of the available adolescent literature would fill not a chapter, but a large book, and since it would be immediately out of date we will forego that alternative as well. A close analysis of a few works would be both too narrow and too detailed to be useful. Whatever course we choose, we must compromise between breadth and depth and between permanence and currency.

We'll compromise by examining several works grouped according to two of the most controversial themes in contemporary adolescent literature, and follow that discussion with introductory bibliographies, also organized thematically. That arrangement will accomplish several aims. First, it will allow us to organize a sprawling and disorderly collection of books into manageable categories. Second, the categories, since they represent some of the issues confronted during adolescence, may help the teacher find appropriate books for specific students. Finally, the thematic approach will allow us to look closely at a few texts and may suggest connections between these works and the standard English curriculum.

Thematic grouping has three serious drawbacks. First, individual works are often hard to categorize. A book may develop many themes, and as we have argued, different themes often emerge for different readers. Thus, in a sense, placing a book in a thematic slot means trying to respond and think for someone else. But if we agree to keep in mind that the assignment to categories is simply one reader's judgment, not meant as a substitute for anyone's own reading of the books, then the arbitrariness of the placement will remain obvious and harmless.

A second drawback lies in the categories themselves. They too will seem arbitrary, and they will be. Countless ways of ordering the material are possible, and each one will incline us to see certain features of the works and neglect others. We might, for instance, tend to overlook a good book that does not fit neatly into one of our categories, just as a biologist discussing cats and dogs may not be happy with the cheetah, which has some features of both. A different set of categories might encourage us to focus on that same book, as the biologist discussing predators that stalk and those that chase would use the cheetah as one of his principal illustrations. The categories will both emerge from and shape the reading of the works. Again, we should simply remain aware of that to avoid deceiving ourselves into thinking that there is anything inevitable about the way we choose to arrange the literature.

A third drawback of the thematic arrangement is the number of possible categories: sexuality, coming of age, race and ethnic identity, family, alienation, illness, death, suicide, insanity, fantasy, science fiction, gothic romance, the occult, power, independence, handicaps, adventure, westerns, religious experience, violence, humor. . . . The list could go on indefinitely. For brevity's sake we will discuss only two possible groups and only a few of the works that might be placed within each one. We'll then list other recommended works of adolescent literature that fit the theme, make some suggestions about keeping up with this rapidly growing body of literature, and end with a short bibliography of both adolescent literature and popular adult fiction in several other categories mentioned above.

SEXUALITY

Someone once commented that if biographers were to do justice to the sexual lives of their subjects, their biographies would have to be two or three times longer than they usually are. Much of that additional text would have to be given to adolescence, when the preoccupation with sexuality seems to be as strong and distracting as it will ever be. As the restraints on writers for adolescents have eased, it is not surprising that many of them have chosen to write about the turmoil of emerging sexuality. Nor is it surprising that some have found their books tucked securely away in a dark corner of the librarian's desk. Sexuality is clearly a sensitive issue no matter how it may be treated, and the current adolescent fiction treats it in a variety of ways.

Consider, for example Judy Blume's *Forever . . .* , a novel that has probably aroused more debate than any other work of adolescent fiction dealing with the issue of sex. It was first published in 1975, and it had angered some readers by the time they finished the first sentence. It begins, "Sybil Davison has a genuis I. Q. and has been laid by at least six different guys."[1]

This sentence was not calculated to slide unnoticed past watchful guardians of youth, virtue, and virginity, whose protests alerted young readers to the possibility that there was something interesting here. There is, as any English teacher knows, no surer way to entice a student to read a book than to warn him of its sinful, wicked content. *Forever . . .* became immensely popular.

The book is about a young girl's first sexual experience. Katherine, the protagonist and narrator, meets Michael, they fall in love, their friendship grows and then dies. Much of the book is devoted to the sexuality of the relationship, which is treated frankly and directly. The affair is neither idyllic nor catastrophic, neither glamorous nor sordid, neither solemn nor comical. Blume seems to have taken care to present the story with a minimum of intrusive comment. There is, for instance, no obvious moralizing about the rightness or wrongness of Katherine's sexual involvement. Even her parents, who could so easily be cast in the role of guardians of traditional morality, make no speeches about the virtue of virtue. Although they are appropriately concerned for Katherine's happiness and safety, they seem also to respect her autonomy and integrity. Katherine's mother discusses sex with her openly, if nervously. She advises Katherine to think carefully and act cautiously, but beyond that, she is unwilling to prescribe how her daughter should behave:

> "It's up to you to decide what's right and what's wrong. . . . I'm not going to tell you to go ahead but I'm not going to forbid it either. It's too late for any of that. I expect you to handle it with a sense of responsibility though, either way."[2]

The absence of a strong condemnation of the sexual activity annoys some critics. They find nothing in the book, either in the beliefs the characters express or in the outcome of events, to frighten young readers about sexuality. Katherine does not get pregnant, does not contract venereal disease, is not ostracized by her friends, thrown out of school, or otherwise tramatized by her experience with Michael. The more vehement critics of the book would wish on her at least one or two of those misfortunes to punish her affair.

If Blume does not condemn the sexual involvement, neither does she glamorize it. Michael and Katherine's first experiences are clumsy rather than ecstatic. They do have to worry about pregnancy, discovery, and their own ineptness. Their first effort is rudely interrupted by Michael's overexcitement, and they must dress and drive to the drugstore to buy more condoms before they can try again. The evening leaves Michael embarrassed and Katherine disappointed, but relieved:

> "I'm no longer a virgin. I'll never have to go through the first-time business again and I'm glad—I'm so glad it's over! Still, I can't help feeling let down. Everybody makes such a big thing out of actually doing it. But Michael is probably right—this takes practice."[3]

Her experience is not the fireworks display of old, third-rate romantic films. It is not perfect or other-worldly. But it is a beginning, and they go from there to more satisfactory experiences.

Blume's treatment of sex is balanced. She represents it neither as pure evil nor as pure pleasure, but as a natural though confusing and complicated process. Her failure to condemn angers those who view literature as an instrument for indoctrination, rather than an art form to promote thought. They see her unwillingness to condemn as tacit approval, or even advocacy, of sexual experimentation, and they conclude that the book is immoral. It could be argued, however, that *Forever . . .* neither condemns nor advocates, but simply describes the early sexual experiences of one girl. What it does seem to advocate is the sense of responsibility mentioned by Katherine's mother. Katherine does act responsibly. She is careful and considerate of both Michael and herself; she neither uses him nor is used by him. Ultimately, she is responsible enough to withdraw from the relationship when she decides it can no longer be satisfactory for both of them. But she does not regret it—it has done her no harm and has presumably helped her grow.

Regardless of what the book advocates or fails to advocate, it is likely to provoke thought and discussion. It deals clearly and vividly with an issue that interests almost every adolescent. If the teacher's concern is not to shape the attitudes of his students but to teach literature, then he may be able to use students' interest in the sexual content to involve them in the literature. Curious about first sexual experiences, the students may be led to look carefully at the characters, examining their motives and their behavior. They may wish to consider whether the portrayal is realistic, whether it neglects some aspects of the experience and overemphasizes others. They may know of, or may have experienced, sexual encounters similar to or different from Blume's story. Their parents may have attitudes toward their children's maturing that can profitably be compared with those of Katherine's parents. If students can be enticed to consider some of these issues, they will be engaging in literary analysis of the most significant sort—analysis inspired by a desire to understand. To judge how realistic the work is they will have to consider their own notions about sexual experience. Blume's novel raises enough of the issues, and treats them delicately enough, that it may be considered an invitation to think rather than an effort to indoctrinate.

Another book dealing with adolescent sexuality has been accused of presenting a less balanced view. Head's *Mr. and Mrs. Bo Jo Jones*, written about ten years before Blume's *Forever . . .* , concerns not so much the developing sexuality of the characters as its result—an unwanted pregnancy. Where Blume is direct and explicit in describing Katherine's first sexual experience, Head is roundabout:

> . . . when Bo Jo said, "Let's go have a look at the ocean,"
> I don't even remember feeling daring about it or giving it
> a thought one way or another. I trusted Bo Jo. I trusted
> myself. I had no idea that there actually is a point of no
> return.
>
> Afterwards I was shattered. And furious with Bo Jo.
> And furious with myself.[4]

Somewhere in between those two paragraphs is July's first sexual encounter, signaled by the word "afterwards." To realize what has occurred, the reader must pull together several clues, for nowhere up to this point in the story has the narrator referred to sex. She does refer to love and marriage, but she says only that she has strong ideas about them. She speaks of "my downfall" without telling us precisely what it is. Then, in the passage quoted above, she mentions a "point of no return" and says that afterwards she was shattered. For the reader to infer that July's downfall is sex, he must be able to share, at least imaginatively, the attitudes toward sex implicit in her words. He must make the imaginative leap from "shattered" to sexuality. The "mock reader," to borrow Gibson's term for the reader implied by the text,[5] is one who shares July's vision that sex is downfall, shattering, shameful, too offensive to be spoken of directly. Only that vision organizes and interprets those insubstantial clues.

Some of Head's readers, perhaps more now than in 1967 when the book was first released, find the attitudes it reflects uncomfortable and demeaning. They argue that sex need not be seen as degrading and destructive, that it need not result in pregnancy, as it does in this story, and that it need not be spoken of coyly and obliquely. It does not have to just happen as it does in Head's book; people can judge their own readiness for it and can foresee and control the possible consequences. They may point out that Head's book presents a very narrow view—her characters never consider contraception, or afterwards abortion or adoption. Instead, their path seems preordained: sex will lead to pregnancy, which will lead to marriage and all the complications it must involve for adolescents. In short, some readers argue that the book sustains an antiquated notion of sex, promoting the foolish belief that carefully cultivated ignorance and abstinence are the best safeguards for the young.

Forever . . . and *Mr. and Mrs. Bo Jo Jones* show dramatically different attitudes toward sexuality, but there are other interesting differences between the two books. The adult characters contrast neatly. In *Forever . . .* , Katherine's mother speaks openly with her about sex, showing respect for Katherine's judgment and responsibility. Her grandmother is also helpful, giving her information about contraception and encouraging her to think. Her parents do not abdicate all responsibility, and late in the novel arrange for Michael and Katherine to be separated for a time, but they do not try to control her completely. The parents in *Mr. and Mrs. Bo Jo Jones*, on the other hand, try repeatedly to engineer their children's lives. July's parents, when they hear that she is pregnant and married, push for annulment of the marriage and adoption for the baby. They decide between themselves, " 'Whatever your answer . . . we are agreed that an annulment is still the only solution.' "[6] They are planning for their children, not with them. Katherine's parents, although they have opinions, are willing to discuss them with their daughter. The parents in *Mr. and Mrs. Bo Jo Jones* come to their children with decisions made—they speak to inform or persuade, not to discuss.

The differences between the two novels—in the motives and reasoning of the characters, the logic of events, and the relationships —should promote thought about both the fictional worlds and the real world. If the adolescent readers are interested in sexuality, as they usually are, then they are very likely to be interested in the characters and events of these stories. This interest will make them more likely to read sensitively and carefully.

Of course, there is some danger that provocative works like *Forever . . .* and *Mr. and Mrs. Bo Jo Jones* will be lost in the discussion they stimulate. The talk can drift from the issues raised by the text to issues and anecdotes in general, growing aimless and shallow. Some of that drift is inevitable in a class that tries to deal with individual students' responses, but too much of it reduces the discussion to cocktail conversation. The teacher must keep in mind that his job is not to teach about sex, but about literature. If sex is an issue in the literature, it must be considered, but the primary point is to teach students to find pleasure and wisdom in reading. To do that, they must test the fictional world against their own. If students lose themselves in daydreams and reminiscences, they may have to be encouraged to weigh those thoughts against the work. If the discussion yields only stale arguments and memorized platitudes, then gentle questioning, to raise doubts about prefabricated visions of the world, may be necessary.

Testing one work against another establishes a context in which the encouragement and questioning come more easily. July and Katherine might be compared with one another. How do their attitudes toward sex differ? Do they want the same things out of life? (Students may notice that July is happy to work as a secretary to put her husband through college, while Katherine seems determined to make a life for herself and will not accept a secondary role.) How do Michael and Bo Jo compare? What are the differences in their attitudes toward sex and toward the girls? Are they both responsible? Are they responsible in the same way? How might each view the actions of the other? What can you infer about the attitudes of the authors and how they compare? (Students might be asked to write or act out a discussion between the two writers, perhaps with a third student as moderator.) How might Michael and July have reacted to one another; how might Bo Jo and Katherine? Would either of these recombinations work?

More specific questions might also yield good discussion. For example, the class could be asked how Michael and Katherine might have dealt with pregnancy. Would they have told anyone? How might they break the news to their parents? How might their parents respond?

Delicacy is, of course, demanded. Some students, even entire classes, may be reluctant to talk about these matters, and their reticence should be respected. Literature classes should not intrude on students' privacy. The literary work itself helps guard against intrusiveness by providing other people and events to talk about. Students need not speak of their own attitudes—they can instead explore those of the characters. This enables them to discuss delicate matters like sexuality without uncomfortable disclosures about themselves. Occasionally a teacher may notice students talking about the actions of a fictional character with a conviction that suggests strong personal feelings, although they may never refer to what they believe or how they would act. That talk may be useful and interesting for the students despite their care to keep their comments safe and objective.

If, however, students are comfortable with the group and confident in their opinions, there is no reason to keep them from speaking of their own beliefs and values. They may want to compare their attitudes with those of the characters, to consider how they would handle problems that arise in the books. Here again, though, delicacy is demanded. The teacher should, if possible, help students avoid revealing thoughts or experiences that may later embarrass them. They will have to continue to work and play with the others in the class, and, as in any social group, they may find the information used maliciously. If the teacher senses that students are speaking too openly, revealing too much about themselves or their families, then he should find some way of tactfully interrupting or diverting the conversation.

A well-timed request to write rather than discuss is often useful in such cases. The energy produced by the discussion can be transferred to the task of writing. Students may not be eager to abandon the ease of talk for the labor of composition, but if they do it they may find that they write with unaccustomed vigor and consider what they have written important. Putting ideas on paper rather than speaking them also allows the students time to decide rationally whether their thoughts should be shared or whether it is wisest to keep them for journal entries and private conversations.

Both *Forever . . .* and *Mr. and Mrs. Bo Jo Jones* have enough merit to stand on their own in the English curriculum, but they might also be grouped with more traditional works. Hawthorne's *The Scarlet Letter* is the most obvious possibility, since it too deals with sexuality. Much more complex and sophisticated than either of the contemporary works, *The Scarlet Letter* nonetheless raises many of the same questions: What is responsible behavior in a society? How completely must an individual conform to the expectations of his society, especially in matters that are largely private? To what extent do these private matters affect the society as a whole?

The three works might be brought together in several different ways. The class might be asked to read all three, perhaps beginning with *Forever . . .* , since it is most contemporary and most explicit and therefore probably most provocative, moving then to *Mr. and Mrs.*

Bo Jo Jones, less explicit and contemporary, and ending with *The Scarlet Letter*, the most distant in style and time. Such a plan would allow the teacher to encourage response to the works and at the same time invite comments on the changing expectations of the reader.

If less time is available, or if it seems desirable to separate the class into groups, the teacher might assign each book to a third of the class. The discussion might be based on broad questions applicable to each of the works, questions like, "What are the attitudes and values of the book's heroine?" Such a question could well develop out of students' early comments on the works, when they are likely to report approving or disapproving of the heroine's actions. They could be asked to explain further, illustrating with references to the text full enough to be comprehensible to others in the class who have not read the book. The need to explain to those others may help stem a student's tendency to lapse into vagueness and uncertainty.

Discussions among groups that have read different works are difficult to run, but not impossible. The teacher will have to judge how much help the students need. Some classes can simply begin to talk about the interesting issues, allowing details of plot and characterization to emerge as they are called for. Others might work better if each group summarizes its book, answering questions about the story line, before they begin to explore the differences in content and style.

Another possible arrangement of the three works is to have the class concentrate on one for close reading and analysis in the classroom, and read one or both of the others outside class. As students discuss issues in the main text, they may be asked to consider the same issues in the texts they are reading independently. If a class working on *The Scarlet Letter* discusses the relationship between a social group and an individual within it who does not share its mores or abide by its customs, the students might be asked to consider the relationship between society and the individual in either *Mr. and Mrs. Bo Jo Jones* or *Forever* . . . , perhaps writing a brief paper on the issue. Such a paper would require them to apply the analytic skills they are developing in class to something they have read outside and would thus measure the extent to which they are learning to respond to and analyze literature.

Works of adolescent literature taught along with the standard curriculum might make the classics more accessible to students by helping them see through the differences to the fundamental similarities. Hester Prynne may speak differently, wear different clothes, and live in a society with different beliefs, customs, and laws, but her problem is not unlike that faced by many young women today. Students who have considered the issues in the contemporary setting of *Forever* ... may be more receptive to such a book as *The Scarlet Letter*.

We have discussed two works of adolescent literature at some length to illustrate their potential and show how they might be related to one another and to other items in the English program. Some schools, of course, will not allow a book like *Forever* ... even in the library, much less in the classroom. And students uncomfortable with the subject matter should not, of course, be forced to deal with it. Finally, some teachers will find that they cannot teach such a book without embarrassment. Recognizing that, they should bypass it for other works. Since schools, students, and teachers differ widely across the country, no recommendations about teaching these books would be suitable in all settings, so it is probably more useful to suggest possible patterns for instruction, indicate the range of material available, and then leave the details to the imagination of each teacher.

Works that concern love, romance and sexuality are numerous —too numerous to list here with any pretense of completeness. The following titles, however, provide a quick sampling of books for adolescents on these issues. Many others will be found in the list at the end of the chapter.

LOVE, ROMANCE, AND SEXUALITY

Baldwin, James. *If Beale Street Could Talk*. New York: Dial, 1974.

Beckman, Gunnel. *Mia Alone*. New York: Viking, 1975.

Boissard, Janine. *A Matter of Feeling*. Trans. Elizabeth Walter. Boston: Little, Brown, 1980.

Birisoff, Norman. *Bewitched and Bewildered: A Spooky Love Story*. New York: Dell, 1982.

Burchard, Peter. *First Affair*. New York: Farrar, Straus, & Giroux, 1981.

Callan, Jamie. *Over the Hill at Fourteen*. New York: New American Library, 1982.

Carr, Josephine. *No Regrets*. New York: Dial, 1982.

Chambers, Aida. *Breaktime*. New York: Harper & Row, 1979.

Christman, Elizabeth. *A Nice Italian Girl*. New York: Dodd, Mead, 1976.

Cleary, Beverly. *Jean and Johnny*. New York: Dell, 1981.

_____. *Sister of the Bride*. New York: Dell, 1981.

Conford, Ellen. *To All My Fans with Love, from Sylvie*. Boston: Little, Brown, 1982.

Davis, Gibbs. *Swann Song*. New York: Bradbury, 1982.

Dizenzo, Patricia. *Phoebe*. New York: McGraw-Hill, 1970.

Elfman, Blossom. *The Butterfly Girl*. New York: Houghton Mifflin, 1980.

———. *The Girls of Huntington House*. New York: Houghton Mifflin, 1972.

———. *A House for Jonnie O*. New York: Houghton Mifflin, 1977.

Eyerly, Jeannette. *Bonnie Jo, Go Home*. Philadelphia: Lippincott, 1972.

———. *Drop-Out*. New York: Berkley, 1969.

Foley, June. *It's No Crush, I'm in Love*. New York: Delacorte, 1982.

Garden, Nancy. *Annie on My Mind*. New York: Farrar, Straus, & Giroux, 1982.

Greene, Constance. *Double-Dare O'Toole*. New York: Viking, 1981.

Guest, Elissa Haden. *The Handsome Man*. New York: Dell, 1981.

Guy, Rosa. *Mirror of Her Own*. New York: Delacorte, 1981.

———. *Ruby*. New York: Viking, 1977.

Hahn, Mary. *The Plantain Season*. New York: Norton, 1976.

Hall, Lynn, *Sticks and Stones*. Chicago: Follett, 1972.

Hanes, Mary. *The Child Within*. Wheaton, Ill.: Tyndale, 1979.

Hannay, Allen. *Love and Other Natural Disasters*. Boston: Atlantic-Little, Brown, 1982.

Hart, Bruce, and Carole Hart. *Waiting Games*. New York: Avon, 1982.

Hayes, Sheila. *Me and My Mona Lisa Smile*. New York: Elsevier-Nelson, 1981.

Holland, Isabelle. *Summer of My First Love*. New York: Fawcett/Juniper, 1981.

Jordan, June. *His Own Where*. New York: Crowell, 1971.

Kennedy, Raymond. *Columbine*. New York: Farrar, Straus, & Giroux, 1980.

Klein, Norma. *It's OK If You Don't Love Me*. New York: Dial, 1977.

Konigsburg, E. L. *Journey to an 800 Number*. New York: Atheneum, 1982.

Langone, John. *Like, Love, Lust*. New York: Avon, 1981.

Laymon, Carl. *Your Secret Admirer*. New York: Scholastic, 1980.

Leahy, Syrell Rogovin. *Circle of Love*. New York: Putnam, 1980.

Levitin, Sonia. *The Year of Sweet Senior Insanity*. New York: Atheneum, 1982.

Mandel, Sally. *Quinn*. New York: Delacorte, 1982.

Mazer, Harry. *I Love You, Stupid*. New York: Crowell, 1981.

Mazer, Norma Fox. *Summer Girls, Love Boys and Other Short Stories*. New York: Delacorte, 1982.

_____. *Up in Seth's Room.* New York: Dell, 1981.

_____. *When We First Met.* Englewood Cliffs, N.J.: Four Winds-Scholastic, 1982.

Murari, Timeri. *Fields of Honor.* New York: Simon & Schuster, 1981.

Murphy, Barbara Beasley. *One Another.* New York: Bradbury, 1982.

Peck, Richard. *Close Enough to Touch.* New York: Delacorte, 1981.

Pevsner, Stella. *I'll Always Remember You . . . Maybe.* New York: Clarion-Houghton Mifflin, 1981.

Peyton, K. M. *Dear Fred.* New York: Putnam/Philomel, 1981.

Plain, Belva. *Random Winds.* New York: Delacorte, 1980.

Platt, Kin. *Flames Going Out.* New York: Methuen, 1980.

Polland, Madeleine. *The Heart Speaks Many Ways.* New York: Delacorte, 1982.

Ray, Karen. *The Proposal.* New York: Delacorte, 1981.

Renvoise, Jean. *A Wild Thing.* Boston: Little, Brown, 1971.

Robinson, Barbara. *Temporary Times, Temporary Places.* New York: Harper & Row, 1982.

Scoppettone, Sandra. *Long Time Between Kisses.* New York: Harper & Row, 1982.

Snyder, Anne. *Counter Play.* New York: New American Library, 1981.

Snyder, Zilpha Keatley. *A Fabulous Creature.* New York: Atheneum, 1981.

Springstubb, Tricia. *Give and Take.* Boston: Atlantic-Little, Brown, 1981.

Sunshine, Tina. *An X-Rated Romance.* New York: Avon/Flare, 1982.

Trew, Anthony. *Sea Fever.* New York: St. Martin, 1981.

Trivelpiece, Laurel. *In Love and in Trouble.* New York: Archway/Pocket Books, 1981.

Wakefield, Dan. *Under the Apple Tree.* Boston: Seymour Lawrence, 1981.

Wolff, Virginia Euwer. *Rated PG.* New York: St. Martin's, 1980.

Wood, Phyllis Anderson. *Pass Me a Pine Cone.* Philadelphia: Westminster, 1982.

Yolen, Jane. *The Gift of Sarah Barker.* New York: Viking, 1981.

VIOLENCE

As a society we seem to be more comfortable with violence than with sex. *Lady Chatterley's Lover* must fight its way through the courts; *Forever . . .* is banished from the shelves of junior and even senior high school libraries; and magazines like *Playboy* come under attack from public prosecutors in relatively cosmopolitan cities like Atlanta; but the maiming and killing in books and movies continues with few protests from anyone. The public school English curriculum has never shied away from the violent, even the gruesome. *Hamlet* litters the stage in the final act with four bloody corpses; "The Cask of Amontillado" seals a man live in a tomb; *Beowulf* rips arms off of monsters; *The Red Badge of Courage* slaughters soldiers on the battle field; "The Most Dangerous Game" hunts a man down as if he were an animal; *The Lord of the Flies* transforms a group of schoolboys into savages who torment and kill each other. All that bloodshed and brutality has created barely a ripple compared to the waves of angry objection to books like *Mr. and Mrs. Bo Jo Jones* and *Forever*. . . . Sexuality seems to offend us more than slaughter.

In adolescent literature, what violence there is comes close to the adolescent's experience. Hinton's *The Outsiders* deals with the violence of street gangs in a community divided between the affluent and those close to poverty. Platt's *Headman,* also about gangs, views them from the perspective of a boy who both needs the gang and wants to escape from its influence. *The Chocolate War* portrays the violence resulting from one young man's resistance to the pressures of his schoolmates. Dizenzo's *Why Me? The Story of Jenny* and Scoppettone's *Happy Endings Are All Alike* both consider rape and its effects on the victim. Duncan's *Killing Mr. Griffin* examines the issue of responsibility for a violent act not fully intended by its perpetrators. In all of these stories, as in most of the adolescent fiction dealing with violence, the central characters are themselves adolescents, and the issues raised are likely to be significant for adolescent readers.

Duncan's *Killing Mr. Griffin.* for instance, tells about a group of high school students who decide to frighten their strict and demanding English teacher. Led by the demonic Mark, they agree to kidnap Mr. Griffin and haul him off to a secluded spot in the woods where they will humiliate and terrify him, forcing him to beg for his life. It will be, they think, suitable repayment for his harshness in the classroom. But the plan goes astray. The students fail to account for Mr. Griffin's courage; he refuses to beg for his release despite his helplessness. The kidnappers, after some arguing among themselves, decide to leave him bound and blindfolded, hoping that the long, cold night in the woods will break him. But they have also failed to account for his health, and Mr. Griffin, suffering from a heart condition and unable to take the nitroglycerin on which he depends, dies during the night, turning the kidnapping into murder.

The story raises some interesting questions about violence and responsibility. Are the students equally responsible? Mark is clearly the leader—without him the kidnapping would not have been attempted. Still, all of the group participate willingly in an obviously criminal act resulting in death. Shouldn't they all share equally in the responsibility for that act? And what is it that the students are responsible for? They kill a man, but they do not mean to. They do not shoot him or knife him—they only try to frighten him, and unfortunately he dies. Some readers may argue that his death is not the students' responsibility, since it results from the heart problem, of which they are ignorant; others will hold that the kidnapping, which is not beyond their control, puts Mr. Griffin in a situation that causes his death, and that the students are thus guilty of killing him.

The issue is not simple. Readers will have to consider distinctions between "murder" and "killing," examine their notions of "responsibility," and consider the implications of either forgiving the stunt or punishing it. They will have to look closely at the students' relationships among themselves and with Mr. Griffin. The book invites both introspection and analysis. Each reader must ask himself how forgiving he is, how strictly he wishes to hold people accountable for their actions. And as he asks those questions about his own values, he may also examine the text to see how Duncan has influenced him.

Most readers will notice, for instance, that in the beginning of the book Mr. Griffin is little more than tyrannical. He humiliates his students, penalizes them for the slightest errors, and rewards their efforts with only minimal praise and with exhortations to do still better. Those first pages encourage sympathy for the students and anger at Mr. Griffin. But in Chapter Five Duncan takes us into Mr. Griffin's home. He is now "Brian," not just "Mr. Griffin." We see his wife, who is expecting their first child, and hear them talk about, among other things, his students and his teaching. Mr. Griffin has given up college teaching because he thought he could contribute more to his students in the high school. His strictness is well-meant; he wants his students to succeed, even if his demands make him unpopular. In this setting Brian Griffin is a more likable character—a perfectionist, perhaps, and thus annoying at times, but not the cruel man his students think he is. His wife's perspective helps to soften us:

> . . . it made him suddenly so human, so vulnerable, that she wanted to hug him. It was terrible to be married to a man whose weaknesses were his virtues.[7]

Chapter Five changes the perspective for the reader. It is not a subtle change—one advantage of adolescent literature is that the books are accessible to students, both in theme and in technique. Students can see the writer's craft here, while in a more subtle work they may have difficulty understanding it even when it is explained to them. Seeing the change in perspective in Chapter Five, students can be led to speculate about its purpose, and should quickly realize that Duncan has complicated matters. There are no good guys and bad guys. Neither Mr. Griffin nor his students (with the possible, and awkward, exception of Mark) can be considered entirely evil or virtuous, and thus judgments about the events in the story require a bit more intellectual labor.

The violence in the book may be examined from several points of view. Its disastrous consequences raise questions about the appropriateness of violence. Was kidnapping the right tool for accomplishing the students' objectives? What were their objectives? Did they hope to improve the situation in Mr. Griffin's classroom, or did they simply want revenge? If the former, was there a better way for them to proceed? If the latter, was revenge justified? Had Mr. Griffin done enough to them to warrant a violent response?

The readers may also want to consider the psychological violence of which Mr. Griffin seems to be guilty. Can he be said to treat his students violently in refusing to tolerate mistakes, punishing even accidental offenses like Jeff's loss of his paper in a windstorm, and forcing Mark to beg to be allowed to retake the course after failing it? If so, does that in any way justify the students' action? Could another way out of the situation have been found? Would Mr. Griffin's wife, who exhorted him to offer something besides criticism, have been able to find a better solution?

Students might also want to speculate about the momentum of violent acts in this book. Mr. Griffin's harsh treatment leads to the kidnapping, which becomes a killing that requires a cold-blooded murder to cover it up. Is life really like that, students may ask, and if it is, how does one interrupt the sequence of events before too much damage has been done?

Another issue, related to the question of responsibility, is that of autonomy. Throughout the book characters allow others to make decisions for them. Readers may be asked if there are friends who hold sway over them as Mark does over his friends. Can they be as easily influenced, and if so, why and how? Issues such as these may be too personal and embarrassing to discuss publicly; if so, the class could consider them in journal entries.

Duncan's *Killing Mr. Griffin* is an excellent work dealing with violence and its consequences, but in some ways it is less problematic than other books in this category. Its violent scenes are not especially graphic or shocking—the kidnapping itself, for instance:

Jeff had the car door open in an instant and had hurled himself upon the thrashing figure. From his position in the backseat, David was holding the bag down with difficulty as the man in front twisted and shoved at it with frantic hands. Jeff grabbed for his wrists and struggled to bring the arms down to the sides, finding it far less easy than he had anticipated.[8]

Some parents will think that allowing students to read such a passage encourages violence against teachers. Even those parents will find far less to object to in Duncan's work than in Scoppettone's *Happy Endings Are All Alike*, a book that complicates the lives of librarians and teachers in conservative communities by dealing with both lesbianism and rape. The rape scene is gruesome:

This time he hit her again.
     The sound of flesh and bone connecting with flesh and bone magnified inside her head to a deafening pitch. The intensity of noise almost obliterated pain. . . .
     She saw the fist come toward her. She moved too slowly and it caught her squarely on the bridge of her nose. There was a crunch, then warm, gushing liquid flowed over her lips, chin. Blood. Pain.
     Abruptly, painfully, he entered her. She could not help crying out. The knife slid down the side of her neck, cold, pointed. Was she cut?[9]

The vivid narration of events like this one, and the candid, though less graphic depiction of the lesbian relationship, may make the book difficult to discuss in the classroom. Some teachers and students may find addressing such issues in a large group awkward and embarrassing, in which case the book might better be read individually or discussed in small groups.
     However it is handled, the book invites us to think about the presence in society of violent and irrational people like the rapist, Mid. It offers some insight into the strange patterns of thought that infect them, and also reminds us that the infection can spread. Mid is clearly a despicable character, capable of feeling that Jaret's homosexuality justifies his brutal rape. His perverted logic may allow students to dismiss him easily, labeling him as evil or sick or demented. But when his thoughts are echoed by the police chief, supposedly a responsible and competent adult, they are harder to forget. Perhaps

the most frightening scene in the book is the exchange between the
chief and Jaret's parents after the rape:

"He's confessed. Howsoever, there are complications."
He took out a handkerchief and mopped his forehead.
"This weather," he mumbled.

Kay and Bert exchanged glances. The air condition-
ing was cooling the room nicely.

Foster cleared his throat. "You see, the Summers
boy claims the two girls . . . ah, your daughter and the
Danzinger girl, are ah. . . ." He gave an odd, nervous
laugh, wiped his hands with the handkerchief. "Ah . . .
intimate wth each other."

Kay lit a cigarette, bit the inside of her lip.

. . . .

"I don't see what their relationship has to do with
anything."

The chief jerked his head in surprise. "Well, now."

"I mean," Kay went on, "is their relationship sup-
posed to be some sort of defense for him?"

"If I may say so, Mrs. Tyler, you seem to be taking
perverted behavior in stride, so to speak."

She glanced at Bert. He looked undone. Back to Foster. "First of all I don't think it's perverted, but that's
neither here nor there." She lit a fresh cigarette from the
old one. "Secondly, no matter what their relationship is, it
has absolutely nothing to do with the fact that Jaret was
beaten and raped. Does it?" she challenged him.

Foster shrugged his shoulders. "The Summers kid is
gonna say that seeing them . . . you know, intimate and
all . . . made him crazy."

"That's absurd," Bert said.

"You may think so, Mr. Tyler, but I guarantee you
that this sort of deviant stuff doesn't go over too big in a
nice little town like Gardener's Point." He sniffed.

"And rape does?" Bert said.

Foster ignored this. "The thing of it is that the Summers kid is gonna tell if you press charges. And there's
something else. The Cross boy says he was intimate with
your daughter. She wasn't a virgin," he said righteously.

"So what?" Kay was outraged. "What does that matter?"

. . . .

Foster went on. "Let me put it to you this way. See, we have a hearing and the judge learns that your girl's not a virgin and on top of that she's a lez. Well, he's not gonna think much of her morals. I'm just trying to give you some friendly advice."

"Are you telling me that this bum, this scum of the earth, is going to get away with what he did if we press charges?" Bert asked.

"Could very well be."[10]

Foster reveals that Jaret's sexual preference and the fact that she is not a virgin are, for him and probably for the court, extenuating circumstances—if they do not fully justify the rape, they at least offer some excuse for it. The fact that he can express such thoughts with no awareness of their irrationality and their vulgar disregard for the individual's rights suggests that Mid is only an extreme instance of something more widespread, something that may contaminate the minds of people who are accepted as normal and rational. Students may need help in seeing the importance of this scene in the book, but it is an excellent passage for teaching them to make significant connections between parts of a literary work.

Thus Scoppettone's book brings violence close to the young reader in two ways. First, it shows the adolescent as both the victim and the predator, and second, it suggests that the predator's mentality may be shared to some degree by many others. It is a frightening notion, but students may be able to think of incidents from their own experience that confirm it.

Scoppettone's book ends on a fairly optimistic note. Jaret seems strong enough to cope with the physical violence she has suffered and the psychological violence she will suffer during the trial. Several of Cormier's books are less hopeful. *The Chocolate War*, one of the best works written for adolescents, depicts the violence of a group toward an individual within it. Set in a Catholic high school, the novel describes the tactics of a secret fraternity and a sadistic teacher who band together during the school's yearly chocolate sale to force students to cooperate with the project. The Vigils, the secret fraternity, and their leader, Archie, devise "assignments" for non-members to carry out. The assignments are pointless stunts, invented primarily for the purpose of exercising power over others. Archie, making one of the assignments, is described as "carried on marvelous waves of power and glory." Jerry, the central character, decides not to submit to that power, not to sell the chocolate, and thus makes himself the target of both the fraternity and the teachers.

The violence Jerry suffers is at first psychological—he is harassed and humiliated—but as he and others resist, matters gradually slip out of control, culminating in a contrived parody of a boxing match arranged by Archie. The savage beating Jerry receives breaks him, and he tries to tell his only remaining friend not to resist as he has tried to:

> He had to tell Goober to play ball, to play football, to run, to make the team, to sell the chocolates, to sell whatever they wanted you to sell, to do whatever they wanted you to do. . . . They tell you to do your thing but they don't mean it. They don't want you to do your thing, not unless it happens to be their thing, too. It's a laugh, Goober, a fake. Don't disturb the universe, Goober, no matter what the posters say.[11]

The book ends with the hero broken, physically and psychologically, and with Archie and Brother Leon triumphant.

The book is a study of one young man's effort to assert his autonomy in the face of tremendous pressure to submit. It raises interesting questions about the relationship of the individual to the group, the rationality of human behavior, and the nature and effect of violence. Students might discuss their own values and expectations—would they, for instance, be willing to stand with someone like Jerry in a confrontation with someone like Brother Leon or Archie? Would they feel capable of standing alone, as Jerry did, in such a situation? Is the right to be who and what you want to be worth the possible suffering? Can connections be made between *The Chocolate War* and their own experiences? Most schools have projects of some sort that students are expected to take part in—have the students felt illegitimate pressure to participate in "voluntary" activities? If so, how did they feel and how did they respond?

Cormier's sharply drawn characters will suggest comparisons, too. Archie, the sadistic manipulator of others, might be compared with Mark in Duncan's *Killing Mr. Griffin*, Urek in Stein's *The Magician*, Jack in Golding's *Lord of the Flies*. Brother Leon might be compared with Mr. Hoyt, the headmaster in Kirkwood's *Good Times, Bad Times*. One benefit of such comparisons is that they draw attention to the writer's craft. The class can compare specific paragraphs, observing the prose style, the point of view, and the focus of the various writers. Some authors of books for adolescents are accomplished stylists—Cormier is one—while others border on the illiterate. Direct comparisons, with careful analysis of short passages, will reveal these differences to the students.

A great many other works address the issue of violence. Two of Cormier's other books, *I Am the Cheese* and *After the First Death*, deal with the violence of governments against their own citizens. Many works depict the violence of gangs—one of these, Hinton's *The Outsiders*, has become a classic contemporary problem novel for adolescents. There are books about violence within the family, war, and violence against nature, as well as mysteries and adventures like Zindel's *The Undertaker's Gone Bananas*. Again, a complete list is impossible here, but a few titles will illustrate the range.

VIOLENCE

Aaron, Chester. *Gideon*. Philadelphia: Lippincott, 1982.

Annixter, Paul and Jane. *The Lost Monster*. New York: Harcourt Brace Jovanovich, 1980.

Barwick, James. *The Hangman's Crusade*. New York: Coward, 1981.

————. *Shadow of the Wolf*. New York: Coward, 1979.

Brancoto, Robin. *Don't Sit Under the Apple Tree*. New York: Knopf, 1975.

Burke, Alan Dennis. *Fire Watch*. Boston: Atlantic-Little, Brown, 1980.

Butterworth, W. E. *LeRoy and the Old Man*. Englewood Cliffs, N.J.: Four Winds-Scholastic, 1980.

Coleman, Charles. *Sergeant Back Again*. New York: Harper & Row, 1980.

Cormier, Robert. *The Chocolate War*. New York: Pantheon, 1974.

Dickinson, Peter. *The Seventh Raven*. New York: Unicorn/Dutton, 1981.

Ellis, Mel. *No Man for Murder*. New York: Holt, Rinehart & Winston, 1973.

Forman, James. *The Pumpkin Shell*. New York: Farrar, Straus, & Giroux, 1981.

Godey, John. *Nella*. New York: Delacorte, 1981.

Golding, William. *Lord of the Flies*. New York: Coward, McCann, 1954.

Grey, Anthony. *Saigon*. Boston: Little, Brown, 1982.

Harris, Davie. *I Shoulda Been Home Yesterday*. New York: Delacorte, 1976.

Hayes, Billy. *Midnight Express*. New York: Dutton, 1977.

Henschel, Lee. *Short Stories of Vietnam*. Guthrie, Minn.: Guthrie Publishing, 1982.

Hinton, S. E. *The Outsiders*. New York: Viking, 1967.

_____. *Rumble Fish*. New York: Delacorte, 1975.

_____. *That Was Then, This Is Now*. New York: Viking, 1971.

Hubert, C. *Dreamspeaker*. New York: Avon, 1980.

Kellogg, Marjorie. *Like the Lion's Tooth*. New York: Farrar, Straus, & Giroux, 1972.

Kirkham, George. *Signal Zero*. Philadelphia: Lippincott, 1976.

Kirkwood, James. *Good Times, Bad Times*. New York: Fawcett, 1968.

Koehn, Ilse. *Tilla*. New York: Greenwillow, 1981.

Korschunow, Irina. *Who Killed Christopher?* Trans. Eva L. Mayer. New York: Putnam/Philomel, 1980.

Lewitt, Maria. *Come Spring*. New York: St. Martin's, 1982.

Lord, Gabrielle. *Fortress*. New York: St. Martin's, 1981.

MacLennan, Hugh. *Voices in Time*. New York: St. Martin's, 1981.

Moeri, Louise. *The Girl Who Lived on the Ferris Wheel*. New York: Dutton, 1980.

Morris, Michelle. *If I Should Die Before I Wake*. Los Angeles: Tarcher, 1982.

Murphy, Jim. *Death Run*. New York: Clarion-Houghton Mifflin, 1982.

Myers, Walter Dean. *Hoops: A Novel*. New York: Delacorte, 1981.

Paier, Robert. *The Pied Piper*. New York: McGraw-Hill, 1979.

Peyton, K. M. *Prove Yourself a Hero*. New York: Dell, 1980.

Platt, Kin. *The Boy Who Could Make Himself Disappear*. New York: Dell, 1971.

_____. *Headman*. New York: Dell, 1977.

Rosenberg, Stuart. *When the Bough Breaks*. New York: Crowell, 1976.

Samuels, Gertrude. *Run, Shelley, Run!* New York: New American Library, 1975.

Scoppettone, Sandra. *Happy Endings Are All Alike*. New York: Laurel Leaf, 1979.

Stachow, Hasso G. *If This Be Glory*. New York: Doubleday, 1982.

Swarthout, Glendon. *Bless the Beasts and Children*. New York: Doubleday, 1970.

Terry, Douglas. *The Last Texas Hero*. New York: Doubleday, 1982.

CHARACTERISTICS OF ADOLESCENT LITERATURE

The corpus of adolescent literature is large, diverse, and growing. To generalize about such a massive collection of works may seem foolhardy; still, we can identify characteristics that many of the currently available books share. This will be useful, if only as a crude outline of the field into which we may fit the individual books we encounter.

Adolescent fiction is first of all likely to have adolescents as its central characters. As Carlsen says,

> Today's young reader wants what *Seventeenth Summer* gave an earlier generation; an honest view of the adolescent world from the adolescent's point of view; a book that holds a mirror up to society so that readers can see their own world reflected in it.[12]

The books discussed earlier in this chapter all share this feature, as do some earlier works of literature that, though not written specifically for adolescents, were seized by adolescent readers for their own. *Catcher in the Rye, Lord of the Flies,* and *A Separate Peace* all focus on adolescent characters.

In many of the books, an adolescent is also the narrator. Duncan's *Killing Mr. Griffin* is necessarily in the third person, since part of the author's strategy is to show the reader a side of Mr. Griffin's life that the students cannot see, but *Forever . . .* is narrated by the heroine, Katherine, and it seems quite likely that the book's popularity is partly a result of Blume's ability to write convincingly in the young girl's voice. Even those books not narrated in the first person must owe much of their appeal to portraying the thoughts and feelings of the adolescent characters. Young readers, working through the confusing growth of adolescence, are naturally interested in the experiences of others approximately their own age and going through similar stages.

LANGUAGE

One problem with using an adolescent narrator is adolescent language. In skillfully written books like *Forever . . .* the problem is minor—the voice Blume has created for her heroine, Katherine, is smooth and palatable. In some works, however, the voice may be grating:

> If you knew I was a seventeen-year-old handsome guy hacking out this verbose volume of literary ecstasy, you'd probably think I was one of those academic genii who run home after a titillating day at school, panting to commence cello lessons. I regret to inform you, however, that I do not suffer from scholasticism of the brain. In fact, I suffer from it so little I dropped out of my puerile, jerky high school exactly eleven months ago.[13]

Adult readers, and probably many younger readers too, will find they can tolerate only so much of that sort of prose. Granted, the problem may be more acute for the teacher than for the student, and such extremes may help to create a character; still, the language of some of the books can be a barrier for the teacher beginning to explore this literature.

Even in third-person narratives, where it is not necessary to imitate the adolescent voice, we often find stumbling prose. Stylistic clumsiness, however, may be useful for students who lack confidence with more sophisticated writing. Even a fairly poor student can see the awkwardness in, "Another undercurrent that was lingering on was the fact that he felt a lot of guilt that he had put together. . . ."[14] and in, "The only thing that was unfortunate was that Bobby had put the stick shift into reverse,"[15] and can suggest other phrasings.

Because the central characters are adolescents, the central concerns are those of adolescence. Even in Cormier's *After the First Death*, which involves kidnapping, murder, and terrorism, the crux of the story is the relationship between father and son and the discovery the son makes about himself—issues significant to most adolescents. In *The Undertaker's Gone Bananas*, essentially a mystery story, the adolescents' relationships with others are a major issue. The content of adolescent fiction is now largely unrestricted—homosexuality, suicide, rape, cancer, death, mental illness, child abuse, divorce. That content, however, is usually viewed through the eyes of an adolescent.

There are some interesting exceptions and variations. Childress, in *A Hero Ain't Nothin but a Sandwich*, uses multiple narrators to tell the story of Benjie's difficulties with drugs. The focus is on Benjie's problems, but we see them from the perspective of others around him as well as from his own. Richard Peck's *New York Time* goes even further from the norm, describing events in the life of a woman in her thirties. If we admit to the category of adolescent literature those works of adult fiction that have found popularity with younger readers, the exceptions are more numerous still.

The "problem novel," as our discussion must suggest, has dominated the field of adolescent literature in recent years. Many students, however, still seek lighter fiction—the comedy of Peck's *Secrets of the Shopping Mall*, the horror of Aiken's *A Touch of Chill,* or the fantasy of L'Engle's *A Wrinkle in Time.* Adolescents are reading westerns, detective stories, romances, tales of the occult, and nonfiction as well. Teachers should not forget, in recommending books to students, the wide range available; presenting only books that address problems would narrow the students' conception of literature unnecessarily.

The better adolescent literature, despite its adolescent perspective, tries to avoid the simple-minded stereotypes and patterns found in much popular fiction. Teachers are not always tyrannical and uninformed, parents not always domineering and stupid. Good and evil are not so clearly and simplistically delineated. There is, of course, a wide range in the quality of adolescent fiction, as there is in adult fiction. Some works, like Cormier's *Chocolate War* and Swarthout's *Bless the Beasts and Children,* can be expected to survive for a long time—others will disappear quickly and quietly.

Adolescent literature is usually short; most of the books run between one hundred and two hundred pages in paperback. As a result, the story usually progresses quickly, a feature that is appreciated by many readers but poses problems for the authors. Fewer characters can be introduced, and they cannot be so fully drawn as in a longer novel. This may tempt the writer to rely more than he might wish on stereotypes or formulas. Description, setting, and background must be handled with economy; digressions, even important ones, must be held to a minimum. Some authors achieve impressive subtleties even within the confines of the short novel. *After the First Death,* for instance, establishes an interesting parallel between the young, innocent boy, sacrificed by his father, and the assassin—both young men strive to satisfy the expectations of mysterious fathers, and both fail. Few writers, however, manage to accomplish what Cormier accomplishes in his books.

SUMMATION AND REFERENCES

Adolescent literature is a vast and sprawling collection. This chapter has sought only to introduce it, to discuss a few representative books, and to sketch its general characteristics. Reading several of the books discussed or listed here will provide a taste of the literature. Beyond that, there are several excellent sources of information about literature for adolescents:

BOOKS ABOUT ADOLESCENT LITERATURE AND WRITERS

G. Robert Carlsen's *Books and the Teenage Reader: A Guide for Teachers, Librarians, and Parents,* rev. 2nd ed., New York: Harper & Row, 1980. Aimed at a broad audience, as the subtitle indicates, Carlsen's book discusses the nature of reading, the development of reading interests, and the wide assortment of books—

including adolescent novels, adult books, classics, and the various genres—useful with young readers.

Kenneth L. Donelson and Alleen Pace Nilsen's *Literature for Today's Young Adults*, Glenview, Ill.: Scott, Foresman, 1980. This is an impressive scholarly text discussing the history of literature for adolescents, the nature of contemporary works for adolescents, and the issues faced by teachers and librarians who hope to present the literature to their students.

Sheila Schwartz's *Teaching Adolescent Literature: A Humanistic Approach*, Rochelle Park, N.J.: Hayden, 1979. Schwartz begins with a brief discussion of methodology, and then analyzes a large number of adolescent books grouped according to theme.

Daniel Kirkpatrick's *Twentieth Century Children's Writers*. New York: St. Martin's, 1978. For about six hundred writers of literature for children and adolescents, this guide presents a brief biography, bibliographies, and an essay of critical evaluation.

BOOKLISTS

Jerry L. Walker, Editorial Chairman, and the Committee on the Junior High School Booklist, *Your Reading: A Booklist for Junior High Students*, Urbana, Ill.: National Council of Teachers of English, 1975.

Robert C. Small, Chair, and the Committee on the Senior High School Booklist, *Books for You: A Booklist for Senior High Students*, Urbana, Ill.: National Council of Teachers of English, 1982.

JOURNALS AND OTHER PUBLICATIONS

Keeping up with adolescent literature is impossible, but there are several publications that may help:

The English Journal.
>National Council of Teachers of English, 1111 Kenyon Road, Urbana, Ill., 61801.

The ALAN Review.
>Assembly on Literature for Adolescents, National Council of Teachers of English, 1111 Kenyon Road, Urbana, Ill., 61801.

Best Books for Young Adults.
>Yearly list from Young Adult Services Division of American Library Association, 50 E. Huron St., Chicago, Ill., 60601.

Booklist.
>American Library Association, 50 E. Huron St., Chicago, Ill., 60601.

Books for the Teen Age.
New York Public Library, Fifth Ave. and 42nd St., New York, N.Y., 10018.

Bulletin of the Center for Children's Books.
Univ. of Chicago Graduate Library School, Univ. of Chicago Press, 5801 Ellis Ave., Chicago, Ill., 60637

School Library Journal.
R. R. Bowker Company, 1180 Avenue of the Americas, New York, N.Y., 10036

Wilson Library Bulletin.
H. W. Wilson Co., 1950 University Ave., Bronx, N.Y., 19452.

The Horn Book.
The Horn Book, Inc., Park Square Building, 31 St. James Ave., Boston, Mass., 92116

Kirkus Review.
Kirkus Service, Inc., 200 Park Ave. South, New York, N.Y., 10003.

Kliatt Paperback Book Guide.
425 Watertown St., Newton, Mass., 92158.

New York Times Book Review.
Times Square, New York, N.Y., 10036.

Voice of Youth Advocates.
10 Landing Lane, New Brunswick, N.J., 08901.

A POSTSCRIPT ON CATEGORIES AND LISTS

In this chapter we have looked at two prominent themes in current adolescent fiction, discussing several representative works and listing others. We could have considered other categories or other works, and any of the works mentioned could have been placed elsewhere. Cormier's *After the First Death*, for instance, mentioned as a book about violence, could have been said to deal with the theme of parent-child relationships—the father, knowing that his son will break quickly under pressure, sends him off to negotiate with terrorists, planted with false information he is expected to reveal. It could as well have been classified with books about self-knowledge or coming of age—the boy discovers that he cannot withstand mild torture and was not expected to be able to, and the knowledge drives him to suicide. Or it could have been grouped with works that investigate the relationship between the individual and his society— here, the boy is sacrificed to protect a secret government project. The categories, in other words, are arbitrary and contrived, and may as much limit thought about the work as assist it. The various books and articles about adolescent literature subdivide it in different ways. Schwartz's *Teaching Adolescent Literature* offers seven categories: The Outsider/The Other, Minorities, Regions and Locales, Teenagers and Sex, Violence: Real and Vicarious, Family Life and Lifestyles, and Science Fiction as Prophecy. Donelson and Nilsen, in *Literature for Today's Young Adults,* in addition to chronological categories, offer the following groups: Parent/Child Relationships, Body and Self, Sex and Sex Roles, Friends and Society, Adventure-Romances, Love-Romances, Adventure Stories, Westerns, Mysteries, Stories of the Supernatural, Historical Fiction, Science Fiction, Fantasy, Utopias, Biographies, Quiet Heroes, Heroes in War, Heroes in Sports, Books About the World Around Us, Books About Physical and Mental Health, Books About Sex, Books About Drugs, How-To Books, Books About Work, Fun Facts, and The New Journalism. Walker's *Your Reading* offers a different set of groups, Small's *Books for You* another, and Carlsen's *Books and the Teenage Reader* still another. The bibliographies in those works are extensive and useful.

Our purpose here is not to argue for still another system of organization, but simply to encourage reading some of the adolescent literature and considering its possible appeal to secondary school students. What follows, then, is a list of representative adolescent works and adult works popular with adolescents, arranged by theme or genre, from which the reader may select a sampling.

RECOMMENDED ADOLESCENT AND POPULAR ADULT LITERATURE

ADVENTURE

Alexander, Lloyd. *The Kestrel.* New York: Dutton, 1982.

_____. *Westmark.* New York: Laurel Leaf, 1981.

Anthony, Evelyn. *The Avenue of the Dead.* New York: Coward, 1982.

_____. *The Defector.* New York: Coward, 1981.

Benchley, Nathaniel. *Only Earth and Sky Last Forever.* New York: Harper & Row, 1972.

Benchley, Peter. *Jaws.* New York: Doubleday, 1974.

Bethancourt, T. Ernesto. *Doris Fein: The Mad Samurai.* New York: Holiday, 1981.

_____. *Doris Fein: Phantom of the Casino.* New York: Holiday, 1981.

_____. *Doris Fein: Quartz Boyar.* New York: Holiday, 1980.

———. *Doris Fein: Superspy*. New York: Holiday, 1980.

Borland, Hal G. *When the Legends Die*. Philadelphia: Lippincott, 1963.

Branscum, Robbie. *Me and Jim Luke*. New York: Doubleday, 1971.

Bridgers, Sue Ellen. *Home Before Dark*. New York: Knopf, 1976.

Bykov, Vasil. *Pack of Wolves*. Trans. Lynn Solotaroff. New York: Crowell, 1981.

Caras, Roger. *The Custer Wolf: Biography of an American Renegade*. Boston: Little, Brown, 1966.

Carroll, James. *Family Trade*. Boston: Little, Brown, 1982.

Charriere, Henri. *Papillon*. New York: Morrow, 1970.

Clark, Mary Higgins. *A Cry in the Night*. New York: Simon & Schuster, 1982.

Cleaver, Vera, and Bill Cleaver. *The Kissimmee Kid*. New York: Lothrop, 1981.

Cohen, Peter Zachary. *Deadly Game at Stony Creek*. New York: Dial, 1978.

Collins, Larry, and Dominique Lapierre. *The Fifth Horseman*. New York: Simon & Schuster, 1980.

Cooney, Caroline B. *Rear-View Mirror*. New York: Random House, 1980.

Craven, Margaret. *I Heard the Owl Call My Name*. New York: Doubleday, 1973.

Crichton, Michael. *Congo*. New York: Knopf, 1980.

———. *The Great Train Robbery*. New York: Knopf, 1975.

Cronley, Jay. *Quick Change*. New York: Doubleday, 1981.

Degens, T. *Transport 7-41-R*. New York: Viking, 1974.

Elder, Lauren, and Shirley Streshinsky. *And I Alone Survived*. New York: Dutton, 1978.

Ellis, Mel. *The Wild Horse Killers*. New York: Holt, Rinehart & Winston, 1976.

Estey, Dale. *A Lost Tale*. New York: St. Martin's, 1980.

Feegel, John R. *The Dance Card*. New York: Dial, 1981.

Follett, James. *Churchill's Gold*. New York: Houghton Mifflin, 1981.

Forsyth, Frederick. *The Day of the Jackal*. New York: Viking, 1971.

———. *The Odessa File*. New York: Viking, 1972.

Francis, Dick. *Reflex*. New York: Putnam, 1981.

Garbo, Norman. *Spy*. New York: Norton, 1980.

Garfield, Brian. *Checkpoint Charlie*. New York: Mysterious, 1982.

Gosling, Paula. *The Zero Trap*. New York: Coward, 1980.

George, Jean Craighead. *Julie of the Wolves*. New York: Harper & Row, 1972.

Glaskin, G. M. *Flight to Landfall*. New York: St. Martin's, 1980.

Haugaard, Erik Christian. *Chase Me, Catch Nobody*. New York: Houghton Mifflin, 1980.

Holland, Isabelle. *Heads You Win, Tails I Lose*. Philadelphia: Lippincott, 1973.

———. *Of Love and Death and Other Journeys*. Philadelphia: Lippincott, 1975.

Hughes, Monica. *Beyond the Dark River*. New York: Atheneum, 1981.

Hunt, Irene. *Across Five Aprils*. Chicago: Follett, 1964.

Hyde, Christopher. *The Icarus Deal*. New York: Houghton Mifflin, 1982.

Jones, Douglas C. *Elkhorn Tavern*. New York: Holt, Rinehart & Winston, 1980.

Kluge, P. F. *Eddie and the Cruisers*. New York: Viking, 1980.

Lee, Mildred. *Fog*. New York: Seabury, 1972.

———. *One Fat Summer*. New York: Harper & Row, 1977.

Ludlum, Robert. *The Bourne Identity*. New York: Bantam, 1981.

———. *The Holcroft Covenant*. New York: Bantam, 1979.

———. *The Matarese Circle*. New York: Bantam, 1980.

Lyle, Katie Letcher. *Finders Weepers*. New York: Coward, 1982.

MacBeth, George. *The Katana*. New York: Simon & Schuster, 1981.

MacLean, Alistair. *Breakheart Pass*. New York: Doubleday, 1974.

———. *Circus*. New York: Doubleday, 1975.

Mayerson, Evelyn. *If Birds Are Free*. Philadelphia: Lippincott, 1980.

Mazer, Harry. *The Island Keeper*. New York: Dell, 1982.

———. *Snow Bound*. New York: Delacorte, 1973.

Mazer, Norma Fox. *Dear Bill, Remember Me?* New York: Delacorte, 1974.

McKinley, Robin. *The Blue Sword*. New York: Greenwillow, 1982.

Messner, Reinhold. *The Big Walls*. New York: Oxford Univ. Press, 1978.

Meyer, Nicholas, and Barry J. Kaplan. *Black Orchid*. New York: Bantam, 1978.

Miller, Stanley. *The Mary Celeste: A Survivor's Tale*. New York: St. Martin's, 1981.

Morrell, David. *Blood Oath*. New York: St. Martin's, 1982.

Moyes, Patricia, *Angel Death*. New York: Holt, Rinehart & Winston, 1981.

Myers, Walter Dean. *The Legend of Tarik*. New York: Viking, 1981.

Namioka, Lensey. *Village of the Vampire Cat*. New York: Delacorte, 1981.

Peck, Richard. *Through a Brief Darkness*. New York: Viking, 1973.

Peck, Robert Newton. *Eagle Fur*. New York: Knopf, 1978.

Petersen, P. J. *Nobody Else Can Walk It for You*. New York: Delacorte, 1982.

Potok, Chaim. *The Chosen*. New York: Simon & Schuster, 1967.

_____. *My Name Is Asher Lev*. New York: Knopf, 1972.

Robbins, Tom. *Still Life with Woodpecker*. New York: Bantam, 1980.

Rodoreda, Merce. *The Time of the Doves*. Trans. David H. Rosenthal. New York: Taplinger, 1980.

Rogers, Barbara. *Project Web*. New York: Dodd, 1980.

Seymour, Gerald. *Archangel*. New York: Dutton, 1982.

_____. *Contract*. New York: Holt, Rinehart & Winston, 1981.

Sherman, D. R. *The Lion's Paw*. New York: Doubleday: 1975.

Siegel, Benjamin. *The Adventures of Richard O'Boy*. Philadelphia: Lippincott, 1980.

Simpson, George E., and Neal R. Burger. *Fair Warning*. New York: Delacorte, 1980.

Sletor, William. *Blackbriar*. New York: Dutton, 1972.

Snyder, Howard H. *The Hall of the Mountain King*. New York: Scribner, 1973.

Steiner, George. *The Portage to San Cristóbal of A. H.* New York: Simon & Schuster, 1982.

Sutcliff, Rosemary. *The Light Beyond the Forest*. New York: Dutton, 1980.

_____. *The Road to Camlann: The Death of King Arthur*. New York: Dutton, 1982.

_____. *The Sword and the Circle*. New York: Dutton, 1981.

Thayer, James Stewart. *The Earhart Betrayal*. New York: Putnam, 1980.

Vliet, R. G. *Rockspring*. New York: Viking, 1974.

Wells, Lee. *Night of the Running Man*. New York: St. Martin's, 1981.

Westall, Robert. *Fathom Five*. New York: Greenwillow, 1980.

_____. *The Scarecrows*. New York: Greenwillow, 1981.

White, Robb. *Deathwatch*. New York: Doubleday, 1972.

Wibberley, Leonard. *Flint's Island*. New York: Farrar, Straus, & Giroux, 1972.

Williams, Paul O. *The Fall of the Shell*. New York: Ballantine, 1982.

Wisler, G. Clifton. *The Trident Brand*. New York: Doubleday, 1982.

Wood, Bari. *The Tribe: A Novel*. New York: New American Library, 1982.

COMING OF AGE/ESTABLISHING IDENTITY:

Aldridge, James. *A Sporting Proposition*. New York: Laurel Leaf, 1975.

Anderson, Mary. *You Can't Get There from Here*. New York: Atheneum, 1982.

Avi. *A Place Called Ugly*. New York: Pantheon, 1981.

Bach, Alice. *Mollie Make-Believe*. New York: Dell, 1976.

———. *They'll Never Make a Movie Starring Me*. New York: Laurel Leaf, 1975.

Blume, Judy. *Are You There, God? It's Me, Margaret*. New York: Bradbury, 1970.

Branscum, Robbie. *Johnny May*. New York: Avon, 1976.

Butterworth, W. E. *A Member of the Family*. Englewood Cliffs, N.J.: Four Winds-Scholastic, 1982.

Calvert, Patricia. *The Snowbird*. New York: Scribner, 1980.

Childress, Alice. *Rainbow Jordan*. New York: Coward, 1981.

Cleaver, Vera, and Bill Cleaver. *A Little Destiny*. New York: Bantam, 1982.

Cohen, Barbara. *King of the Seventh Grade*. New York: Lothrop, 1982.

Conlon, Kathleen. *Forgotten Season*. New York: St. Martin's, 1981.

Conroy, Pat. *Lords of Discipline*. New York: Bantam, 1982.

Danziger, Paula. *There's a Bat in Bunk Five*. New York: Delacorte, 1980.

Davis, Terry. *Vision Quest*. New York: Viking, 1979.

Demas, Vida. *First Person, Singular*. New York: Laurel Leaf, 1975.

Demetz, Hana. *The House on Prague Street*. New York: St. Martin's, 1980.

Dodson, Susan. *Have You Seen This Girl?* New York: Scholastic, 1982.

Duncan, Frances. *Finding Home*. New York: Avon, 1982.

Dygard, Thomas J. *Point Spread*. New York: Morrow, 1980.

Epstein, Jacob. *Wild Oats*. Boston: Little, Brown, 1979.

Fox, Paula. *A Place Apart*. New York: Farrar, Straus, & Giroux, 1980.

Garfield, Leon. *Footsteps.* New York: Delacorte, 1980.

Gold, Robert S. *Stepping Stones: An Anthology.* New York: Dell, 1981.

Greene, Bette. *Morning Is a Long Time Coming.* New York: Dial, 1978.

———. *Philip Hall Likes Me, I Reckon Maybe.* New York: Dial, 1974.

Greene, Constance C. *Dotty's Suitcase.* New York: Viking, 1980.

Greenwald, Sheila. *Blissful Joy and the SAT's: A Multiple Choice Romance.* Boston, Atlantic-Little, Brown, 1982.

Hautzig, Deborah. *Hey, Dollface.* New York: Morrow, 1978.

Hemingway, Ernest. *Islands in the Stream.* New York: Scribner, 1970.

Hesse, Herman. *Beneath the Wheel.* New York: Bantam, 1970.

Hogan, William. *The Quartzite Trip.* New York: Atheneum, 1980.

Hunt, Irene. *William.* New York: Scribner, 1977.

Kerr, M. E. *Is That You, Miss Blue?* New York: Harper & Row, 1975.

Klein, Norma. *Domestic Arrangements.* New York: Evans, 1981.

Kotzwinkle, William. *Jack in the Box.* New York: Putnam, 1980.

Lee, Mildred. *Fog.* New York: Seabury, 1972.

———. *The People Therein.* New York: Clarion-Houghton Mifflin, 1980.

Leffland, Ella. *Last Courtesies and Other Stories.* New York: Harper & Row, 1980.

LeGuin, Ursula K. *Very Far Away from Anywhere Else.* New York: Bantam, 1982.

Lehrman, Robert. *Juggling.* New York: Harper & Row, 1982.

L'Engle, Madeleine. *Camilla.* New York: Delacorte, 1981.

Lipsyte, Robert. *The Summerboy.* New York: Harper & Row, 1982.

Lyle, Katie Letcher. *I Will Go Barefoot All Summer for You.* New York: Dell, 1974.

Madison, Winifred. *Bird of the Wing.* New York: Laurel Leaf, 1975.

MacLeish, Roderick. *The First Book of Eppe.* New York: Random House, 1980.

Mazer, Norma Fox. *Summer Girls, Love Boys, and Other Short Stories.* New York: Delacorte, 1982.

McHargue, Georgess. *The Horseman's Word.* New York: Delacorte, 1981.

Namioka, Lensey. *Who's Hu?* New York: Vanguard, 1981.

Newton, Suzanne. *M. V. Sexton Speaking.* New York: Viking, 1981.

Paterson, Katherine. *Jacob Have I Loved.* New York: Crowell, 1980.

Peck, Richard. *Representing Superdoll.* New York: Viking, 1974.

Peck, Robert Newton. *Justice Lion.* Boston: Little, Brown, 1981.

Portis, Charles. *True Grit.* New York: Signet, 1968.

Rawls, Wilson. *Where the Red Fern Grows*. New York: Doubleday, 1961.

Rees, David. *Silence*. New York: Elsevier-Nelson, 1981.

Rodowsky, Colby. *A Summer's Worth of Shame*. New York: Watts, 1980.

Rossner, Judith. *Emmeline*. New York: Simon & Schuster, 1980.

Rubenstein, Robert E. *When Sirens Scream*. New York: Dodd, Mead, 1981.

Sargent, Sarah. *Secret Lies*. New York: Dell, 1982.

Sebestyen, Ouida. *Far from Home*. Boston: Atlantic-Little, Brown, 1980.

Shreve, Susan. *Loveletters*. New York: Bantam, 1981.

Simons, Wendy. *Harper's Mother*. Englewood Cliffs, N.J.: Prentice-Hall, 1980.

Singer, Marilyn. *The First Few Friends*. New York: Harper & Row, 1981.

Springstubb, Tricia. *The Moon on a String*. Boston: Atlantic-Little, Brown, 1982.

Trahey, Jane. *Thursdays 'til 9*. New York: Harcourt Brace Jovanovich, 1980.

Wells, Rosemary. *When No One Was Looking*. New York: Dial, 1980.

Whelan, Gloria. *The Pathless Woods*. Philadelphia: Lippincott, 1981.

Windsor, Patricia. *Diving for Roses*. New York: Harper & Row, 1976.

Winthrop, Elizabeth. *Walking Away*. New York: Harper & Row, 1973.

Yglesias, Rafael. *The Game Player*. New York: Doubleday, 1978.

FAMILY

Anderson, Mary. *The Rise and Fall of a Teen-Age Wacko*. New York: Atheneum, 1980.

Angell, Judie. *Dear Lola: Or How to Build Your Own Family*. New York: Dell, 1982.

Bach, Alice. *A Father Every Few Years*. New York: Harper & Row, 1977.

Bethancourt, T. Ernesto. *Where the Deer and the Cantaloupe Play*. San Diego: Oak Tree, 1981.

Bickham, Jack M. *I Still Dream about Columbus*. New York: St. Martin's, 1982.

Blume, Judy. *It's Not the End of the World*. New York: Bradbury, 1972.

Bridgers, Sue Ellen. *Home Before Dark*. New York: Knopf, 1976.

_____. *Notes for Another Life.* New York: Knopf, 1981.

Byrd, Elizabeth. *I'll Get By.* New York: Viking, 1981.

Colman, Hila. *What's the Matter with the Dobsons?* New York: Crown, 1980.

Cleaver, Vera, and Bill Cleaver. *Queen of Hearts.* New York: Bantam, 1979.

_____. *Trial Valley.* New York: Harper & Row, 1977.

Danziger, Paula. *The Divorce Express.* New York: Delacorte, 1982.

Day, Ingeborg. *Ghost Waltz.* New York: Viking, 1980.

Desai, Anita. *Clear Light of Day.* New York: Harper & Row, 1980.

Donovan, John. *I'll Get There. It Better Be Worth the Trip.* New York: Harper & Row, 1969.

_____. *Remove Protective Coating a Little at a Time.* New York: Harper & Row, 1973.

Engebrecht, P. A. *Under the Haystack.* Nashville: Thomas Nelson, 1973.

Fitzbagh, Louise. *Nobody's Family is Going to Change.* New York: Farrar, Straus, & Giroux, 1974.

Forest, Antonia. *The Ready-Made Family.* Riverside, Colo.: NACAC, 1980.

Gaines, Ernest J. *In My Father's House.* New York: Knopf, 1978.

Gerber, Merrill Joan. *Please Don't Kiss Me Now.* New York: Dial, 1981.

Grant, Cynthia. *Joshua Fortune.* New York: Atheneum, 1980.

Greenburg, Joanne. *A Season of Delight.* New York: Holt, Rinehart, & Winston, 1981.

Guest, Judith. *Second Heaven.* New York: Viking, 1982.

Guy, David. *Football Dreams.* New York: Seaview, 1981.

Hall, Lynn. *The Leaving.* New York: Scribner, 1980.

Hamilton, Virginia. *Sweet Whispers, Brother Rush.* New York: Putnam/Philomel, 1982.

Harris, Mark Jonathan. *With a Wave of the Wand.* New York: Lothrop, 1981.

Irwin, Hadley. *What about Grandma?* New York: Atheneum, 1982.

Kerr, M. E. *Dinky Hocker Shoots Smack.* New York: Harper & Row, 1972.

_____. *Gentlehands.* New York: Harper & Row, 1978.

_____. *Little, Little.* New York: Harper & Row, 1981.

_____. *The Son of Someone Famous.* New York: Harper & Row, 1974.

Kherdian, David. *Finding Home.* New York: Greenwillow: 1981.

_____. *The Road from Home*. New York: Greenwillow, 1980.

Kingman, Lee. *The Year of the Raccoon*. New York: Houghton Mifflin, 1966.

Klein, Norma. *Mom, the Wolfman, and Me*. New York: Pantheon, 1972.

_____. *Taking Sides*. New York: Avon, 1976.

Lifton, Betty Jean. *I'm Still Me*. New York: Knopf, 1981.

Lorimer, L. T. *Secrets*. New York: Holt, Rinehart & Winston, 1981.

Loury, Lois. *Find a Stranger, Say Good-Bye*. New York: Houghton Mifflin, 1978.

Lyle, Katie Letcher. *Dark but Full of Diamonds*. New York: Coward, 1981.

Mazer, Harry. *The Dollar Man*. New York: Delacorte, 1974.

_____. *Guy Lenny*. New York: Delacorte, 1971.

Mazer, Norma Fox. *A Figure of Speech*. New York: Dell, 1975.

Mendonca, Susan. *Tough Choices*. New York: Dial, 1980.

Milofsky, David. *Playing from Memory*. New York: Simon & Schuster, 1981.

Moeri, Louise. *The Girl Who Lived on the Ferris Wheel*. New York: Dutton, 1979.

Morgenroth, Barbara. *Will the Real Renie Lake Please Stand Up?* New York: Atheneum, 1982.

Myers, Walter Dean. *It Ain't All for Nothing*. New York: Viking, 1978.

Ney, John. *Ox: The Story of a Kid at the Top*. Boston: Little, Brown, 1970.

Nostlinger, Christine. *Marrying Off Mother*. Trans. Anthea Bell. New York: Harcourt Brace Jovanovich, 1982.

Oppenheimer, Joan. *Which Mother Is Mine?* New York: Bantam, 1980.

Peck, Robert Newton. *A Day No Pigs Would Die*. New York: Knopf, 1972.

Platt, Kin. *Chloris and the Creeps*. New York: Dell, 1974.

_____. *Chloris and the Freaks*. New York: Bantam, 1976.

_____. *Chloris and the Weirdos*. New York: Bantam, 1980.

Roth, Arthur. *The Caretaker*. Englewood Cliffs, N.J.: Four Winds-Scholastic, 1980.

Rushforth, Peter. *Kindergarten*. New York: Knopf, 1980.

Salassi, Otto R. *On the Ropes*. New York: Greenwillow, 1981.

Smith, Robert Kimmel. *Jane's House*. New York: Morrow, 1982.

Stolz, Mary. *The Edge of Next Year*. New York: Harper & Row, 1974.

_____. *Leap Before You Look*. New York: Harper & Row, 1972.

Tamar, Erika. *Blues for Silk Garcia*. New York: Crown, 1983.

Troop, Elizabeth. *Darling Daughters*. New York: St. Martin's, 1981.

Wallin, Luke. *The Redneck Poacher's Son*. New York: Bradbury, 1981.

Wells, Rosemary. *None of the Above*. New York: Avon, 1977.

Wheaton, Phillip. *Razzamatazz*. New York: Everest House, 1980.

Winthrop, Elizabeth. *A Little Demonstration of Affection*. New York: Harper & Row, 1975.

Wolitzer, Hilma. *Hearts*. New York: Farrar, Straus, & Giroux, 1980.

Zindel, Paul. *Confessions of a Teenage Baboon*. New York: Harper & Row, 1977.

FRIENDSHIP

Angell, Judie. *Ronnie and Rosey*. New York: Dell, 1979.

_____. *Secret Selves*. New York: Bradbury, 1979.

Armstrong, William. *Sounder*. New York: Harper & Row, 1972.

Asher, Sandy. *Daughters of the Law*. New York: Beaufort, 1980.

Bates, Betty. *Picking Up the Pieces*. New York: Holiday, 1981.

Bethancourt, T. Ernesto. *New York City Too Far from Tampa Blues*. New York: Holiday, 1975.

Blume, Judy. *Tiger Eyes*. New York: Bradbury, 1982.

Bond, Nancy. *The Voyage Begun*. New York: Atheneum, 1981.

Bradford, Richard. *Red Sky at Morning*. Philadelphia: Lippincott, 1968.

Brancoto, Robin. *Something Left to Lose*. New York: Bantam, 1979.

_____. *Sweet Bells Jangled Out of Tune*. New York: Knopf, 1982.

Branfield, John. *The Fox in Winter*. New York; Atheneum, 1982.

Bridgers, Sue Ellen. *All Together Now*. New York: Knopf, 1979.

Cheatham, K. Follis. *Bring Home the Ghost*. New York: Harcourt Brace Jovanovich, 1980.

Cleaver, Vera, and Bill Cleaver. *Where the Lilies Bloom*. Philadelphia: Lippincott, 1969.

Danzinger, Paula. *Can You Sue Your Parents for Malpractice?* New York: Delacorte, 1979.

_____. *The Cat Ate My Gymsuit*. New York: Delacorte, 1974.

_____. *The Pistachio Prescription*. New York: Delacorte, 1978.

Davis, Gibbs. *Swann Song*. New York: Bradbury, 1982.

Degens, T. *Friends*. New York: Viking, 1982.

DeJongh, James, and Charles Cleveland. *City Cool*. New York: Random House, 1978.

Delton, Jina. *Two Blocks Down*. New York: Harper & Row, 1981.

Donovan, John. *Remove Protective Coating a Little at a Time*. New York: Harper & Row, 1973.

Elfman, Blossom. *The Return of the Whistler*. New York: Houghton Mifflin, 1981.

Gerson, Corinne. *Passing Through*. New York: Dell, 1980.

Gilbert, Anna. *Flowers for Lillian*. New York: St. Martin's, 1981.

Guy, Rosa. *Edith Jackson*. New York: Viking, 1978.

____. *The Friends*. New York: Holt, Rinehart & Winston, 1973.

Hamilton, Virginia. *M. C. Higgins the Great*. New York: Macmillan, 1974.

____. *The Planet of Junior Brown*. New York: Laurel Leaf, 1979.

____. *Zeely*. New York: Macmillan, 1967.

Hammer, Richard. *Mr. Jacobson's War*. New York: Harcourt Brace Jovanovich, 1981.

Hayes, Sheila. *Me and My Mona Lisa Smile*. New York: Elsevier-Nelson, 1981.

Hentoff, Nat. *I'm Really Dragged But Nothing Gets Me Down*. New York: Simon & Schuster, 1968.

Herbert, Frank. *SoulCatcher*. New York: Putnam, 1972.

Hinton, S. E. *That Was Then, This is Now*. New York: Viking, 1971.

Holland, Ruth. *The Room*. New York: Delacorte, 1973.

Hughes, Dean. *Switching Tracks*. New York: Atheneum, 1982.

Hunter, Kristin. *The Soul Brothers and Sister Lou*. New York: Scribner, 1968.

Kerr, M. E. *Is That You, Miss Blue?* New York: Harper & Row, 1975.

____. *The Son of Someone Famous*. New York: Harper & Row, 1974.

Knowles, John. *A Separate Peace*. New York: Macmillan, 1960.

Kullman, Harry. *The Battle Horse*. Trans. George Blecher and Lone Thygesen-Blecher. New York: Bradbury, 1981.

Levin, Jennifer. *Water Dancer*. New York: Poseidon, 1982.

Levoy, Myron. *Alan and Naomi*. New York: Harper & Row, 1977.

____. *A Shadow Like a Leopard*. New York: Harper & Row, 1981.

Magorian, Michelle. *Good Night, Mr. Tom*. New York: Harper & Row, 1982.

Mazer, Harry. *The War on Villa Street*. New York: Delacorte, 1978.

Mazer, Norma Fox. *A Figure of Speech*. New York: Delacorte, 1973.

Meriwether, Louise. *Daddy Was a Number Runner*. Englewood Cliffs, N.J.: Prentice-Hall, 1970.

Mohr, Nicholas. *El Bronx Remembered*. New York: Harper & Row, 1975.

_____. *In Nueva York*. New York: Dial, 1977.

Myers, Walter Dean. *Fast Sam, Cool Clyde, and Stuff*. New York: Viking, 1975.

_____. *Won't Know Till I Get There*. New York: Viking, 1982.

Nostlinger, Christine. *Luke and Angela*. New York: Harcourt Brace Jovanovich, 1981.

O'Dell, Scott. *Kathleen, Please Come Home*. New York: Houghton Mifflin, 1978.

Peck, Richard. *Close Enough to Touch*. New York: Delacorte, 1981.

Phipson, Joan. *A Tide Flowing*. New York: Atheneum, 1981.

Potok, Chaim. *The Chosen*. New York: Simon & Schuster, 1967.

_____. *In the Beginning*. New York: Knopf, 1975.

_____. *My Name Is Asher Lev*. New York: Knopf, 1972.

Reader, Dennis J. *Coming Back Alive*. New York: Random House, 1982.

Salinger, J. D. *The Catcher in the Rye*. Boston: Little, Brown, 1951.

Schmidt, Michael. *Green Island*. New York: Vanguard, 1982.

Sherman, D. R. *The Lion's Paw*. New York: Doubleday, 1975.

Somerlott, Robert. *Blaze*. New York: Viking, 1982.

Springstubb, Tricia. *Give and Take*. New York: Dell, 1981.

Stein, Sol. *The Magician*. New York: Delacorte, 1971.

Strachan, Ian. *Moses Beech*. New York: Oxford Univ. Press, 1982.

Swarthout, Glendon. *Bless the Beasts and Children*. New York: Doubleday, 1970.

Taylor, Mildred. *Roll of Thunder, Hear My Cry*. New York: Dial, 1976.

Voigt, Cynthia. *Tell Me If the Lovers Are Losers*. New York: Atheneum, 1982.

Walker, Mary Alexander. *Maggot*. New York: Atheneum, 1980.

Wharton, William. *A Midnight Clear*. New York: Knopf, 1982.

Wood, Phyllis Anderson. *This Time Count Me In*. Philadelphia: Westminster, 1980.

Yep, Laurence. *Kind Hearts and Gentle Monsters*. New York: Harper & Row, 1982.

Zindel, Paul. *Pardon Me, You're Stepping on My Eyeball.* New York: Harper & Row, 1976.

_____. *The Pigman.* New York: Harper & Row, 1968.

_____. *Let Me Hear You Whisper.* New York: Harper & Row, 1974.

HISTORICAL

Abel, Robert H. *Freedom Dues.* New York: Dial, 1980.

Auel, Jean M. *The Clan of the Cave Bear.* New York: Bantam, 1981.

Benchley, Nathaniel. *Beyond the Mists.* New York: Harper & Row, 1975.

Bickham, Jack M. *I Still Dream about Columbus.* New York: St. Martin's, 1982.

Bograd, Larry. *The Kolokol Papers.* New York: Farrar, Straus, & Giroux, 1981.

Bradley, David. *The Chaneysville Incident.* New York: Harper & Row, 1981.

Brindel, June Rachuy. *Ariadne.* New York: St. Martin's, 1980.

Brown, Dee. *Killdeer Mountain.* New York: Holt, Rinehart & Winston, 1983.

Burnford, Lolah. *The Vision of Stephen.* New York: Macmillan, 1972.

Burton, Hester. *Kate Ryder.* New York: Crowell, 1973.

_____. *To Ravensrigg.* New York: Crowell, 1977.

Clavell, James. *Shogun.* New York: Atheneum, 1975.

Collier, James, and Christopher Collier. *The Bloody Country.* Englewood Cliffs, N.J.: Four Winds-Scholastic, 1976.

Coleman, Terry. *Thanksgiving.* New York: Simon & Schuster, 1981.

Davis, Paxton. *Three Days.* New York: Atheneum, 1980.

Doctorow, E. L. *Ragtime.* New York: Random House, 1975.

Fast, Howard. *April Morning.* New York: Crown, 1961.

_____. *The Hessian.* New York: Dell, 1980.

_____. *The Immigrants.* New York: Houghton Mifflin, 1977.

Fox, Paula. *The Slave Dancer.* New York: Bradbury, 1973.

Gaan, Margaret. *Little Sister.* New York: Dodd, Mead, 1982.

Garfield, Leon. *Black Jack.* New York: Pantheon, 1969.

_____. *The Confidence Man.* New York: Viking, 1979.

_____. *Devil-in-the-Fog.* New York: Pantheon, 1966.

_____. *The Pleasure Garden.* New York: Viking, 1976.

_____. *The Prisoners of September.* New York: Viking, 1975.

_____. *The Strange Affair of Adelaide Harris*. New York: Pantheon, 1971.

Haugaard, Erik Christian. *Cromwell's Boy*. New York: Houghton Mifflin, 1978.

_____. *A Messenger for Parliament*. New York: Houghton Mifflin, 1976.

Heidish, Marcy Moran. *Witnesses*. New York: Houghton Mifflin, 1980.

Highwater, Jamake. *The Sun, He Rises*. Philadelphia: Lippincott, 1980.

Howe, Fanny. *The White Slave*. New York: Avon, 1980.

Hunt, Irene. *No Promises in the Wind*. Chicago: Follett, 1970.

Hunter, Mollie. *The Stronghold*. New York: Harper & Row, 1974.

Keith, Harold. *This Obstinate Land*. New York: Crowell, 1977.

Keneally, Thomas. *Confederates*. New York: Harper & Row, 1980.

Llywelyn, Morgan. *The Horse Goddess*. New York: Houghton Mifflin, 1982.

Lord, Bette Bao. *Spring Moon*. New York: Harper & Row, 1981.

McCullough, Colleen. *The Thornbirds*. New York: Harper & Row, 1977.

Meggs, Brown. *The War Train: A Novel of 1916*. New York: Atheneum, 1981.

Michener, James A. *Centennial*. New York: Random House, 1974.

Namioka, Lensey. *The Samurai and the Long-Nosed Devils*. New York: Dell, 1980.

_____. *White Serpent Castle*. New York: Dell, 1980.

O'Dell, Scott. *Carlota*. New York: Dell, 1980.

_____. *The Hawk That Dare Not Hunt by Night*. New York: Houghton Mifflin, 1975.

_____. *Island of the Blue Dolphins*. New York: Houghton Mifflin, 1960.

Peck, Robert Newton. *Millie's Boy*. New York: Dell, 1975.

Renault, Mary. *The Bull from the Sea*. New York: Vintage, 1975.

_____. *The King Must Die*. New York: Atheneum, 1958.

_____. *The Last of the Wine*. New York: Pocket Books, 1964.

_____. *The Persian Boy*. New York: Bantam 1974.

_____. *The Praise Singer*. New York: Pantheon, 1978.

Sutcliff, Rosemary. *Frontier Wolf*. New York: Elsevier-Nelson, 1981.

_____. *The Lantern Bearers*. New York: Walck, 1959.

_____. *The Shield Ring*. New York: Walck, 1957.

_____. *The Silver Branch*. New York: Walck, 1958.

_____. *Song for a Dark Queen*. New York: Crowell, 1979.

_____. *The Sword and the Circle: King Arthur and the Knights of the Round Table*. New York: Dutton, 1981.

West, Jessamyn. *The Massacre at Fall Creek*. New York: Harcourt Brace Jovanovich, 1975.

MYSTERY

Aiken, Joan. *Nightbirds on Nantucket*. New York: Dell, 1981.

_____. *The Wolves of Willoughby Chase*. New York: Dell, 1981.

Anderson, Mary. *. . . Forever, Ahbra*. New York: Atheneum, 1981.

Anthony, Evelyn. *The Janus Imperative*. New York: New American Library, 1981.

Ball, John. *In the Heat of the Night*. New York: Harper & Row, 1965.

Benedict, Stewart H. *The Crime Solvers*. New York: Dell, 1966.

Bennett, Jay. *The Birthday Murderer*. New York: Delacorte, 1977.

_____. *The Dangling Witness*. New York: Delacorte, 1974.

_____. *Deathman, Do Not Follow Me*. Chicago: Meredith, 1968.

_____. *The Executioner*. New York: Avon, 1982.

_____. *The Long Black Coat*. New York: Delacorte, 1972.

_____. *Say Hello to the Hit Man*. New York: Delacorte, 1976.

Borthwick, J. S. *The Case of the Hook-Billed Kites*. New York: St. Martin's, 1982.

Branscum, Robbie. *Johnny May*. New York: Doubleday, 1975.

Cameron, Eleanor. *Beyond Silence*. New York: Dutton, 1980.

Christian, Mary Blount. *Deadline for Danger*. Chicago: Albert Whitman, 1982.

Christie, Agatha. *And Then There Were None*. New York: Dodd, Mead, 1940.

_____. *The Murder of Roger Ackroyd*. New York: Dodd, Mead, 1926.

_____. *Murder on the Orient Express*. New York: Dodd, Mead, 1981.

Clark, Mary Higgins. *The Cradle Will Fall*. New York: Dell, 1981.

_____. *A Stranger Is Watching*. New York: Dell, 1979.

_____. *Where Are the Children?* New York: Dell, 1979.

Cook, Robin. *Brain*. New York: Putnam, 1981.

Corlett, William. *The Dark Side of the Moon*. New York: Bradbury, 1977.

De Andrea, William L. *The Lunatic Fringe: A Novel Wherein Theodore Roosevelt Meets the Pink Angel*. New York: Evans, 1980.

Dickens, Charles, and Leon Garfield. *The Mystery of Edwin Drood*. New York: Pantheon, 1981.

Dibdin, Michael. *The Last Sherlock Holmes Story*. New York: Pantheon, 1978.

Duncan, Lois. *Daughters of Eve*. New York: Dell, 1980.

———. *Down a Dark Hall*. New York: New American Library, 1975.

———. *Five Were Missing*. New York: New American Library, 1980.

Follett, Ken. *Triple*. New York: New American Library, 1980.

Garfield, Brian. *The Threeperson Hunt*. New York: Evans, 1974.

Gosling, Paula. *The Zero Trap*. New York: Coward, 1980.

Greenburg, Dan. *Love Kills*. New York: Harcourt Brace Jovanovich, 1978.

Hamilton, Virginia. *The House of Dies Drear*. New York: Laurel Leaf, 1979.

Hillerman, Tony. *The Blessing Way*. New York: Harper & Row, 1970.

———. *Dance Hall of the Dead*. New York: Harper & Row, 1973.

———. *The Listening Woman*. New York: Harper & Row, 1978.

James, P. D. *The Black Tower*. New York: Scribner, 1972.

———. *Death of an Expert Witness*. New York: Scribner, 1977.

———. *An Unsuitable Job for a Woman*. New York: Scribner, 1972.

Kemelman, Harry. *Friday the Rabbi Slept Late*. New York: Crown, 1964.

———. *Monday the Rabbi Took Off*. New York: Putnam, 1972.

———. *Thursday the Rabbi Walked Out*. New York: Morrow, 1978.

———. *Wednesday the Rabbi Got Wet*. New York: Morrow, 1976.

Kittredge, William, and Steven M. Krauzer. *The Great American Detective*. New York: Mentor, 1978.

Le Carré, John. *The Spy Who Came In from the Cold*. New York: Coward, 1964.

L'Engle, Madeleine. *Dragons in the Waters*. New York: Dell, 1982.

MacDonald, John D. *The Dreadful Lemon Sky*. Philadelphia: Lippincott, 1975.

———. *The Green Ripper*. New York: Fawcett, 1979.

McDonald, Gregory. *Who Took Toby Rinaldi?* New York: Putnam, 1980.

Madsen, David. *Black Plume: The Suppressed Memories of Edgar Allan Poe*. New York: Simon & Schuster, 1980.

Marsh, Ngaio. *Light Thickens*. Boston: Little, Brown, 1982.

Martin, George R. R. *Fevre Dream*. New York: Poseidon, 1982.

Mazer, Norma Fox. *Taking Terri Mueller*. New York: Morrow, 1981.

Melville, James. *The Ninth Netsuke*. New York: St. Martin's, 1982.

Meyer, Nicholas. *The Seven-Per-Cent Solution*. New York: Dutton, 1974.

———. *The West End Horror: A Posthumous Memoir of John H. Watson, M. D.* New York: Dutton, 1976.

O'Toole, G. J. A. *Poor Richard's Game*. New York: Delacorte, 1982.

Peters, Elizabeth. *The Curse of the Pharaohs*. New York: Dodd, Mead, 1981.

Platt, Kin. *Run For Your Life*. New York: Dell, 1979.

Pronzini, Bill, ed. *The Edgar Winners: 33rd Annual Anthology of the Mystery Writers of America*. New York: Random House, 1980.

Rendell, Ruth. *No More Dying Then*. London: Hutchinson, 1971.

———. *A Sleeping Life*. New York: Doubleday, 1978.

———. *Some Lie and Some Die*. London: Hutchinson, 1973.

Saul, John. *Comes the Blind Fury*. New York: Dell, 1980.

Schellie, Don. *Maybe Next Summer*. New York: Scholastic, 1980.

Smith, Martin Cruz. *Gorky Park*. New York: Random House, 1981.

Zindel, Paul. *The Undertaker's Gone Bananas*. New York: Harper & Row, 1978.

SCIENCE FICTION, FANTASY, AND SUPERNATURAL

Adams, Douglas. *The Hitchhiker's Guide to the Galaxy*. New York: Crown, 1980.

———. *Life, the Universe, and Everything*. New York: Crown, 1982.

Alexander, Lloyd. *The High King*. New York: Holt, Rinehart & Winston, 1968.

———. *Taran Wanderer*. New York: Holt, Rinehart & Winston, 1967.

Anderson, Poul. *The Dancer from Atlantis*. New York: Doubleday, 1971.

———. *Fantasy*. New York: Pinnacle, 1981.

Anson, Jay. *The Amityville Horror*. Englewood Cliffs, N.J.: Prentice-Hall, 1977.

Beagle, Peter. *A Fine and Private Place*. New York: Viking, 1960.

———. *The Last Unicorn*. New York: Viking, 1969.

Berger, Thomas. *Arthur Rex*. New York: Delacorte, 1978.

Blatty, William P. *The Exorcist*. New York: Harper & Row, 1971.

Bova, Ben. *Voyagers*. New York: Doubleday, 1981.

Bradbury, Ray. *Fahrenheit 451*. New York: Doubleday, 1951.

———. *The Illustrated Man*. New York: Doubleday, 1951.

_____. *The Martian Chronicles.* New York: Doubleday, 1950.

_____. *The Stories of Ray Bradbury.* New York: Knopf, 1980.

Campbell, Ramsey. *The Parasite.* New York: Macmillan, 1980.

Card, Orson Scott. *Songmaster.* New York: Dial, 1980.

_____. *Unaccompanied Sonata and Other Stories.* New York: Dial, 1981.

Carr, Terry, ed. *Dream's Edge: Science Fiction Stories about the Future of Planet Earth.* New York: Sierra Club Books, 1980.

Clarke, Arthur C. *Childhood's End.* New York: Ballantine, 1953.

_____. *2010: Odessey Two.* New York: Ballantine, 1982.

Cooper, Susan. *The Dark Is Rising.* New York: Atheneum, 1973.

_____. *Greenwitch.* New York: Atheneum, 1974.

_____. *The Grey King.* New York: Atheneum, 1975.

_____. *Over Sea, Under Stone.* New York: Harcourt Brace Jovanovich, 1966.

_____. *Silver on the Tree.* New York: Atheneum, 1977.

Coyne, John. *The Searing.* New York: Putnam, 1980.

Crichton, Michael. *The Andromeda Strain.* New York: Knopf, 1969.

Donaldson, Stephen R. *The Wounded Land: The Second Chronicles of Thomas Covenant—Book One.* New York: Ballantine, 1980.

Duncan, Lois. *A Gift of Magic.* Boston: Litle, Brown, 1976.

_____. *Summer of Fear.* Boston: Little, Brown, 1976.

Engdahl, Sylvia Louise. *The Doors of the Universe.* New York: Atheneum, 1981.

Farmer, Philip Jose. *The Magic Labyrinth.* New York: Berkley, 1980.

Goldman, William. *Magic.* New York: Delacorte, 1976.

Gordon, John. *The Ghost on the Hill.* New York: Viking, 1977.

Hamilton, Virginia. *The Gathering.* New York: Greenwillow, 1981.

_____. *Justice and Her Brothers.* New York: Greenwillow, 1978.

Harris, Marilyn. *The Conjurers.* New York: Random House, 1974.

Heinlein, Robert A. *The Number of the Beast.* New York: Fawcett/Columbine, 1980.

_____. *Stranger in a Strange Land.* New York: Putnam, 1961.

Herbert, Frank. *Dune.* Radnor, Pa.: Chilton, 1965.

_____. *God Emperor of Dune.* New York: Putnam, 1981.

King, Stephen. *The Firestarter.* New York: Viking, 1980.

_____. *The Shining.* New York: Doubleday, 1977.

Knight, Damon. *The World and Thorinn.* New York: Putnam, 1981.

Konvitz, Jeffrey. *The Sentinel.* New York: Simon & Schuster, 1974.

Kurtz, Katherine. *Deryni Checkmate*. New York: Ballantine, 1972.

———. *Deryni Rising*. New York: Ballantine, 1970.

———. *High Deryni*. New York: Ballantine, 1973.

Le Guin, Ursula K. *The Beginning Place*. New York: Harper & Row, 1980.

———. *The Dispossessed*. New York: Harper & Row, 1974.

———. *The Farthest Shore*. New York: Atheneum, 1972.

———. *The Left Hand of Darkness*. New York: Ace, 1969.

———. *The Tombs of Atuan*. New York: Atheneum, 1971.

———. *A Wizard of Earthsea*. Berkeley, Calif.: Parnassus, 1968.

Martin, George R. R., and Lisa Tuttle. *Windhaven*. New York: Pocket Books, 1982.

McCaffrey, Anne. *Dragondrums*. New York: Atheneum, 1979.

———. *Dragonsinger*. New York: Atheneum, 1977.

———. *Dragonsong*. New York: Atheneum, 1976.

———. *The Ship Who Sang*. New York: Walker, 1969.

McKillip, Patricia A. *The Forgotten Beasts of Eld*. New York: Atheneum, 1974.

———. *Harpist in the Wind*. New York: Atheneum, 1979.

McKinley, Robin. *Beauty*. New York: Harper & Row, 1978.

Miller, Walter M. *A Canticle for Leibowitz*. Philadelphia: Lippincott, 1959.

Newman, Sharon. *Guinevere*. New York: St. Martin's, 1981.

Niven, Larry, and Jerry Pournelle. *The Mote in God's Eye*. New York: Simon & Schuster, 1974.

Niven, Larry, and Steven Barnes. *Dream Park*. New York: Ace, 1981.

Norton, Alice Mary [Andre Norton]. *Dark Piper*. New York: Harcourt Brace Jovanovich, 1968.

———. *Gryphon in Glory*. New York: Atheneum, 1981.

———. *Moon of Three Rings*. New York: Atheneum, 1976.

———. *Wraiths of Time*. New York: Atheneum, 1976.

O'Brien, Robert. *Z for Zachariah*. New York: Atheneum, 1975.

Peck, Richard. *The Ghost Belonged to Me*. New York: Viking, 1975.

———. *Ghosts I Have Been*. New York: Viking, 1977.

Pohl, Frederik. *Beyond the Blue Event Horizon*. New York: Ballantine, 1980.

Pohl, Frederik, et. al., eds. *The Great Science Fiction Series*. New York: Harper & Row, 1980.

Sargent, Pamela. *Watchstar*. New York: Simon & Schuster, 1980.

Schiff, Stuart David, ed. *Mad Scientists: An Anthology of Fantasy and Horror.* New York: Doubleday, 1980.

Scithers, George, ed. *Isaac Asimov's World of Science Fiction.* New York: Dial, 1980.

Sherburne, Zoa. *Why Have All the Birds Stopped Singing?* New York: Morrow, 1974.

Siddons, Anne Rivers. *The House Next Door.* New York: Simon & Schuster, 1978.

Silverberg, Robert. *Lord Valentine's Castle.* New York: Harper & Row, 1980.

_____. *Shadrack.* Indianapolis: Bobbs-Merrill, 1976.

_____. *The World Inside.* New York: Doubleday, 1971.

Silverberg, Robert, ed. *Science Fiction Hall of Fame: The Greatest Science Fiction Stories of All Time.* New York: Doubleday, 1971.

Sleator, William. *House of Stairs.* New York: Dutton, 1974.

Stableford, Brian M. *Halcyon Drift.* New York: Daw, 1972.

Stewart, Mary. *The Crystal Cave.* New York: Morrow, 1970.

_____. *The Hollow Hills.* New York: Morrow, 1973.

_____. *The Last Enchantment.* New York: Morrow, 1979.

Stone, Elna. *The Visitation.* New York: St. Martin's, 1980.

Storr, Catherine. *Winter's End.* New York: Harper & Row, 1979.

Straub, Peter. *Shadowland.* New York: Coward, 1980.

Tolkien, J. R. R. *The Hobbit, or There and Back Again.* New York: Houghton Mifflin, 1937; rev. ed., 1965.

_____. *The Lord of the Rings.* New York: Houghton Mifflin, 1954–56.

_____. *The Silmarillion.* New York: Houghton Mifflin, 1977.

Venables, The Reverend Hubert, ed. *The Frankenstein Diaries.* New York: Viking, 1983.

Wangerin, Walter, Jr. *The Book of the Dun Cow.* New York: Harper & Row, 1978.

White, T. H. *The Once and Future King.* New York: Putnam, 1940.

_____. *The Sword in the Stone.* New York: Putnam, 1939.

Wibberley, Leonard. *The Mouse That Roared.* Boston: Little, Brown, 1955.

Windling, Terri, and Mark Alan Arnold, eds. *Elsewhere.* New York: Ace/Grosset, 1981.

Wolfe, Gene. *The Shadow of the Torturer.* New York: Simon & Schuster, 1980.

Zelazny, Roger. *Coils.* New York: Pinnacle, 1982.

_____. *The Last Defender of Camelot.* New York: Pocket Books, 1980.

NOTES

1. Judy Blume, *Forever . . .* (New York: Pocket Books, 1976), p. 9.
2. Blume, p. 93.
3. Blume, p. 116.
4. Ann Head, *Mr. and Mrs. Bo Jo Jones* (New York: New American Library, 1967), pp. 8–9.
5. Walker Gibson, "Authors, Speakers, Readers, and Mock Readers," *College English,* 11, No. 5 (Feb. 1950), 265–69.
6. Head, p. 47.
7. Lois Duncan, *Killing Mr. Griffin* (New York: Dell, 1978), p. 59.
8. Duncan, pp. 69–70.
9. Sandra Scoppettone, *Happy Endings Are All Alike* (New York: Dell, 1978), pp. 114–15.
10. Scoppettone, pp. 160–62.
11. Robert Cormier, *The Chocolate War* (New York: Dell, 1974), p. 187.
12. G. Robert Carlsen, *Books and the Teenage Reader: A Guide for Teachers, Librarians, and Parents,* 2nd rev. ed. (New York: Harper & Row, 1967), p. 59.
13. Paul Zindel, *I Never Loved Your Mind* (New York: Bantam, 1972), p. 1.
14. Paul Zindel, *The Undertaker's Gone Bananas* (New York: Bantam, 1979), p. 45.
15. Zindel, *Undertaker,* p. 151.

Visual Literacy 6

Film and television are forms of literature. We might quarrel over their merits, arguing that some films and most television are too bad to be called literature; however, the same could be said of much of what passes for literature in the bookstores. Bookstores themselves sometimes make the distinction, labeling one section "literature"—the good stuff—and another "fiction"—the popular stuff. But we can't dispute the parallels between much of film and television and the more traditional literature, both fiction and drama.

The typical movie or television show (excluding, of course, news programs, game shows, and the like) is clearly dramatic fiction. It has characters, as do the novel and the play. It places those characters in some conflict, which they must resolve; thus, it has a plot, with beginning, middle, and end (except the soap opera, which has only a middle). It is divided into scenes, with some of the same techniques for transition between them that would be found in a stage play. It may develop a theme, or at least focus on some controlling idea. It shares, in brief, many features of fiction and perhaps most features of dramatic literature.

Further, it works as both fiction and drama work. It evokes responses from viewers—sympathy for one character, dislike for another, anxiety in the suspenseful moments, and satisfaction when the tension is resolved. It leaves characters and situations only partially described, requiring viewers to fill in imaginatively. The incompleteness of literature, both visual and printed, is at best a productive ambiguity allowing readers to add something of themselves to the reading, and at worst the shallow stereotyping that provides hardly any unique detail at all. Whether best or worst, however, the technique is virtually the same for the visual and the printed—a representation is offered to the viewers, who flesh it out imaginatively, respond to it, and perhaps think about it.

163

The visual literature is also as value-laden as the written. Dealing with human life as it does, it cannot be otherwise. It continually reveals its values in its choice of some subjects—crime, violence, romance—rather than others—philosophy, art, scholarship. Further, it probably serves to inculcate those values in its audience, as written literature does, subtly suggesting to them what is important and how they ought to view things. Ellis has pointed out that, for instance, our view of love tends to be closer to the vision offered in popular novels, songs, television commercials, and movies than to the facts of love and marriage as recorded by the sociologists and psychologists. Love, Ellis observes, does not conquer all, as the divorce rate suggests. It must be nurtured and cared for, not simply "fallen into."[1] Yet people tend to accept unreflectively the simpler visions presented in fiction.

This last similarity—the embodiment and communication of values—constitutes the strongest argument for granting film and television a place in the curriculum. Television, especially, is the literature we are immersed in for three to four hours a day, on the average. If film and television do function as written literature does, communicating a vision of the world, and if viewers do absorb from them ideas of good and bad, possible and impossible, true and false, then it is appropriate that the schools teach children to watch them intelligently. So far the schools have largely neglected this task. Few courses focus on the visual media, and fewer still grant them a place, even a small one, beside the written literature. Students are trained to enjoy and analyze written literature all through public school, while the visual literature that occupies much more of their time and may influence them more subtly is ignored.

Students are sometimes urged not to waste their time watching television, but the appeal is a moral rather than an intellectual one, since it is usually presented as a premise, not as a reasoned conclusion. It is assumed that television is a waste of time. In the schools, at least, the student sees no investigation or questioning of the medium, but only the cautioning of a teacher who wants the students to have time for the literature she teaches. It is an exhortation easily ignored.

And it should be. Children should question a teacher's ungrounded assertions just as they should the messages of television or the enticements of advertising. To accept those messages uncritically is to accept discipleship, to place one's mind in the control of someone else. The schools should work instead to create thinking, skeptical, rational people.

It seems reasonable, then, to invite students to examine the visual media. They fill much of the students' lives anyway, and will continue to do so whether the schools pay attention to them or not. They reflect certain ideas of the world, and thus ought to be thought about rather than simply absorbed. And they are simple and accessible enough that students should be able to understand and analyze them thoroughly.

What, then, should students be expected to learn about the visual media? First, they might analyze their own habits and patterns. Film and television are an important part of almost everyone's life. Even homes without books, newspapers, and indoor plumbing have television, maybe even with cable service. In almost every home, students will find that television is part of the habit and ritual of the day. Second, they might learn that watching film and television can be much like reading a literary work; they can respond to and think about the visual just as they would the written. Third, they may learn something about the technical elements of visual literature and their differences from techniques of written literature.

EXAMINATION OF HABITS

Let us begin with the first issue—the habits of the students. Were we to investigate their reading habits, we might find a tremendous range. Some students, especially in the middle or junior high schools, are voracious readers, devouring books at a rate they will never again equal as adults. Others may proudly state that they have never read a book and never hope to. Some of those who do read may choose a wide variety of books, while others may stick to books about horses, books by Judy Blume, or some other narrow category.

On the other hand, if we examine the viewing habits of our students (and let us ignore film for the moment), we will find that nearly all spend a fairly large amount of time watching television. There are non-readers, but there seem to be almost no non-viewers. Different students will watch different shows, but they will watch something. Perhaps surprisingly, the teenage audience watches an average of only 3½ hours per day, half an hour less than the other age groups. Roberts attributes this difference to the competing demands of school, social life, and other media.[2] Nonetheless, 3½ hours a day is a lot of time—almost eight thousand hours during the six years of secondary school—and it should provide plenty of material for discussion.

THE TELEVISION LOG

Students might assess the role of television in their lives by keeping a log for a week or two. They can devise the log themselves, deciding what information they are interested in obtaining, but it should include the title of the program, its time and station, the nature of the show (comedy, mystery, soap opera), its sponsors, and perhaps some notes on its content and their reactions to the show. This sort of information can be analyzed in several ways. The students might begin by summarizing the data across the class to determine the most and least popular shows. They might then examine those lists and speculate about the characteristics of the shows that account for their rank. They might even be asked to watch several shows closely, perhaps armed with a checklist or set of questions, in order to confirm or refute their guesses.

An exercise such as this is useful practice in gathering and interpreting data, set in the context of the students' own lives rather than the more academic areas to which many assigned research papers lead. Because this research focuses on an aspect of the students' world, it is more likely to stimulate reflection and talk.

Analyzing tastes and preferences can lead students to insights into themselves, the others in the class, and the medium itself, as do discussions of response to written literature. Students fond of M*A*S*H may observe that they are amused by the interplay of vastly different characters like Colonel Potter, Hawkeye, and Klinger, curious about their ability to work comfortably together, and encouraged by the show's constant message that human life is valuable and its suffering to be sympathized with and alleviated. By noting such reactions, students come to understand themselves and the show better. If they say simply, "I like the show," or perhaps say nothing at all, but only sit down regularly to watch it for reasons unexamined, they miss an opportunity to learn something.

Similarly, hearing such comments made by others might teach students something about their classmates, revealing aspects of their minds and personalities that were hidden in the dimmer light of the daily routine. Such discoveries might show the students new ways of seeing the world. Those who see M*A*S*H as a dull war story with not enough fighting and killing may learn from their classmates another way of looking at the show that offers pleasures their own habits of thought have locked out.

The television log is, then, a basis for discussing responses. Unable to bring television shows into the classroom, except with a great deal of difficulty, the teacher can nonetheless begin with the perceptions and reactions of the students, rather than with information on form, production, history, industrial organization, and the like. The focus is on the students themselves—their reactions to the medium serve as windows into their own minds and those of their classmates.

Students may also learn something about the group. They might find, for instance, that the boys in the class tend to watch certain shows while the girls prefer others. Identifying the distinguishing characteristics of these shows might be revealing. Further, they may think about the shows they watched several years ago, or better still, collect data from younger students, and compare the interests of the different age groups. Again, the objective is not the list of shows, but an analysis of students' reactions and the features of the shows that seem to cause them.

Such analysis should lead fairly smoothly into a discussion of conception and technique. The teacher can ask students what it is they like about a show; with some urging, they may begin to talk about details. When students have reached that point, they are less passive and mindless in their viewing. The talk can then proceed in one of two directions, both worth pursuing. Students might be led to consider either the vision of the world they are being offered or the technical elements of the medium itself. Of these two issues, the first will arouse more interest.

TELEVISION'S WORLD VIEW

The public and the press have been concerned for some time about the effects of television on the young. Violence and sex are the central concerns. The fear is that viewers will imitate the behavior they witness, and the typical response to that fear is condemnation and censorship. The past several decades have seen increasing complaints from such groups as the National Citizens' Committee for Broadcasting, the National Gay Task Force, and Action for Children's Television. Large or small, rational or not, they all want to establish some control over television and thus over the thinking of the people who watch it. Even the National Rifle Association has found occasion to object to the content of television broadcasting, criticizing a CBS special, "The Guns of Autumn," which suggested that hunting is not a kind and gentle recreation.

The issue is not simple. There is evidence that both children and adults can be influenced by what they watch. The theory that television is cathartic, allowing viewers to release their aggressions vicariously, has been abandoned by most researchers. As Berkowitz remarked in his opening address to a Media Violence Conference in Stockholm, " . . . most authorities are . . . fairly well agreed that the viewers do not discharge their own pent up aggressive impulses simply through watching other people beat each other up."[3] Berkowitz cites instances in which the fictional violence of television and film has been obviously and directly imitated, and reports research indicating that aggression on film can increase the viewer's willingness to act aggressively and her tendency to see aggression as justified. He points out that even "well socialized, well behaved university students" can be stimulated by violent movies to "stronger attacks upon an available target." "The argument," he says, "by and large, is over. Media violence can have bad effects and can stimulate aggressive behaviour."[4]

The arguments, of course, continue. One is over the broadcast industry's responsibility. On the one hand, it is argued that very few people are disturbed enough to be stimulated to violence by watching a violent television program, and these people are likely to commit violent acts without that added stimulus. Those who hold this position argue that the harm done by censorship will far outweigh the minuscule good achieved. On the other hand, there are those who think the networks should be held legally responsible for acts that can be linked to their shows. An eleven million dollar suit was filed against NBC in 1978, charging it with responsibility for a sexual assault committed in apparent imitation of a scene from the movie *Born Innocent*. Some time later, a lawyer defending a young man accused of murder argued that his client had watched so many violent television shows that his judgment was hopelessly distorted, and that therefore television, and not he, was guilty. The defense was, of course, ludicrous; if successful, it would have effectively relieved everyone of the responsibility for her own behavior if she could find a model for it somewhere. Still, that the argument could be made at all is instructive. It illustrates the difficulty of determining the roles of viewer and medium in shaping behavior and suggests that responsibility is an important issue in the debate.

Rather than argue the appropriateness of public control over the broadcast media, or the merits of censorship boards, or even the value of television's image of the world, it seems best to try to define the school's role in teaching about a medium that can influence the viewer's conception of the world and her behavior. In any society that purports to respect freedom of thought, censorship is inappropriate. There is no set of beliefs and values that all citizens will agree on, no code of behavior that everyone will happily abide by, no certified standard of right and wrong that everyone will subscribe to. Lacking that unanimity, we can either impose some standard, censoring and prohibiting whatever departs from it, or accept diversity, arguing for our own views but tolerating or even welcoming those of others. The second alternative seems more promising. The world's experiments with totalitarianism have not been happy ones.

If we are to teach students to deal with diversity of opinion, then we must confront them with that diversity and encourage them to think about it carefully. In other words, they need to learn to reflect on what they see—something they rarely do. Watching television is usually a passive activity, often accompanied by other activities such as eating or doing homework. Most families do not talk much about television, and thus its more subtle messages tend to go unexamined. Our failure to analyze makes us susceptible to the indirect messages of the medium. Fiske and Hartley observe:

> The world of television is clearly different from our real social world, but just as clearly related to it in some ways. We might clarify this relationship by saying that television does not represent the manifest actuality of our society, but rather reflects, symbolically, the structure of values and relationships beneath the surface.[5]

It is this structure of values, and what it may do to the viewer, that concerns Gerbner and Gross, who discuss the possible long-range effects of television viewing. Their analysis of the content of television programs leads them to the following observations and conclusions:

> Night after night, week after week, stock characters and dramatic patterns convey supposed truths about people, power and issues. . . .
> Unlike the real world, where personalities are complex, motives unclear, and outcomes ambiguous, television presents a world of clarity and simplicity. In show after show, rewards and punishments follow quickly and logically. Crises are resolved, problems are solved, and justice, or at least authority, always triumphs. The central characters in these dramas are clearly defined: dedicated or corrupt; selfless or ambitious; efficient or ineffectual. To insure the widest acceptability, (or greatest potential profitability) the plot lines follow the most commonly accepted notions of morality and justice, whether or not those notions bear much resemblance to reality.
> In order to complete a story entertainingly in only an hour or even half an hour, conflicts on TV are usually personal and solved by action. Since violence is dramatic, and relatively simple to produce, much of the action tends to be violent. As a result, the stars of prime-time network

TV have for years been cowboys, detectives, and others whose lives permit unrestrained action.[6]

Gerbner and Gross also study the views held by the American public and conclude that heavy viewers tend to have distorted notions that can be traced to television. For instance, most leading characters in shows are, quite naturally, American. Heavy viewers are much more likely than others to overestimate what percentage of the world's population lives in the United States. Among occupations, the professions are twice as heavily represented on television as in the real world. Again, heavy viewers asked to estimate the real proportions are much more likely than light viewers to overestimate. Both cases seem to reflect the influence of television's view of the world.

Television not only influences our culture, Leonard argues, it "*is* our culture, the only coherence we have going for us, naturally the repository of our symbols, the attic of old histories and hopes, the hinge on the doors of change." It both reflects us and trains us:

> The sitcom, after a lot of thrashing about with events and personalities, instructs the members of its "family"—and the rest of us—on appropriate behavior, helps them internalize the various decencies, define the wayward virtues, modulate peeves, legislate etiquette, compromise the ineffability of self with clamors of peer groups.
>
> In the Fifties, that flabby decade, the sitcom proposed as a paradigm the incompetent father, the dizzy mother, the innocent child. In the Sixties, it proposed the incompetent father, the dizzy mother, the innocent child, war as a fun thing and young women with supernatural powers (witch genie, magical nanny, flying nun) who could take care of their men and their children, look cute, and never leave the house. In the Seventies, it proposed the incompetent father, the dizzy mother, innocent child —all sitting around discussing abortion, infidelity, impotence, homosexuality, drug addiction, and death—and the career girl (have talent, need sex). The inability of the American father to lace up the shoes of his own mind without falling off his rocker has been constant, perfectly reflecting and perpetuating our cultural expectations.[7]

If television offers us that sort of perception, then we must teach students to receive it critically and skeptically, not simply to absorb it. Were we to accept uncritically the visions offered us, we would be burdened with a narrow and unrealistic view of the world and of huge groups of people. If we were to impose on the real world the expectations cultivated by television, we would find ourselves committing a serious injustice.

But stereotypes are not invulnerable. They can be identified, examined, and dealt with. The structure of values Fiske and Hartley refer to may be complex, subtle, and quietly interwoven into the story, but it is not totally inaccessible or fixed. Looking back, we remember a time when television showed women only in the home, or perhaps as teachers or librarians—not in the courtroom, the operating room, or the police car. Similarly, we remember when a black man or woman could be a laborer or a maid, but not a scientist, scholar, or judge. Television reflects and perpetuates the visions of existing culture but it can not sustain these views in the face of other forces.

The questions for students now are "What impressions of the world, and what system of values, is television promoting?" and "How do your own perceptions and values differ from those you find on television?" They may differ a little or a great deal, but the student must identify those differences to gain control over them and avoid absorbing the perceptions he is offered.

Television changes quickly in some ways, and it would be difficult to predict the shape of television's world in the future. Stein complained in 1979 that television portrays businessmen and military men as evil and gives the inaccurate impression that most killing is committed by a white middle-class person upon a white middle-class victim.[8] By 1989 the patterns it reveals may be vastly different. Whatever they are at any moment, however, students can investigate them fairly easily, using their discussion of preferences as a basis.

They could, for instance, choose several shows, each to be analyzed by a small group of students. The class might be asked to plan a series of questions, or a checklist of features, to use in the study. Its content would vary according to the interests and sophistication of the class, but it should include questions about the nature of protagonists and antagonists, the patterns in the plot, and the typical outcome. Consider the following very brief set of questions:

1. Who is the protagonist? What are her most appealing traits? What are her least appealing traits?
2. Who is the antagonist? What are her characteristics?
3. What is the central element of conflict in the show? Is it about money, power, love, something else?
4. How is the issue resolved? By fighting, reasoning, chance, something else?

As simple as the list is, it can help to stimulate further investigations. For instance, the description of the protagonist might suggest a second set of questions. If the students' notes show that most of the heroes they observed are male, white, middle-class, single, tall, clean-shaven, with non-routine jobs, they might then look at all the prime time shows and ask,

1. What is the hero's sex?
2. What is the hero's race?
3. His economic status?
4. His employment?
5. Physical features?
6. Marital status?

The data yielded by this second set of questions might reveal a bias in television's conception of the world. Perhaps the students will discover that most heroes in the adventure shows—the comedies will differ—*do* share those characteristics they first noticed. What, they might be encouraged to ask themselves, does that mean? Why does that particular image dominate? Do they find themselves or others emulating the characters they see portrayed? What might those not cast in the same mold think about the image of the hero? Are there respectable, happy patterns and personalities not represented? Would they actually want to live as the television heroes live?

Such questions may lead students to consider several issues, not the least significant of which is the commercial nature of television. One reason for the predominance of certain character types is simply financial. A show is a device that sells a product, and its success is determined by how many people watch the show and may thus be influenced to buy the product. Consequently, shows are designed for wide appeal. Heroes are created, and actors chosen, to capture the largest possible audience. What features, the teacher may ask her students, would they give the hero of a show intended to attract the bulk of the viewing audience in this country? Perhaps they could even design shows and propose them to another class, who would play the role of network or potential sponsor and select those they predict would be financially worth producing.

It may be easier to talk about the rationale for presenting the public with a rather uniform hero than about the possible effects of that image on viewers, but the question may nonetheless be raised. It might be easier to start with one show or a small group of shows than to try to generalize about all television. The teacher might ask: "What characteristics seem to be presented as good traits in the main characters of ____?" Students could then consider whether they respect those characteristics and whether they think many people do. The ruthlessness of the heroes of *Dallas*, for instance—is it to be admired? Is it also present in other shows? Media studies reveal that it is. Police programs, for example, often show their heroes performing in ways that would, in the real world, be considered gross violation of police procedure, though they are dramatic and effective in the fictional world of television. Do they, too, glorify a kind of ruthlessness? Fiske and Hartley, referring to several studies of television and social values, argue that "the main difference between heroes and villains is the greater efficiency of the heroes and the sympathy with which they are presented. Otherwise, there are few clear-cut distinctions, particularly in morality or method."[9]

Students investigating the values present in the shows they watch may reach similar conclusions. They may wonder how constant, unreflective viewing of shows that promote such values might affect the thinking of the watchers. Could people gradually and unwittingly absorb those same values? The teacher might point out that adults have been killed and injured imitating the reckless driving style of the Burt Reynolds movies or the *Dukes of Hazzard* television show, although the stunts are obviously dangerous and clearly demolish the cars used in them. If adults are so easily deceived, how will they fare with more subtle ethical questions? How, we may ask, can we avoid the grip of these unhealthy conceptions?

We have suggested some questions that could be asked about the heroes on television. Students might ask similar questions about the villains. Do they also follow a pattern, and if so, what does that indicate? Or we might ask about typical plots. Students might divide the shows into genres—police procedurals, detective shows, adventures, situation comedies, and so on—and identify repeating patterns in each. Do they find that in the private detective shows there is usually a slightly strained but working relationship between the hero and the police, and that the police are handicapped by their unimaginative adherence to established procedures, while the independent and free-wheeling detective manages, in his inventive and unorthodox way, to triumph? If that pattern is observable, does it vary greatly from show to show or from episode to episode? How well does it conform to the real world? How predictable are the shows? And if they are predictable, then what is their appeal?

TECHNICAL ELEMENTS

These questions bring us closer and closer to the technical elements in the visual media, so we might now consider how to introduce these elements in the classroom. Once they have analyzed a show in some detail, students might try to invent a story line that would suit the show. In teams, they might design plots consistent with the patterns noted, working with the values they have identified as implicit in the show's content. They could then work together to write dialogue and stage directions. If time permits, and if the equipment is available, the scripts might actually be performed and video-taped. This will demand attention to the technical elements of television production—blocking, timing, sound, manipulation of the camera, and the like.

Meadows describes a similar strategy in which he has students adapt a well-known tale—his examples are "Little Red Riding Hood" and "Goldilocks"—to the format of a television show chosen by the students. He lists six steps: dividing the class into five-person committees, each of which chooses a show; observing and taking notes on the show; writing the script; rehearsing; producing the video-tape; and evaluating. The students who undertake this activity, he notes, become more critical and skeptical viewers, more aware of the patterns and stereotypes and sentimental appeals than they were before the activity.[10]

The stories and poems in the literature program are good candidates for this treatment. How, for instance, might "The Most Dangerous Game" be adapted for television? On what shows would it fit? How would it be different if adapted for different shows? Could Robinson's "Richard Corey" be rewritten for, perhaps, Lou Grant? Could Reed's "Lessons of War" inspire an episode of M*A*S*H? Could any of Poe's detective stories be used in one of the police series, or any of O. Henry's tales in a situation comedy? Comparisons such as these suggest ways of including television in the context of a traditional literature course.

Other methods will come readily to mind. When analyzing the television hero, for instance, students might be asked about characters in the literature they have studied during the year (or any other literature they may have read). Which characters would be most suitable for the lead in a television show or series? Is there one they could propose successfully to the networks? What features would make her popular? How is she like other television heroes? How is she different? The class might even invent a series around such a character, specifying the setting, other regular characters, kinds of episodes, the tone of the show (serious, comic), the established shows with which it would compete, and perhaps even the sort of sponsor it might attract and possible strategies for selling it to a backer. Students might suggest actors who could play the main roles and, if especially sophisticated, even discuss which producers and directors might be interested in the series.

Such close study of television, first identifying its values and then adapting other stories to the established format, will involve students in the technical aspects of the medium. The character's appearance itself is a matter of technique. In a short story we would call it description and ask how it reveals character, attitude, motivation, and status. In the visual media, which usually function without a narrator, we don't read or hear a description; rather, we see the character dressed in certain clothes, walking and speaking in a certain way. These details must reveal character without the intervention of an interpreter. Or rather, the camera serves as interpreter. It must catch expressions and touch on significant features so that they catch our notice. Thus it guides our attention, as the narrator does in a short story. The absence of a narrator accounts for another difference between the visual and the written media. Writing is better suited for handling extended thought, while the visual media are better for action and movement. Thus, a more philosophical work may not translate well to the screen. Long passages of introspection have no vehicle in the visual media; a long monologue disrupts the forward motion of a film and seems out of place. So ideas must somehow be conveyed in the action, or developed in dialogue, and that limitation makes film and television less intellectual media than the essay, novel, and short story can be.

But the writer can never convey the violence of a fight, the tumult of a stampede, or the power of a volcano quite so effectively as the film can, with its visual and aural resources. Perhaps it is this fact that has led the visual media to concentrate on human violence. A cowboy can fill the screen with his brawling for hours, while his potential in the essay would be exhausted after a page or two. Because the visual media are biased in that way, it is even more important that students in our schools be trained to see the power of all the media, visual and written. To be immersed in the visual, as so many of the present generation are, is to neglect other important modes of thinking about the world and its experiences.

As character description is presented visually, so is setting. It is there for us to see, perhaps with the addition of a line in the dialogue to name the city or specify the date. But description and setting are elements in the visual media, just as they are in the written. They are achieved in different ways, but their principles are the same.

Still, the grammar is different. In discussing written literature we may talk about diction and sentence structure—with film and television we would talk instead about camera angle, movement, distance from the subject, and focus. These elements may go virtually unnoticed at first. Students can learn to look for them in both film and television by noting their responses and then trying to see how those responses were achieved. The most dramatic moments are the most accessible. Suspense and fright are emotions whose source is easily analyzed, and the analysis will introduce students to the methods of the visual media.

Students may even be able to reconstruct from memory the techniques of especially powerful scenes. In *Psycho*, the ominous presence of the stuffed animals, the quiet, eerie voice of the innkeeper, the peep-hole into the motel room adjoining the office, the dark, looming mansion, the long period of near silence leading up to the killing, and finally the killer's silhouette through the shower curtain all contribute to the building tension. From other films, students may recall brightly lit shots of the unsuspecting victim alternating with dimly lit shots, perhaps of only the killer's feet steadily and quietly approaching. The cuts may grow gradually more rapid to suggest the imminence of the crime and heighten still further the tension of the audience.

The discussion of scenes like these will call attention to the use of sound, light, and movement, both by the actors and by the camera. It will invite comment on the camera operator's selection of her subject (only the feet of the stalking killer), on the editor's timing of cuts (slow in one scene and quick in another), and on other aspects of filming.

If films can be obtained for use in the class, the study can be much more vivid and lively. Students can time scenes to note the pacing of different events—the violent scenes with many cuts, perhaps so rapid that images remain on the screen for less than a second, and the leisurely scene-setting shots, with fewer cuts and gentler transitions.

For these purposes it might be useful to distinguish between film and television. Although similar, they have some important differences, and pacing is a case in point. Television pacing is bound by certain external constraints. The show is limited, for one thing, to a specific length. On the major networks, the time is cut into half-hour units, and shows are planned to fit neatly into one or several of those units. Further, the program must accommodate regular breaks for commercials. The script must divide neatly and logically into scenes, so that the audience will not feel disrupted by the advertising.

The students' efforts to write scripts suitable for television will tell them much about the difficulties of the medium. They may notice that the necessity of dividing the show into segments limits them. They cannot write scenes that require a steady building of tension longer than the twelve minutes or so between commercials. Watching a movie not made for television, but shown on television interrupted by soap, new cars, hardware sales, and announcements of forthcoming shows, will reveal the same problem. The movie, edited without the constraint of commercial interruptions, will often fit badly into the small slots. Breaks will come at inopportune moments, disrupting the flow of the story.

Comparing television and film will reveal other technical differences. Film, because of the large screen, is able to handle wide vistas and huge battlefield scenes. On the small screen such images are much less impressive. A lone rider, moving slowly along a ridge in the distance, seems on the movie screen diminished by the grandeur of the country; on the television he may be only a speck moving through a blur. Television, on the other hand, is intimate. It is in the home, accessible and controllable. The viewer can alter the volume, tune the picture and discuss the show with others while it is in progress. And television seems to deal intimately with its subject matter. Much of the drama on television takes place inside a room. That seems to be the perspective television manages well. Students may note other points of comparison.

In both film and television, as well as writing, focus is an important issue. In a short story we may be shown an event through its effect on one of the characters. Similarly, a scene in a film may focus on some minor character, whose reaction shows us the significance of the event or tells something about the main character. Thus, awe in the faces of the office-workers informs us that the person walking through is a powerful figure in the company; silence falling over a saloon tells us that the man who has just entered is to be feared; terror in the faces of the victims suggests the horrible visage of the monster, and so on. Focus falls temporarily someone other than the main character, describing through effect rather than directly. Focus is a tool of both writers and directors.

Similarly, both the written and the visual media can show much through details. In Jackson's short story "After You, My Dear Alphonse," the little offers Johnny's mother makes to Boyd reveal her prejudice, or at any rate, her stereotyping of Boyd. In *Psycho*, the fly sitting unharmed on Perkin's hand at the end of the film suggests the depth of his psychosis. In both cases much is done with little, and so sensitivity to details is very important for the reader and the viewer.

Films based on literary works are useful for comparing visual and written literature. Many have been made especially for use in the classroom. More recently, commercial television has begun to adapt classics and contemporary literature into short television movies for young viewers. Such items offer both a second look at the work itself and a glimpse into the nature of each medium. Films made as pedagogic tools are often unsatisfying—a mixture of drama and lecture, they leave the viewer with the feeling that she has tasted the story but not digested it. But the films and television specials that attempt to recreate a work and not just teach about it provide an interesting chance to see how written and visual media treat the same story.

Recently, there has been a great deal of cross-fertilization between the print and the visual media. Whereas in the past books were made into films, now we also find films made into books, films made into television series, and television series made into books. Some works are now available in several media, providing interesting possibilities for teaching. Let us look at one such pair, the film *Death Wish*, which we discussed briefly in Chapter Two, and the novel from which it was made.

A comparison of the film and the book will reveal both technical and conceptual differences. One obvious difference is in how the killers are presented. In the book they remain faceless, unidentified, part of the mass of New York's humanity. In the film they are shown clearly—the camera comes close to the dirty, leering faces, and we hear the quiet, sadistic voices. Their repulsiveness is nearly tangible.

Why that difference? Why would the writer choose one strategy and the director the other? Part of the answer may be the different potential of the two media. Film, with its strong visual impact, can shock and repel us quickly. It can tell us much about the characters through their dress, expressions, and bearing. In *Death Wish*, the film, we quickly see that the killers are corrupt and sadistic, without redeeming features. In print, it would take longer to convey that repugnance. The writer, Garfield, is not interested in looking into the killers' minds or explaining their degeneracy; he is concerned with the consequences of their actions on the main character, Paul Benjamin, whose wife and daughter they assault. In the film they can appear, be clearly identified as villains, and vanish quickly—in the book, they might take more time and trouble than they are worth. Further, they might arouse our own hatred enough to interfere with our perception of Benjamin's response. Better, perhaps, to treat them as Garfield does, as menacing apparitions, hovering, ominous, but never clearly seen and confronted.

So, at any rate, might the discussion go. Students could also consider the effect of having the villains remain faceless in the movie too, or of making them full characters in the novel. The difference between the two works is crucial and easily traced throughout.

Another difference, perhaps related, is in the transformation of Benjamin himself. In the novel he changes gradually. His unfocused anger seeks out objects and begins to find them. The first is an addict who tries to rob him late at night on the streets—a fairly clear instance of self-defense. But it is also something more. Benjamin has thrown himself in the addict's way, seeking an excuse to satisfy his rage, taking a misplaced revenge for the deaths of his wife and daughter.

His second killing is slightly different. He finds a man robbing a drunk in the park and confronts him. When the man flees, Benjamin stops him and shoots him while his hands are raised in surrender. The killing is not self-defense this time; it is not even a defense of the drunkard. The victim has been stopped from committing a crime, but he is no longer a threat—he has given up. Benjamin is satisfied with less justification for this killing than for the first.

The progression continues. Two teenage boys prepare to strip his car, and he shoots them from hiding. This time he does not confront his victims. Then he kills a man stealing a television set from an apartment. The crimes grow less threatening and further removed from him, but they still provoke him to kill. Finally, he murders three of four teenagers he finds throwing bricks at a passing subway train.

At the beginning of the novel Benjamin is a justifiably angry man who unfortunately has no target for his anger. By the end, he is one of the predators, corrupted by the tragedy he has suffered and by his unsatisfied desire for vengeance. When he kills his first victim, he is still a hero; when he kills his last, he has been transformed into someone disturbingly like the savages he hates.

The movie follows a different path. There is no gradual change in the encounters here; each one seems justified and laudable. Benjamin begins as a hero and ends as a hero. The public applauds his one-man war against crime, and the papers report decreasing street crime as the vigilante begins to intimidate the criminals. The ineffectiveness of the police serves as background and contrast to his efficiency. He becomes a contemporary Robin Hood, defending the weak in a society with too many predators and too few police. Finally he is forced to leave town, but he leaves as a hero. In the final scene, arriving in a new city, he helps a young girl who has been knocked down by one of the local ruffians, and with his final gesture, a finger pointed like a gun at the culprit, shows his intention to continue his private war.

The book chronicles Benjamin's deterioration from victim to killer; the film chronicles his resurrection from victim to killer. It is an interesting contrast—the same story presenting two opposing visions. Garfield himself has repudiated the film:

> The movie was all right, but it wasn't my book and there wasn't anything I could do about it. I had written about

a man whose rage turned into paranoia. He ended up shooting unarmed teenagers on the street because he didn't like their looks. It's what I saw as the ultimate result of the vigilante mentality.

In the movie, they made him into a white knight, cleaning up New York City without regard to what's right or wrong or what's legal.[11]

The contrast, although it may be less obvious to young students than to more experienced readers, is probably sharp enough to be sensed, and that feeling may lead students to try specifying the difference. It may suggest questions like those we have discussed—How do the killings differ between novel and film? How does the main character differ? The answers will call attention to both the technique and the artistic conception of each work.

Pairing books and films allows for this sort of investigation. Just as students might compare how two poems treat one theme, so might they compare the different treatments of one story in two media, print and film.

Other potentially interesting pairings are possible. The film M*A*S*H might be compared with the television show. The television show Star Trek might be compared with the books based on it, with the film, or perhaps with the movie Star Wars, which is in some ways similar. For the lower grades, where something like Death Wish would be inappropriate, the books in Wilder's Little House series might be compared with the television show, Little House on the Prairie. And of course, every so often a story will show up in the form of a television episode or a children's special, or, like Roots, a special with wider appeal.

It seems appropriate for the English teacher to encourage intelligent viewing of film and television. They are similar enough to the printed literature from which they have sprung that dealing with them should not be difficult. The basic strategy is the same—begin with responses, look for the sources of those responses in the person and in the work, compare responses to clarify and enrich them, and compare works to see still other features.

There will, of course, be problems. One is obtaining films, or arranging for the classes to see them at a theater. Some students will be unable to watch a particular show that you want to discuss, either because parents forbid it or because they insist on watching something else. There is the problem of having to discuss something from memory or notes without being able to refer directly to it. That, however, might be seen as an opportunity rather than a disadvantage, because it might motivate students to learn to take careful notes as they watch.

Then there is the problem of censorship, as absurd as it may seem in a twentieth-century democracy. In many communities the showing of a film like *Death Wish* would be considered grounds for firing a teacher. These communities are willing to gamble that keeping children ignorant will keep them pure and safe. This idea seems to be spreading, as efforts increase to pull books off library shelves, close movie theaters, and harass magazine publishers; and teachers will have to deal with it as best they can.

Teachers who hope to incorporate some film and television into the English courses will have to note these problems, consider the nature of the community and school, and perhaps get the advice and support of supervisors and principals if possible. At the very least, they should probably communicate with parents, telling them about purposes and plans for including the visual media. Informing them may forestall some problems and even win allies for teachers.

One further purpose of informing the parents is to gently encourage a change in the patterns of viewing in the homes of your students. Television is discussed in few families. Both children and adults sit in front of the set, absorb what it presents, and then go about their business, never analyzing what they have seen. Suggesting to the parents that television may have a subtle influence on the ideas of its viewers, and that it is useful to help students learn to resist and control that influence, may draw them into the circle. They may agree to watch with their children occasionally, reflecting on the questions teacher and students have devised and offering their own responses and judgments. Ideally, students and their parents might develop the habit of talking about shows, trading reactions and opinions. That habit might help sustain the goals of the instruction after the students have left your class.

If that habit catches on in the families of some students, it is possible that they might even learn to read books together and discuss them in the same way. At the very least, some parents might begin to think about the education their children are receiving and participate in it in some small way.

SPECIAL COURSES

We have not discussed special courses in film and television, since we have been most concerned with how they function as literature and with their place in the literature curriculum. Special courses are possible, however, though they may require extra funding and other assistance. Film courses need films, which have to be rented and shipped. They also require adjustments in the schedule—one class period is usually not long enough. Television courses, unless they depend on memory and note-taking, will require video-tape equipment and tapes of the shows to be discussed. But if there is sufficient interest among students and teachers, and if the climate in the school and the community is favorable, such courses can be very good. They can generate a great deal of enthusiasm and hard work.

Courses in television production or film-making can be especially valuable. In preparing a show or film, students will have to exercise many of the skills English courses are expected to teach. They will have to talk among themselves, negotiating their ideas, predicting, and planning. They will have to write—letters asking for information or permission, scripts, programs, advertisements, production schedules. And that work will be in the context of a real activity, not to satisfy some arbitrary assignment or invented task. If the equipment can be obtained, such courses are excellent additions to the curriculum.

THE INDUSTRY

Intensive courses would also allow time to investigate another side of the media—the commercial side. Although knowledge of the industry behind film and television isn't necessary to intelligent viewing, the industry is fascinating, and students may want to know more about it. Almost inevitably, discussion of film and television leads to talk about money, about the advertisers who control so much of what happens and about the people involved in the business. An awareness of that huge and complicated industry is useful in understanding the visual media. Students interested in looking into its dark corners will find suitable material in the following list of readings.

A BRIEF LIST OF RECOMMENDED BOOKS ON MEDIA

Agee, Warren K., Phillip H. Ault, and Edwin Emery. *Introduction to Mass Communications.* 6th ed. New York: Harper & Row, 1979.

Aldrich, P. *The Impact of Mass Media.* Rochelle Park, N.J.: Hayden, 1975.

Atwan, Robert, Barry Orton, and William Vesterman, eds. *American Mass Media: Industries and Issues.* New York: Random House, 1978.

Bobker, Lee R. *Elements of Film.* 3rd ed. New York: Harcourt Brace Jovanovich, 1979.

Brown, Les. *Television: The Business Behind the Box*. New York: Harcourt Brace Jovanovich, 1972.

Budd, Richard W., and Brent D. Ruben. *Beyond Media: New Approaches to Mass Communication*. Rochelle Park, N.J.: Hayden, 1979.

Chafee, Steven H., and Michael J. Petrick. *Using the Mass Media: Communication Problems in American Society*. New York: McGraw-Hill, 1975.

Giblin, Thomas R., ed. *Popular Media and the Teaching of English*. Pacific Palisades, Calif.: Goodyear, 1972.

Fiske, John, and John Hartley. *Reading Television*. London: Methuen, 1978.

Foster, Harold M. *The New Literacy: The Language of Film and Television*. Urbana, Ill.: National Council of Teachers of English, 1979.

Kuhns, William. *Exploring Television*. Chicago: Loyola Univ. Press, 1971.

Lacey, Richard A. *Seeing with Feeling: Film in the Classroom*. Philadelphia: W. B. Saunders, 1972.

Mayer, Martin. *About Television*. New York: Harper & Row, 1967.

Maynard, Richard A. *The Celluloid Curriculum: How to Use Movies in the Classroom*. New York: Hayden, 1971.

McLuhan, Marshall. *Understanding Media*. New York: Signet, 1966.

McLuhan, Marshall, Kathryn Hutchon, and Eric McLuhan. *Media, Messages and Language: The World as Your Classroom*. Skokie, Ill.: National Textbook Co., 1980.

Monaco, James. *How to Read a Film*. New York: Oxford Univ. Press, 1977.

Newcomb, Horace, ed. *Television: The Critical View*. 2nd ed. New York: Oxford Univ. Press, 1979.

Pember, Don R. *Mass Media in America*. 3rd ed. Chicago: Science Research Associates, 1981.

Rodman, George. *Mass Media Issues: Analysis and Debate*. Chicago: Science Research Associates, 1981.

Sandman, Peter M., David M. Rubin, and David B. Sachsman. *Media: An Introductory Analysis of American Mass Communications*. 2nd ed. Englewood Cliffs, N.J.: Prentice-Hall, 1976.

Sheridan, Marion C., et al. *The Motion Picture and the Teaching of English*. New York: Appleton-Century-Crofts, 1965.

Sohn, David A. *Film: The Creative Eye*. Dayton, Ohio: A. Pflaum, 1970.

Voelker, Francis H., and Ludmila A. Voelker, eds. *Mass Media: Forces in Our Society*. 3rd ed. New York: Harcourt Brace Jovanovich, 1978.

Whitney, Frederick C. *Mass Media and Mass Communications in Society*. Dubuque, Iowa: Wm. C. Brown, 1975.

Wright, Charles R. *Mass Communications: A Sociological Perspective*. New York: Random House, 1959.

NOTES

1. Albert Ellis, *The American Sexual Tragedy* (New York: Twayne Publishers, 1954), p. 98.
2. D. F. Roberts, "One Highly Attracted Public," in *TV and Human Behavior*, ed. G. Comstock (New York: Columbia University Press, 1978), pp. 173–287.
3. Leonard Berkowitz, "Opening Speech to the Media Violence Symposium," in *Report from a Media Violence Symposium in Stockholm, April 25th, 1974* (Stockholm, Sweden: University of Stockholm, September 1974), p. 1–3.
4. Berkowitz, p. 10.
5. John Fiske and John Hartley, *Reading Television* (London: Methuen, 1978), p. 24.
6. George Gerbner and Larry Gross, "The Scary World of TV's Heavy Viewer," *Psychology Today*, 9, No. 11 (April 1976), 44.
7. John Leonard, "And a Picture Tube Shall Lead Them," *Playboy*, 23, No. 6 (June 1976), 204.
8. Benjamin Stein, *The View from Sunset Boulevard* (New York: Basic Books, 1979), pp. 15–28 and 47–56.
9. Fiske and Hartley, p. 29.
10. Robert Meadows, "Get Smart: Let TV Work for You," *English Journal*, 56, No. 2 (1976), 121–24.
11. Brian Garfield, quoted in Terry Brewster, "Best-Selling Author Believes in Taking a Quick Write," *Friends*, 37, No. 10 (1980), 12.

PART III
The Literature Program

The Literature Curriculum 7

Literature has been in trouble ever since Plato banned the poets from his ideal society. Plato thought that, because they dealt in fictions, poets could contribute little to the pursuit of truth and virtue and were probably a threat to the morality of a society's youth. Many people still share Plato's fears, and others who don't are nonetheless unsure that literature serves any valuable purpose. It may be harmless amusement, but little more—it is surely not a serious, useful study, like mathematics, biology, or economics. Even teachers are often vague about its value, making for it nebulous and unconvincing claims. In some ways it is surprising that a subject so weakly supported should be as firmly entrenched in the curriculum as literature seems to be.

Its place in the curriculum is at once tenuous and secure. In the elementary grades instruction in literature is often replaced by instruction in reading, as it is presented in basal reading texts, but in the secondary grades literature seems secure. It is taught from seventh through twelfth grade as a major part of the English program in most schools. Although some critics protest that too much of the English program is devoted to literature and more time should be spent teaching writing, few have seriously suggested that literature is frivolous and not worth teaching at all.

Many take literature seriously enough to wish to control its effect on students. Such people sense that literature might influence its readers and, unwilling to put any faith in students' ability to manage that influence intelligently, try to manage it for them by determining what they may and may not read.

But, despite literature's ubiquity in the schools and the love and fear in which it is held, its role in the curriculum has not been satisfactorily defined. Other disciplines have, in this era, a clear purpose. Mathematics supports all of the sciences as well as business and industry—it is clearly practical and useful. Science contributes to progress and to comfort and security—it too is clearly practical. This is a scientific, mathematical, pragmatic era. The nation's health is measured by its production, its economy, and its military and political stature rather than its accomplishments in art, music, dance, and theater. Literature's role in such an era may be hard to identify.

It does not contribute to the common good in any tangible way. It does not make its readers healthy, secure, rich; it does not conquer disease, settle international conflict, or solve economic problems. In this pragmatic time, literature seems to make few pragmatic contributions. Asked what literature can do for the student, the teacher often has only the vaguest, most abstract, and most unconvincing answers. "It can help students look on life with a broader perspective," we might answer, but that has little weight with someone interested in how to prepare them for a career and what kind of money they will earn in it. Or we might propose that the study of literature "will acquaint students with their cultural heritage," but that too has a hollow ring in a culture dominated by the sciences, a culture that judges success in terms of productivity and acquisition.

That the English program has suffered from this pragmatism and emphasis on science became obvious in the 1960s, when the nation started setting aside funds for basic educational research. In 1961 the government divided up 561 million dollars—71% went to the physical sciences, 26% to the biological sciences, 2% to the psychological sciences, 1% to the social sciences, and nothing to the humanities.[1] English presumably could contribute little to the national defense. It was not worth a chunk of the budget; it was not practical. It would be naive to think that literacy does not contribute to the national security, since the ability to read and write is fundamental to almost every other intellectual achievement, but the reluctance to invest much in literature teaching is less surprising.

THE HISTORY

The problem is much older than the sixties; it dates back to the time English entered the curriculum. English is not as old a subject as many of its teachers imagine, having secured a place in the curriculum only around the turn of the century. Applebee, summarizing the early history of English teaching in the schools, observes:

> By 1865, schools and colleges recognized a variety of loosely related minor studies of the vernacular—rhetoric,

oratory, spelling, grammar, literary history, and reading all had their places, often conflicting with one another for attention. Though many of these studies made use of literary selections, literary study in its own right had yet to find a place or a justification. Rhetorical and grammatical studies often included literary texts, but instruction was designed and carried out in the service of composition, not literature. Literary history, though the schools called it the teaching of literature, was biographical in emphasis and often involved no literature at all.[2]

Literature in the late nineteenth century was not the central element in the curriculum that it is now. It came in gradually, competing for a place with older pedagogic traditions. Of these, in the colleges at least, rhetoric and oratory dominated. They were the significant studies in schools intent on educating future ministers and bureaucrats. Of the related disciplines, classical studies had perhaps the most influence on literature teaching. The classics were studied first for their historical significance and second as a rigorous mental discipline that toughened the sinews of the mind.

As English studies gradually entered the curriculum, they were shaped by the tradition that had emphasized the classics, rhetoric, and oratory. Thus, literature was seen in this context and became a subject to study and know in the same way that the classics were studied and known. The emphasis fell on information, knowledge *about* the literature rather than sensitive reading of the literary works themselves.

> By 1870 the emphasis on information in literary studies was well established. . . . Such studies of facts about literature remain an element in high school instruction to the present day, though their justification has changed from mental discipline to knowledge of our literary heritage.[3]

As the schools moved into the twentieth century, it became apparent that their role was changing somewhat. By the turn of the century not all high school students were college-bound; a great many were going directly to work. The formal, classical training that prepared them for college did not prepare them as well for blacksmithing, bartending, and bricklaying. Pressure to reform the English curriculum ultimately yielded several results; one of the most important was the *Bureau of Education Bulletin Number Two*, compiled by James F. Hosic, a founder of the National Council of Teachers of English.

The report, issued in 1917, was the work of a joint committee formed by the Commission on the Reorganization of Secondary Education (a commission of the National Education Association) and the National Council of Teachers of English (NCTE). It expressed the committee's concern about the growing number of students who did not go on to college, for whom the high school curriculum seemed less and less suitable. For some time the curriculum had been strongly influenced by college entrance criteria, through such organizations as the National Conference on Uniform Entrance Requirements. Hosic and his committee thought that the molding of the high school curriculum by the colleges had produced some unfortunate results. He concluded:

> The English course as a whole tended to formality, scholasticism, and overmaturity, and needed to be vitalized, redirected, and definitely related to the life of the present.[4]

The committee recommended that the English program more carefully consider students' needs. Planning, they thought, should focus somewhat less on scholarship and somewhat more on the psychology of the student. English should be thought of as a tool for effective living, so that students would be prepared, not just for the academic life, but for life in whatever role they might have to play.

Unfortunately, the concept of English as a social instrument did not grant literature a very respectable place. Hosic suggested distinguishing between "English for work" and "English for leisure," the first to teach composition and the second to teach literature.[5] Hosic had granted literature a place in the program, but only as recreation or entertainment. He demoted—or promoted—the reading of literature from the serious, scholarly, but doubtfully relevant, pursuit of knowledge to a source of amusement.

This new conception of the English program had the virtue of being somewhat more consistent with the needs and interests of the students. It recognized that a great many of them would not become ministers or scholars, but would simply need to speak and read and write competently, and it encouraged teachers to respect those needs. In treating English as a set of skills to be developed, rather than a body of facts to be memorized, it began the transition from a curriculum focused on the discipline to one focused on the student.

But along with that virtue—that it considered the students' needs—it had the great defect of conceiving of literature as little more than a pastime. It was "English for leisure," nothing more.

That was to say, essentially, that literature had no serious contribution to make to the students. It was fine for scholars, or to while away the evening hours, but that was all.

The "life-adjustment" principle was to dominate in the schools for several decades, exemplified, for English teachers, by the NCTE's *Experience Curriculum in English*. This curriculum was devoted to relevance, with little concern for significance. It taught telephone manners and how to write thank-you notes, and proposed a model unit in which

> such a purpose as the provision of milk and other needs for the children of an indigent family dominates the work of a group for weeks, subject-matter divisions being ignored and any material used whenever it serves the group purposes.[6]

The activity has obvious merit, but it reveals that the discipline had moved far away from rigorous study of the classics. English was now a social tool—a collection of skills for getting along well in the world.

THE BASIC ISSUES CONFERENCE

This state of affairs persisted until the late fifties. In 1957 the Russians launched Sputnik and precipitated a flurry of activity in the United States. People became worried about the educational system that had failed to produce scientists skillful enough to stay ahead of the Russians. In 1959 the Modern Language Association, the College English Association, and the National Council of Teachers of English met together in a Basic Issues Conference to reassess the state of the art in English teaching. They asked,

> Has the fundamental liberal discipline of English been displaced, at some levels of schooling, by ad hoc training in how to write a letter, how to give a radio speech, manners, dating, telephoning, vocational guidance? Can agreement be reached upon a body of knowledge and set of skills as standard at certain points in the curriculum, making due allowances for flexibility of planning, individual differences, and patterns of growth? This issue seems crucial to this entire document, and to any serious approach to the problem. Unless we can find an answer to it, we must resign ourselves to an unhappy future in which the present curricular disorder persists and the

whole liberal discipline of English continues to disinte-
grate and lose its character.[7]

PROJECT ENGLISH

The Basic Issues Conference marked the beginning of a swing away
from the life-adjustment curriculum and back toward a more rigorous academic approach. The laxity of the curriculum had become
distressing, especially when the national security came into doubt.
The money poured into curriculum development over the next
decade went to projects characterized by close attention to the discipline. Kitzhaber, who directed one of the most productive of the
twelve Project English Curriculum Centers during the sixties, fore-
told the direction English curriculum planning would take when he
observed that one

> respect in which English curriculum is particularly vulner-
> able is its almost complete failure to reflect the present
> state of knowledge in the disciplines from which it draws
> its proper substance—philology and linguistics, rhetoric,
> logic, and the critical study of literature.[8]

The life-adjustment era had overcome the sterility of the classical approach of the late 1800s, but at the cost of losing its scholarly
grounding. It had become insubstantial, almost trivial, and those
who worked on the English curriculum during the sixties tried hard
to re-establish a respectable foundation. Predictably, the English curricula produced by the Project English Centers were serious, scholarly affairs. The Oregon Curriculum Center produced a series of six
massive anthologies, concerned more with the literary heritage—its
great works and its body of scholarship—than with the students'
telephone manners. The Nebraska curriculum was similarly demanding. Carnegie-Mellon's was almost oppressively weighty and
solemn—no one would accuse it of catering to its students or seeking
to make English too light, too relevant, or too easy. So English once
again reversed its field, rejecting the life-adjustment approach and
turning to the scholarly disciplines to structure its curriculum.

This academic era, however, proved to be very brief. Late in the
sixties it was disrupted suddenly by the conclusions of the Dartmouth Seminar. Held in 1966 and attended by about fifty prominent
English educators from the United States, Britain, and Canada, this
meeting cast serious doubts on the direction taken by many of the
Project English Centers and acquainted the representatives from the

United States with the fundamentally different philosophy then current in England.

The British educators were concerned not so much with rigor and intellectually demanding labor in their schools as with making the work personally significant to the students. They spoke, for instance, of encouraging students to respond to the literature read rather than having them analyze it. Dixon, in *Growth Through English*, one of the two major summaries of the Dartmouth Conference, says:

> The essential talk that springs from literature is talk about experience—as *we* know it, as *he* [the student] sees it (correcting our partiality and his; exploring the fullness of his vision, and ours). Conversely, only in a classroom where talk explores experience is literature drawn into the dialogue—otherwise it has no place. The demand for interpretation—was it this or that he meant?—arises in the course of such talk: otherwise it is a dead hand.[9]

Since Sputnik, the U.S. schools had been encouraged to demand rigorous work and impose high standards of scholarship. Now, at Dartmouth, the British recommendations seemed to contradict that philosophy. Britton, in the opening paper for the Literature Study Group, rejected the notion that our purposes in the schools include the "driving out of bad currency"—that is, correcting the child's taste for inferior literature—and argued that we should be trying instead to awaken his appetite for better works. He argued further against the dominance of the critics, who represent, of course, high standards of literary performance:

> The point at which critical statements can be of help to a student is . . . a difficult one to determine. It is even more important, however, to consider the manner in which such help is offered. The voice of the critic must not be allowed to seem the voice of authority; more harm has probably been done to the cause of literature by this means than by any other. It is all too easy for the immature student, feeling that his own responses are unacceptable, to disown them and profess instead the opinions of repected critics. And to many teachers, with their eyes on what may rightly go on in other parts of the curriculum, this looks like good teaching. It may of course be the best kind of preparation for an ill-conceived examination, and this may be the real root of the trouble.[10]

The Dartmouth Conference precipitated a great deal of heated debate among educators alert enough to hear about it. It suggested a set of criteria for English teaching different from those the Project English curriculum planners had had in mind. They had been concerned with intellect; Dartmouth suggested more concern for emotion. They had been thinking of the discipline; Dartmouth suggested that they think of the child. The question of purpose was not so simple or dichotomous as that, but emphasis did seem to be shifting once again from the subject to the student, as it had in the first part of the century under the guidance of Hosic and others.

Miller summarizes this evolution of English currriculum. There have been four stages, he says:

> the Authoritarian, the Progressive, the Academic, and the Humanitarian.
>
> The first of these stages, the Authoritarian, we identify with the arid classicism and rote learning of the nineteenth century; the second, the Progressive, with John Deweyism (something different from the real Dewey), indiscriminate permissiveness, and social adjustment, all running deep into the twentieth century. In more recent times we have been witness to a revolution in our schools which we may, for convenience, date from Russia's Sputnik launching in 1957, and which I have arbitrarily designated Academic. . . .
>
> We are now . . . on the threshold of the fourth stage [1967], which I call the Humanitarian. If we pause for a moment and glance backward, we note that the stages I have described are not clearly defined historical periods but merely the slow swinging of a pendulum between two poles of emphasis which may be variously described as substance and psychology, subject matter and student, or intellectuality and society.[11]

We are, of course, now well into Miller's fourth period, and a great many conflicting pressures weigh on the schools. The humanism evident in the recommendations of the Dartmouth Seminar still runs strong, but is countered by the back-to-basics movement, which espouses the teaching of the least significant language skills in ways least likely to help students and virtually certain to alienate and humiliate them. Whether or not "Humanitarian" is the best term to describe this era in English education remains to be seen. The significant point to be observed in this brief history is that the vacillation back and forth from student-centered to discipline-centered has not produced a conception of literature adequate to support the curriculum. And yet, in those two poles of the pendulum swing, the two crucial elements of such a conception are apparent.

CONCEPTIONS OF THE LITERATURE CURRICULUM

The uncertainty about the fundamental purposes and appropriate focus of the literature curriculum creates problems with planning. In the concluding chapter of his history of English teaching, Applebee identifies some of the remaining defects of English curriculum:

> Teachers of literature have never successfully resisted the pressure to formulate their subject as a body of knowledge to be imparted.[12]
>
> The acknowledged goals of the teaching of literature are in conflict with the emphasis on specific knowledge or content.[13]
>
> There is a need to reconceptualize the "literary heritage" and its implications for patterns of teaching.[14]

These are, of course, the very problems that have plagued us from the first. They betray the inadequate conception of literature on which curricula have been built.

Conceived of as a body of information, the literature curriculum tends to become a course in literary history or genre, as many high school literature textbooks show. For example, a typical curriculum —and there are many exceptions—will focus on American literature in the eleventh grade and British literature in the twelfth. The textbooks, and therefore the courses, are most often arranged chronologically. As a result, the class is likely to concentrate on historical matters, examining the literature in terms of periods, dates, major authors, major works, and so on. The organization of the course predisposes the teacher to focus on information, a pattern inherited from literature's first days in the curriculum.

The tenth grade text is probably organized by genre, with a section for the short story, one for poetry, one for drama—perhaps even one for the short novel. The concept here is slightly different. The literature is arranged to yield not historical information but technical information about the distinguishing characteristics of the genres. If anything, this system is less likely than the historical to appeal to young students.

This common curricular pattern reveals the history Applebee has traced and the problems he has identified. In this arrangement, literature is knowledge—information to acquire, remember, and be tested on.

THE LITERARY HERITAGE

The usual justification for such a curriculum is that students need to become familiar with their literary heritage. The literary heritage model for the literature curriculum is appealing. It suggests that the students will be immersed in great traditions and profit from the best the culture has to offer. The belief in teaching the literary heritage implies a faith that it will produce good results of some sort for the students. Exactly what these results are is often left unspecified. Generally they seem to include moral and intellectual effects such as making students better people and clearer thinkers, and social or cultural effects such as producing a sense of common experience and thought.

Here let us simply observe that literature's moral purpose is either a justification for teaching it or a reason to attack it. Literature's contribution to moral development could be viewed simplistically as didactic and prescriptive—it *gives* students their moral sense; or, granting students more individual freedom and responsibility, we may instead see literature as *suggesting* moral visions for them to consider.

Even among those who favor the teaching of literature, the didactic view has been inadequate. It assumes that contact with the works is the essential thing and consequently focuses on the works themselves rather than on their significance and how they may be taught. Applebee comments,

> Any definition of a literary heritage in terms of specific books or authors distorts the cultural significance of a literary tradition by failing to recognize that what the Great Books offer is a continuing dialogue on the moral and philosophical questions central to the culture itself.[15]

To think of the literature curriculum simply as a list of titles is to miss the central issue. The heritage is not the bibliography itself, but the rich history of evolving perceptions and ideas that the literary works contain. LaConte, describing how he was misled by his efforts to teach the literary heritage, says:

> The problem, of course, is that I was viewing the literary heritage as a body of *works*, classic pieces of literature to

be studied and mastered. It's a view that continues to be very popular. One of the glaring ironies of most courses in the humanities is that they have so little to do with humans. They tend to be concerned with the form, style, historical sequence, and even a bit with the content of the *works*, but seldom do students experience a genuine feeling of identification, of sharing with other humans a "shock of recognition."[16]

Literature courses conceived as repositories of the great works are likely to be more like a walk through a graveyard than an encounter with the minds of great writers and thinkers.

This is not to suggest that the great works do not belong in the curriculum, but simply that they should not be approached with awe and handled with kid gloves. Unless the students see them as exchanges with another mind about significant issues, the great works will be little more than great burdens.

LaConte offers another criticism of the typical literary heritage course—its "narrow ethnic focus."[17] He notes that the literature program closely examines the British heritage but seldom gives much attention to the other cultures that have influenced American life. Some programs have partially corrected that problem by offering courses in world literature and by better representing the literature of minority groups. Still, few curricula are committed to covering the range and variety of thought and perception throughout the world. Our concept of heritage tends to be strongly nationalistic.

COMPETENCE

The Mandel collection in which LaConte's essay appears proposes two other models for the English curriculum. Each deserves some attention. The competence model, immensely popular with those educators committed to segmenting, measuring, and record-keeping, proposes that we think of the subject as a set of behaviors engaged in by students, and thus subdivide the discipline into its smallest discrete units. Advocates of this model argue that specifying the behaviors to be produced gives teaching precision. It enables teachers to plan thoroughly, with a clear sense of purpose and direction, and easily judge the effectiveness of their instruction. It also, unfortunately, inclines them to see English as a collection of separate skills and activities, without regard for the broader though less specific goals of literature teaching.

It is unlikely that the significant goals for the literature program can be expressed in lists of behavioral objectives, because it is unlikely that the effects of reading can be measured in the behavior of students. Literature acts on the mind and the emotions, but how its effects may show themselves is uncertain. Whether they will be seen at all by outside observers is questionable; that they can be produced on demand in the classroom, for each of thirty students, seems unlikely. Some behaviors, of course, can be elicited in this way. We can insist that students learn to spell "Shakespeare" (or "Shakespere," or "Shakspeare"), and if we are sufficiently resolute, we can force most students to show that they have learned it. But can we get them to demonstrate that reading *Macbeth* has helped to shape their understanding of power or temptation? Perhaps some will, but others, equally affected by the reading, may be unable to, or may simply refuse. To limit our teaching to those behaviors we can observe and measure is to disregard most of the substance of literature. Moffett warns,

> In insisting that desirable behaviors be *observable*, the behavioral approach rules out a great deal of learning— too much to merely mention in a cautionary note prefacing the goals. Consider, for example, what may be happening in a more taciturn member of a discussion group. The effects of certain reading, acting, and writing on a student's social, emotional, and cognitive growth tend of course to be long-range and inextricable. Although it helps to acknowledge that many of these effects will occur years later and often out of school, in practice these effects will either not be observed by evaluators or be falsely attributed to more recent school treatment—or, most likely, be ignored because they cannot be causally traced.[18]

Curricula planned with this model in mind tend to contain long lists of activities, many of them useful. But the philosophy that guides them seems deficient. It seldom addresses the major issue: Why does the student study literature? What can it do for him? What contribution does it make to his life? Competence currricula are often very explicit about what is to be learned and how it should be evaluated, but they fail to examine the broader goals of the literature program. Reducing the literature program to a list of activities and objectives, practical as that may seem, obscures the more important purposes for teaching literature.

If, as we have argued, reading helps the student create his world—that part of it, at least, that is symbolic, emotional, and intellectual—then literature is too vast and imprecise a study to submit to the shackles of a competence-based program. Analysis of the various skills and behaviors involved in studying literature may contribute valuable information about the activities possible in the classroom, but unless the fundamental purpose of teaching is kept clearly in mind and allowed to govern the teaching, the value of literature will be as well concealed behind the lists of competences as it has been in the past behind lists of information.

PROCESS

Mandel, in his introduction, speaks of the process model as the "inside out" of the competence model:

> Whereas the competencies approach advocates the introduction of concepts and skills at the appropriate time so that students can master them, the process approach advocates the creation of an environment in which students can "discover" what has heretofore been unknown to them.
>
> For the teacher of process education, the paradigm means the natural, inevitable flowering of an individual's skills and concepts under the guidance of teachers who pose questions that are open-ended and provocative. Needless to say, the "nonteaching" done by process teachers requires great sensitivity, knowledge of cognitive levels, and patience.[19]

As we might gather from Mandel's description, the process model offers limited guidance for curriculum design. In advocating the "natural flowering" of the student's abilities and suggesting open-ended investigation, this model declines to specify exactly what is to be learned and when. Instead, the teacher must become aware of the possibilities and then capitalize on the opportunities that arise.

Such a model relies heavily on the skill of the teacher. If he is good, with thorough knowledge of his subject and insight into the students, then the process model allows him the freedom to respond to the moment, to explore possibilities as they arise in class. It also *demands* that he do so, because it does not give him a reassuring list of objectives or activities to follow. It is based on the belief that the natural processes of learning and growing will provide better guidance, if the teacher trains himself to watch them. As the Stanfords remark, " . . . the process curriculum tends to value the internal judgments about growth made by the individual learner more than external standards established by society."[20]

The pre-eminent concern of those teaching in this model is the natural growth of the child. Rather than seek the structures of curriculum in the discipline itself, teachers drawn to the process model seek them in the psychology of the child, in the interests, problems, and behavior patterns that emerge. The Stanfords note of the typical process curricula that

> it is often organized into integrated units relating to the developmental tasks of adolescence. Thematic units derived from the tasks seem to be more helpful to students than units focusing on isolated skills such as composition, vocabulary development, or public speaking.[21]

They suggest units on such topics as "identity, woman and man, dealing with conflicts, death, communication, generations, values, loneliness, love, and planning for the future."[22]

Their suggestions are reminiscent of what we saw in *An Experience Curriculum in English,* units designed with more attention to the students than to the discipline of English. Such units could have great merit, but they might easily become indulgent, relying too heavily on students' ability to decide what they need. As the Stanfords themselves caution, total student freedom is not the ideal—planning that draws on the best that both students and teacher can offer will be more productive. Clearly students have a great deal to offer, and unless they are somehow involved in planning their work, many opportunities will be lost. But they cannot precisely foresee their adult needs, and although the teacher's guesses about the future may also be far off, his advantage in age, experience, and training should not be overlooked.

One curious thing about the essays in Mandel's collection is that regardless of which model is being promoted, the writer takes steps to qualify it. Those writing about the competence model warn that curricula can become trivial unless planners carefully attend to some of the larger, unmeasurable goals of teaching. Those writing about the process model want to remind the reader not to neglect the demands of the discipline—students do, after all, have to learn to do more than attend to their own emotions. Those writing about the literary heritage do not want classwork to become so academic that it is removed from the issues that preoccupy adolescents. It is as though all are seeking some sort of middle ground that will accommodate the focus of each model. Obviously, students do need to develop the skills that the competence model might teach them; obviously, they should come to understand the cultural tradition that permeates and shapes their lives; obviously, the uniqueness of each student should be taken into account, as the process model suggests. Each pattern offers something valuable.

The reconciliation of the three might be found in Rosenblatt's ideas and the patterns of instruction discussed earlier. Her conception of the poem as a transaction between the reader and the text justifies equal attention to the students and the discipline. Student-centered curricula tend to focus too intently on the students, while discipline-centered curricula overemphasize the subject matter. By promoting one element above the other, both fail to find the mark. But if we look instead at the nature of the transaction between reader and text, between individual and culture, we might achieve a literature program combining the best elements of the various approaches to curriculum design.

TRANSACTIONAL MODEL

What such a curriculum might look like is difficult to predict. In order to be responsive to the changing student body, it would have to remain flexible. It would have to develop over time, contributed to by a large group of students, teachers, and scholars. It could never be as tidy and complete as some of the curricula planned in other models—too much of what it holds important is unpredictable, perhaps even inarticulable. Still, some of its important features may be foreseen.

It would, following Applebee's suggestion, conceive of the literary heritage as more than a list of great books. It would try to focus on the great issues that inspired the great books, and it would attempt to raise those issues at times in the student's development when he is likely to be interested in them, insofar as something as idiosyncratic as that can be predicted.

The "great issues" approach itself is not a new one. The Carnegie-Mellon Project English program, for instance, is predicated on the belief that "literature is mankind's record, expressed in verbal art forms, of what it is like to be alive. . . . [T]he writer of literature deals with universal concerns of every age and every culture. . . ."[23] In fact, most of the Project English Centers tried to develop curriculum along thematic lines, and the themes often seem to represent the great cultural issues. The University of Nebraska Center organized its literature program around such themes as "The Hero" for the eighth grade and "Man and Nature, Society, and Moral Law" for the tenth. The eleventh grade addressed three themes in American literature—individualism and nature, sin and loneliness, and American materialism.

But as Carlsen and Crow point out in their assessment of the Centers as a whole,

> For the most part the Centers have been concerned almost exclusively with the content of English and only incidentally with methodology. . . . [P]erhaps the strangest omission of all is the lack of concern for the learner and how he learns. . . . Many of the Centers make highly questionable assumptions about children and the learning process. . . . The programs are distinguished by their serious and humorless intensity.[24]

They suffered, in other words, from too much attention to the demands of the discipline and too little attention to the needs of the students. They may conceive of the literature in terms of the great cultural questions, but they fail to bring it to bear on the students' lives. There are ways to correlate those broad cultural concerns with the students' development, so that each can be addressed when students are most likely to be receptive to it and in a manner that is likely to interest them. We do know something about how children mature, and it is possible that that information could be brought to bear on the curriculum.

We know, for instance, a fair amount about patterns of reading interest. G. Robert Carlsen's studies have contributed much to our knowledge of the developmental patterns in adolescent reading, but that knowledge has not been employed effectively in curriculum development. Carlsen has concluded that the reading interests of adolescents fall into three stages. The first, which he labels "Early Adolescence," about ages 11 to 14, is characterized by an interest in animal stories, adventures, mysteries, the supernatural, sports, coming of age in different cultures, stories about the home and family life, slapstick, stories set in the past, and fantasy. "Middle Adolescence," roughly 15 to 16, typically selects nonfiction adventure, longer historical novels, mystical romances, and stories of adolescent life. "Late Adolescence," about 17 and 18, is the period of transition to adult reading. The issues for this age group are the search for personal values, social questions, strange experiences and unusual circumstances, and the transition to adult roles.[25]

Carlsen also identifies some issues students are typically not interested in reading about:

> Generally, the concerns of the great middle-aged section of the population have little appeal. Teens rarely care to read about characters who are middle-aged unless, as in

spy stories, the individuals are highly romanticized and lead lives of incredible adventure. They are not interested in the character who has had to compromise with life or who is bowed down by the humdrum. Clyde Griffith in *An American Tragedy*, though young, is branded despicable by the young reader and not worth reading about. . . . Books about the wealthy usually have little attraction for the young. Wealth is tolerated only in a historical romance or story of intrigue. Nor do teenage readers care for stories of the industrial or political world or the trials and tribulations of marriages.[26]

Carlsen's analysis of the stages of reading interest is not sufficient foundation for an entire literature curriculum, but it might well serve as a starting point. Teachers might begin, for instance, by trying to correlate these stages of development with some of the great cultural issues. There is little agreement, of course, on what those issues are, but any formulation acceptable to the planners will do—it can always be modified in the light of further research or reflection. The Stanfords' set of themes (see p. 200) might be a suitable place to begin.

LaConte suggests that the themes identified be stated as polarities—opposites that represent a range of human experience. The example he develops in his essay has clear potential for correlation with the stages of reading interest Carlsen identifies:

By carefully framing polarities and thematic questions to take into account the maturity and interest of the students, we could fashion a program of "developmental exploration" in which students confront more sophisticated and intellectually challenging questions at each grade level. For example, within our loyalty-treachery polarity, the student might start in the seventh grade by exploring the question "How are animals loyal to humans?" and end in the twelfth grade by exploring the question "How can the state betray the individual?"[27]

The question he suggests for the seventh grade fits neatly into Carlsen's pattern—it would allow the students to read animal stories, which Carlsen tells us they are likely to enjoy—and yet the unit would be chosen for its theme, not simply to cater to the students' interests. Similarly, the question suggested for the twelfth grade, involving the relationship between an individual and the state, fits in with the transition to adult roles. Significant literary works could be chosen for each topic. In such units, the students would be discussing issues, and not simply isolated works.

Such a curriculum plan would be imprecise, of course. Still, the example from LaConte's proposal illustrates the possibility of developing curricula that are both academically sound—that is, concerned with significant ideas and literary works—and psychologically sound —that is, based on the maturity and interests of the child.

LaConte goes on to discuss some of the issues curriculum planners must consider. One is the question of selection: How should works be chosen for each of the central themes? LaConte suggests that the works chosen should represent different answers given to the question during different historical periods. He recommends a "three-tiered structure of past, present, and future,"[28] rather than the traditional chronological organization of the literature course. Students can learn to see attitudes and ideas as socially created, evolving constructs by observing their evolution through the past and speculating about their evolution in the future.

He also offers some advice about course organization, suggesting a balance betwen control and freedom. He identifies two basic approaches to planning a thematic curriculum—demonstrative and exploratory—and cautions against relying too heavily on either:

> While demonstrative organization lends itself to a tighter structure and control, exploratory organization affords far richer teaching opportunities. The demonstrative approach can too easily become moral indoctrination, using both literature and theme as object lessons in a particular point of view. The exploratory approach, on the other hand, can degenerate into totally uncontrolled bull sessions with both literature and theme being lost in verbal meandering.[29]

The balance he recommends between the two accommodates both discipline and student. It allows the teacher to decide on some of the issues to be addressed and some of the works to be considered, drawing on his knowledge of the literature, but it also asks him to observe the students and respond to their interests and the relevant digressions they may introduce.

ADOLESCENT LITERATURE IN THE CURRICULUM

The thematic structure would also provide a basis for including adolescent literature in the curriculum. If our purpose is to structure a dialog about important ideas rather than to teach a prescribed reading list, the bibliography for a course need not be limited to works that have achieved a high stature in the eyes of the academic community. Two criteria apply in this curriculum. One, of course, is literary merit and significance; The other is suitability for the group of students being taught. Most literature curricula and secondary school literature textbooks have considered the first of those criteria but neglected the second.

Adolescent literature clearly appeals to secondary school students, but some of its critics consider it a sad compromise with immature taste and cheap popular culture. In a curriculum based on the transaction between the reader and the work, however, the immaturity of students' taste and the deficiencies of popular culture are easy to accept: the first because it is natural—the students are adolescents and thus may be expected to have adolescent tastes—and the second because even shallowness (and, as we've argued before, much of adolescent literature is *not* shallow) may serve a purpose in the classroom, if only to complement the clearer and deeper perceptions of better writers. Students will come to perceive, through both natural maturation and experience in the classroom, which literature is more satisfying.

That is not to suggest that curriculum should rely solely on the students' natural development. If we could do that, schools would be unnecessary. But ignoring the natural patterns of development is equally foolish. If a young girl prefers Janet Dailey to Emily Brontë, insisting that she change her mind is probably a waste of effort. Better to examine the works students are willing to read, questioning and responding to them, and let their virtues and defects emerge in the process. This is the proper attitude for an intellectual dialog, in any case—one of questioning and openness to experience, rather than reliance on accepted authorities. If students learn the questioning process on books of lesser merit, they are nonetheless learning the process and will be able to apply it later to books of greater sophistication and maturity.

To argue for the greatness of a particular work is, of course, to argue for a personal perception. The value of a work for any one reader depends on the quality of his own transaction with the text. We can claim that some texts are more likely, because of certain demonstrable features, to sustain a rewarding transaction. Too often, however, teachers assume that their experience, training, and age give them the authority to judge their students' transactions. And they too seldom take into account the vast difference between their own situations and abilities and those of the students. Texts that are powerful for an adult may not have the same effect on adolescent readers.

The suggestion that adolescent literature be granted a place in the literature curriculum is not a compromise. It does not weaken the curriculum by displacing the great works. Rather, it strengthens it, by offering students the emotional and intellectual experiences of significant reading—the same sorts of experiences that skilled adults may have with the established great books of the culture. It invites them to participate at their own level in the ongoing dialog about the major issues of human life.

OTHER CONSIDERATIONS

In addition to the matters discussed above, planners of literature curricula might keep several other points in mind. We've suggested that they watch their natural tendency to think of curriculum in terms of lists of works, and think instead of the issues—the emotion and thought—that inspire the works, so that they might involve students in the cultural dialog. Essentially, we've suggested that planners consider both the student and the work, focusing on the transaction between the two. Even with the transaction between reader and text foremost in the teacher's mind, however, there is room for dogmatic insistence on one mode, usually interpretation.

The transaction between work and reader may take various shapes. It may be an act of interpretation and inference. The reader may grow curious about the intentions of the author and want to speculate about his meaning and his assumptions. Or he may even become intrigued by the technical workings of a piece and want to discuss how the author achieved his effects. Such a reading may seem highly intellectual, with little of the personal response that we argued for in Part One. There is no reason, however, to deny the legitimacy of a response simply because it is analytical and rational.

On the other extreme, the student's response may resist any connection with the work read. His train of thought may stray so far from the work that it seems irrelevant. Although that sort of response is clearly not a reading of the text, it too is legitimate. It is one of the possible satisfactions to be derived from reading.

Both ends of the spectrum should be respected in the classroom. One we may call self-bound, the other text-bound. The one is introspective and self-satisfying, and the other may ignore the self for the pleasures of investigating something in the text. Students should broaden their repertoire, learning to experience the literature in as many ways as possible. If they remain totally self-bound, they are trapped within their own minds, unable to compare their perceptions with others. If they are entirely text-bound, they may not have the satisfaction of finding personal connections with the works they read. Either extreme is a handicap. A good literature curriculum would ask its teachers to remain alert to this issue, perhaps by keeping some record of the range of students' responses and working to help them expand it.

Just as the curriculum should discuss the relationship between students and the literary work, it should also draw attention to the relationships among the people involved. We have described the appropriate relationship between the teacher and the class. It is not that of the captain to his troops or the informed to the ignorant; it is rather that of the more experienced and wise to the somewhat less experienced and wise. The teacher can offer the benefits of broader reading, but he cannot give students *the* reading, the final, authoritative, correct reading. That can be achieved, if at all, only by the individual for the individual.

Both teacher and students must provide information in the classroom. The teacher, of course, gives information about books, about techniques, and about his own reading. But the students too have very important information to offer, without which the literature course cannot succeed—information about their interests, their reactions to the works read, and their opinions of the responses and interpretations of others. The curriculum must specify an exchange of information in the classroom. Without it, the teacher will know very little about the students' transaction with the text, and thus about the literature they create in the act of reading.

The curriculum should also address the relationship among the students, for they can contribute á great deal to the development of literary insight. They can offer much that the teacher might not, since they are closer in age and experience. Their common ground may allow them to help each other understand the literature and themselves. Students are a resource too seldom used in the schools.

PLANNING THE LITERATURE CURRICULUM

Implicit in much of this chapter is the idea that a variety of people need to be involved in the complex and time-consuming work of planning a literature curriculum. Obviously the teachers need to be involved, though in many school systems they are not. They know the students, and thus have essential information to offer. They also know the constraints under which they work, constraints that are often hard to imagine. They will know, for instance, what it is like to try to teach one hundred and fifty students a day. To expect a teacher to give effective instruction in composition and literature to more than twenty or twenty-five students a day is absurd; to give him a hundred students a day should be considered criminal. The literature teacher is charged with helping students formulate their ideas of the world, of their own potential, and of the relationships among people—and yet he is asked to work with one hundred and fifty students. Teachers will know what limitations these impossible class loads impose on them and will be able to suggest the necessary compromises for the curriculum.

Clearly, also, for the reasons discussed earlier, students need to be included. They too have valuable information to offer. How they can be involved is, of course, a matter for each school or system to decide. In some small schools they might be able to participate as members of planning committees, discussing the purposes of the literature program, the criteria for selecting books, and all the other issues. Larger systems may have to be content with assessing interests and abilities and with finding ways to involve students in planning individual courses.

Parents need to be involved, or at least informed. They often labor under misconceptions about the curriculum, and especially about the English program. They are even less well-informed than most school administrators about the appropriate purposes of teaching literature and composition, and may believe that literature should be used to implant values rather than to investigate them, that teaching grammar will improve students' writing, or that books containing profanity or dealing with sex will poison their minds. There is a desperate need to educate parents about education and help them change their expectations of schools and teachers.

School administrators should also be involved, though in a subordinate role. The administrators responsible for handling money will need to be kept informed of plans made for the curriculum so that, in their enthusiasm, planners don't spend more than the system has. Those charged with scheduling and related duties will also need to know what the English curriculum becomes so that they can offer the necessary support.

Finally, someone should serve as supervisor of English to coordinate the task of curriculum planning. The knowledge of teachers, students, and scholars has to be brought together. The various people who have insights to offer the schools too often remain isolated and ignorant of each other's work. Teachers are uninformed about educational research or literary theory, critics fail to understand the minds and emotions of young children, and students too seldom know the goals of the teachers or grasp the significance of their own labors. The task of coordinating a curriculum development project is formidable.

A FINAL WORD ON THE SHAPE OF THE CURRICULUM

The curriculum should be an evolving, changing document, rather than something rigid and unbending. Guides written over a three-year period, printed, bound, distributed, and then untouched for the next ten years are of dubious value. Too few people participate in their conception and birth, and over too short a time. It would be much more helpful to conceive of the curriculum guide as a file drawer filled with units of instruction, bibliographies, and articles, plus a book shelf containing significant texts and journals. During each year a committee with rotating membership could assess the value of the materials, the effectiveness of the teaching, and the ideas emerging in the journals, and then work during the summer to reformulate aspects of the literature program.

In a school operating this way, the curriculum would be alive, changing and growing as the students and teachers change, responding to developments in literary theory and educational research. The staff would continually redesign and evaluate the curriculum, and would thus feel a sense of ownership and responsibility for it. Because of that responsibility, they would be motivated to continue reading and learning, and thus would continue to find the satisfactions for which they entered the profession.

NOTES

1. Albert R. Kitzhaber, "Project English and Curriculum Reform," in *Iowa English Yearbook*, 9 (Fall 1964) 4.
2. Arthur N. Applebee, *Tradition and Reform in the Teaching of English: A History* (Urbana, Ill.: National Council of Teachers of English, 1974), pp. 13–14.
3. Applebee, p. 11.
4. James F. Hosic, ed., "Reorganization of English in Secondary Schools," in *United States Bureau of Education Bulletin #2* (U.S. Government Printing Office, 1917), p. 14.
5. Hosic, pp. 129–30.

6. *An Experience Curriculum in English,* National Council of Teachers of English Curriculum Commission (New York: Appleton-Century, 1935), pp. 10–11.

7. George Winchester Stone, Jr., ed., *Issues, Problems, and Approaches in the Teaching of English* (New York: Holt, Rinehart and Winston, 1964), p. 7.

8. Albert R. Kitzhaber, "Project English and Curriculum Reform," *Iowa English Yearbook, Number 9* (Fall 1964), p. 6.

9. John Dixon, *Growth Through English* (London: Oxford Univ. Press, 1967), p. 60.

10. James Britton, "Response to Literature," in *Response to Literature,* ed. James R. Squire (Champaign, Ill.: National Council of Teachers of English, 1968), p. 6.

11. James E. Miller, Jr., "Literature in the Revitalized Curriculum," *NASSP Bulletin,* No. 38 (April, 1967), pp. 25–26.

12. Applebee, p. 245.

13. Applebee, p. 246.

14. Applebee, p. 247.

15. Applebee, p. 248.

16. Ronald LaConte, "A Literary Heritage Paradigm for Secondary English," in *Three Language-Arts Curriculum Models: Pre-Kindergarten through College,* ed. Barrett J. Mandel (Urbana, Ill.: National Council of Teachers of English, 1980), p. 126.

17. LaConte, p. 126

18. James Moffett, *Coming on Center: English Education in Evolution* (Montclair, N.J.: Boynton/ Cook, 1981), p. 13.

19. Barrett J. Mandel, *Three Language-Arts Curriculum Models: Pre-Kindergarten through College* (Urbana, Ill.: National Council of Teachers of English, 1980), p. 7.

20. Barbara Stanford and Gene Stanford, "Process Curriculum for High School Students," in *Three Language-Arts Curriculum Models: Pre-Kindergarten through College,* ed. Barrett J. Mandel (Urbana, Ill.: National Council of Teachers of English, 1980), pp. 139–40.

21. Stanford, p. 152.

22. Stanford, p. 153.

23. Erwin R. Steinberg, Robert C. Slack, Beekman W. Cottrell, and Lois S. Josephs, "The Overall Plan of the Curriculum Study Center at Carnegie-Mellon University," in *English Education Today,* ed. Lois S. Josephs and Erwin R. Steinberg (New York: Noble and Noble, 1970), p. 61.

24. G. Robert Carlsen and James Crow, "Project English Curriculum Centers," *English Journal,* 56, No. 7 (October, 1967), pp. 991–92.

25. G. Robert Carlsen, *Books and the Teenage Reader: A Guide for Teachers, Librarians, and Parents*, 2nd rev. ed. (New York: Harper and Row, 1980), pp. 35–42.

26. Carlsen, pp. 42–43.

27. LaConte, p. 135.

28. LaConte, p. 132.

29. LaConte, p. 131.

Evaluation and Testing 8

TESTING AND THE DISCIPLINE

Literature, because it is the meeting of reader and text, is a difficult subject to test. If we could establish the one right reading of a work, as the New Critics tried to do, or if we believed that information about literature is of primary importance, as do those inclined toward a historical approach, or if we were satisfied with comprehension questions, as the writers of basal readers seem to be, then assessing the learning of literature would be easy. Tests would be simple to design, administer, and assess, and we could all feel confident that we know how we are doing. But if reading is the idiosyncratic experience that Rosenblatt and others believe it to be, matters are not quite so simple.

Testing is easiest when we have clear standards for students' performance and acceptable units of measurement. There are, of course, aspects of English that can be accurately measured. We can agree on the spellings of words, test students' ability to remember them, and measure the results. We can agree on most of the principles of punctuation and test them. We can assess the students' knowledge of a body of facts—names, dates, titles, and the like. Thus it is that English has been plagued by a swarm of inappropriate tests and measurements. The teaching profession has succumbed to the temptation to measure what it can, much to the detriment of students and the discipline.

The problem is, of course, that the essential matters are not so easily tested. Spelling and punctuation are useful skills, but they are obviously superficial—they pale into insignificance beside the ability to create, to imagine, to relate one thought to another, to organize, to reason, or to catch the nuances of English prose. Information about literature is also interesting, perhaps even important, but unless students can read sensitively, respond, and consider and compare their responses, the information is just so much useless baggage. But inventing, reasoning, response, and reflection do not lend themselves readily to testing, especially testing that is economical and efficient and that yields precise and manageable numbers. So schools often compromise, testing what seems testable, and hoping for the best with the remainder of the discipline.

The consequences of that compromise are predictable. What is tested becomes the most important part of the curriculum, and what is not tested is neglected. A great many schools have reduced their writing instruction to the testable basic skills of spelling, punctuation, grammar, and usage—skills often foisted on the gullible public as writing. And they have abandoned literature to teach comprehension, vocabulary, identifying words in context, or any of the other testable aspects of reading. Education is thus reshaped, inappropriately, by the pressures of the tests. Elements of the discipline rise to prominence or fade into obscurity not because of their level of importance but because they are easy or difficult to test.

One frequent objection to the response-based literature teaching this book suggests is that it would make testing difficult or impossible. Clearly it *is* difficult to test, in any traditional sense, the students' unique and changing interactions with the literature. But that difficulty does not reduce the importance of those interactions or increase the importance of abilities more easily tested. Too often, the schools conclude that testing something insignificant is more important than teaching something significant. Form, then, outweighs substance, and the rituals of the institution obscure its purposes. Education becomes silly—a pointless game whose significance and pleasure have been lost. Teachers may rightly object that testing is an obligation forced on them by administrators and by tradition, but it nonetheless remains their job to fight its influence and keep in mind the purposes for which they teach literature.

TESTING AND THE STUDENT

The obsession with testing not only tends to distort our vision of the discipline, but it also confuses students about their role in the educational process. By giving the responsibility for judgment to the teacher, continual testing suggests to students that they are not the ultimate judges of their own thoughts and emotions, as of course they must be. Externally imposed assessments are surely appropriate and necessary in other situations, when there are clear standards of correctness or when someone must be certified to do a particular job.

Surgeons, pilots, electricians, and plumbers have to perform certain specified tasks accurately and reliably. They can be tested on the skills and knowledge they are expected to have, and clearly they *should* be tested, to improve the odds that the public will survive their professional services. But literature is more personal, variable, and idiosyncratic than plumbing and wiring. We can test the electrician by connecting the circuit and seeing if anything catches fire or blows up, but to test someone's reading of a literary work we would have to know her better than she is likely to know herself. We would have to understand the interplay of events in her life—the works she has read, the people she has met, and her thoughts and feelings about these experiences. Without that knowledge and insight, we would be unqualified to judge her interaction with the work.

We can judge some of it, of course. A misunderstood word, for instance, is fairly easy to detect. If the text reads "proscribe" and the student reads "prescribe," anyone who knows the two words can point out the error and help the reader correct it. But the more subtle and more essential matters are not so manageable. Questions of values and beliefs, and judgments about the significance of a literary work for the student, only the student herself can decide. And these are, of course, the significant issues in literature.

This is not to suggest that these more difficult and interesting matters should go unexamined, or that the teacher should have no role in their examination. The teacher's help in evaluating beliefs, ideas, and judgments is extremely important. But responsibility for evaluation must lie primarily with the student, since she is the only one with access to the necessary information. She alone knows whether she has thought carefully and honestly; she alone can know what issues matter most to her, what she believes, or what memories are triggered by a literary work. One serious problem with testing is that it often substitutes for this sort of evaluation, just as grades have come to substitute for evaluative comment.

GRADING

Curiously enough, our educational system has managed to convince a good many people that something as insubstantial as a grade actually has meaning. Students will listen impatiently to careful explanations of their abilities and their weaknesses, and then demand, "But what did I get?" as if the letter grade says more than the most elaborate statements about their work. Even some parents, after a lengthy and detailed commentary on their child's work, feel sadly uninformed about what the child is accomplishing until the explanation is reduced to a single letter selected from the first five of the alphabet.

This astounding preference for meaningless simplicity over meaningful complexity would be unfathomable anywhere else but school. A pilot in training, having some difficulty with her landings, would not be satisfied to hear that her efforts were worth a "C." Not even refining the system so that we could say she had earned a "C ," or changing the letter into a number—"79"—would satisfy her, though such pseudo-precision might delude the naive. She would want to know instead what she was doing right and what she was doing wrong, and how she could improve. To substitute a grade for an evaluation would be obviously foolish. And yet, in learning language, a much more complicated task than learning to land an airplane, we are often content with the simple grade.

The problem is not simply that the grade doesn't inform; rather, it misinforms and deceives. It imitates the precision of mathematics, though it is at best only impression and judgment. In so doing it conceals information that might be useful to students and parents, and trains them to accept an empty symbol as surrogate.

Reliance on testing encourages students to look to someone else for final judgments even on important matters. Student come to believe that they must obtain answers from an authority rather than formulate the answers themselves. They are thus likely to pester the teacher for explanations and interpretations—"We've talked about the poem; now tell us what it really means." Students who develop this attitude are insulated from the literature and themselves. By looking outside rather than in, they learn to avoid intelligent reading. Testing thus cultivates dependence, discouraging intellectual responsibility and self-reliance.

EPISTEMOLOGY

Perhaps the most serious problem with extensive testing is that it distorts the students' conception of knowledge. Knowledge becomes what the teacher knows, or what lies in the books. It is a thing, out there in the world, waiting to be found. Such an idea is destructive; it leads students to wait for knowledge to be given to them.

Knowledge is not such a simple matter. It cannot be bought and sold—it must be made. It is the product of the mind's interaction with the world. As such, it can change and grow. If knowledge is out there to be found, there is no possibility for progress—we can only know what is already known. But if knowledge is created, there can be new knowledge, new ways of seeing, thinking, and behaving, and we are not limited to what we now have. To convince students that knowledge is something they can be given ready-made is to trap them, to discourage them from thinking and exploring, to make them gullible.

It is natural, in a scientific era, to imagine that all knowledge is to be found in the physical world. The impressive knowledge nowadays is that of physicists designing powerful weapons and biologists developing potent drugs, and the source of that sort of knowledge *is* the physical world. Its criteria are objective, drawn from scientific method and statistical analysis. The knowledge literature deals with, however, is different. It has to do with the individual and her interactions with the world, and thus it has a personal element. To know about the issues of great literature—love, death, justice, and so on—we must pay attention to our own uniqueness as well as to the observable data of the outside world. We do not weigh and measure these elements as we weigh and measure the raw materials of science, and yet knowledge of them is obviously important. Literature's knowledge is different from that of physics and biology, and harder to parcel out into questions on an exam, but it is no less significant.

ALTERNATIVES

None of this argument against testing and its effects should be construed as an argument against evaluation. Instead, it is an argument against the form evaluation has taken in too many schools. Evaluation has become something the teacher does *to* the students, rather than with them, something imposed rather than shared. But at its best it could be a cooperative venture in which teacher and student share impressions and help each other understand what has happened in the reading of the literature.

The pattern of evaluation should grow logically out of our concern for students' responses to the literature and their analysis of them. At the end of a unit the teacher might ask students questions like the following:

1. Did you enjoy reading the work? Can you identify why you did or did not?
2. Did the literary work offer any new insight or point of view? If so, did it lead you to a change in your own thinking? If not, did it confirm thoughts or opinions you already held?
3. Did the discussion reveal anything about the work, about your classmates, or about yourself?

Such questions ask students to evaluate their own interaction with the text and with other students. They focus on the experience of reading and discussing rather than on the work read. Further, they ask students to watch for changes, suggesting that growth is more important than correctness. They do not, by focusing exclusively on details of the text as many examinations do, declare the students' opinions, feelings, and thoughts irrelevant.

Questions like these could be handled in several different ways. They could be discussed openly in class. If the teacher senses that some students have profited from reading the work and might be willing to talk about their experience, then open discussion might be the most effective way of assessing the group's efforts. Those students who did enjoy the work and think carefully about it would illustrate some of the possibilities for meaningful reading. Of course, they should not be identified as models to imitate—that would effectively silence them.

Students might sometimes be asked to reply to evaluation questions in writing so that the teacher can review them for insight into the students' minds. Over time, she may be able to note patterns in the students' reactions and take them into account in her planning. Perhaps a class continually expresses frustration with the literature selected, reporting that the works give them no pleasure and stimulate little thought. That information could prompt the teacher to review her selection of material and her methods of instruction. Perhaps one student reveals hostility toward adults or toward the authority of the school. The teacher might then choose works that would invite discussion of the relationships between adults and children and the problems of achieving autonomy. The replies of some students may suggest lines of inquiry that had not occurred to the teacher as she read the work herself, or even as she discussed it with her class. Private evaluations may reveal some of the thoughts and feelings that the students were unwilling to articulate before the entire group.

The teacher does, of course, need to analyze the comments students make in these evaluations and in their other work, both written and oral. She needs some way to determine how the students are progressing. One possibility is to devise a checklist for the students' work that touches on the major issues. Such a list might include some of the following questions:

1. Does the student seem willing to express responses to a work, or is she cautious and constrained?
2. Does the student ever change her mind, or is she intransigent?
3. Does the student participate in discussions, listening to others, considering ideas offered, and presenting her own thoughts?

4. Does the student distinguish between the thoughts and feelings she brings to a literary work and those that can be reasonably attributed to the text?
5. Is the student able to distinguish between fact, inference, and opinion in the reading of a literary work?
6. Is the student able to relate the literary work to other human experience, especially her own—that is, can she generalize and abstract?
7. Does the student accept the responsibility for making meaning out of the literature and the discussions? Or does she depend on others to tell her what works mean?
8. Does the student perceive differences and similarities in the visions offered by different literary works, or is she unaware of the subtleties?

This is hardly a complete list, but it suggests helpful criteria that teachers might devise. Consider a hypothetical student whose work we analyze with such a set of questions. For the first question we note that she seldom expresses a response but will sometimes answer questions of fact. Question 2 reveals that if she ever does express an opinion or make an observation she holds to it regardless of other students' objections. Our notes on Question 3 suggest that she does not consider other ideas, unable, in effect, to hear them. Whenever she does participate she opens with "Yes, but. . .," rejecting the statements of others without considering them at all. In her papers we note, for Question 4, that she has difficulty distinguishing between her own ideas and those in the text, often casually attributing her thoughts and opinions to the writer.

If we can make such observations about a student, we have much more information to work with than if we test her on the details of a literary work. We will know that we first need to deal with her refusal to change her mind—not an uncommon problem for students trained in classes that emphasize correctness. Basal readers, with ten comprehension questions following each reading assignment, could not be better designed to persuade students that being right matters more than anything else.

Second, we must help her learn to distinguish between her own thoughts and those of others, including the authors she reads. We might provide her with questions to answer before reading, so that she articulates her own thoughts, and then ask her to observe similarities and differences in the work. If we are teaching Bryan's "So Much Unfairness of Things," we might have her write briefly about her views of cheating—what it is, how important it is, and what the appropriate penalties are. This process may help her to identify the perspectives of the student in the story who cheats, the students who report him, and the teachers who throw him out of school.

In order to record our observations of students more easily, we might recast our list of questions as dichotomous pairs. The first question, for example, might simply be:

open – closed

Others might be:

speaks willingly – – – – – – – – – – – speaks reluctantly
enjoys the reading – – – – – – – – – – dislikes the reading
relates work to self – – – – – – – – – – – – remains distant
listens to others – – – – – – refuses to hear other ideas
rational – – – – – – – – – – – – – – – – – – emotional

Locating students on each continuum may give the teacher useful information about their habits and inclinations.

All of the information gathered from such evaluative questions can be equally valuable to both teacher and student. For the teacher it can suggest directions for the future; for the student it is a record of her own development. In a set of evaluations collected over the course of a school year, the student may be able to see changes in her behavior and in her patterns of response. She may note that interests died away and were replaced by others, that some confusions were clarified, and that other issues about which she had had firm convictions became ambiguous and frustrating. She may discover that her later entries reveal concerns that never surfaced early in the year. The evaluations, which she has written herself, though the teacher will have spoken with her about them and perhaps added comments, may provide concrete evidence of the effects of literature on her life, just as slashes on a tree give evidence of physical growth.

THE RANGE OF AN EVALUATION PROGRAM

Purves, in an essay on testing competence in reading, suggests a distinction useful in discussing evaluation:

Research has shown that there may be quite individual responses—perceptions, feelings, attitudes—to a piece of writing, but at the same time there are certain shared perceptions. . . . These shared perceptions can be thought of as the *meaning*, and the particular or individual understanding as the *significance*.[1]

In another essay[2], perhaps the most complete and thorough analysis of the problems of evaluation in literature, Purves lists various aspects of literature instruction to evaluate. His taxonomy might be useful to teachers interested in devising a balanced testing program.

Purves begins by suggesting that both content and behavior be considered, proposing that they might be plotted as the two axes of a grid. Purves subdivides the category of content into "Literary Works," "Contextual Information," "Literary Theory," and "Cultural Information." These categories are further subdivided. Under "Literary Works" he lists genres to be taught, including both the traditional (poetry, drama, fiction, and nonfiction) and movies, television, and other mass media. "Contextual Information" includes biographical and historical knowledge. "Literary Theory" refers to literary terminology and critical approaches and "Cultural Information" to knowledge of the dominant myths and metaphors of a culture.

The other axis of his grid, behavior, is a checklist of the behaviors that might be elicited from students. These fall into three broad categories of "Knowledge," "Response," and "Participation." "Knowledge" in this context means applying information. It is further subdivided into the various sorts of information one might apply in discussing literature—knowledge of specific works, biographical information, terminology, and so on. "Response" is divided into several categories including recreating the work, expressing feelings, interpreting and judging, and analyzing the work and its parts. "Participation" deals with the willingness to respond.

Such checklists will help teachers evaluate both students and programs. Analyzing a curriculum might reveal, for instance, that poetry is overemphasized or that novels are neglected. Either might be an imbalance in the curriculum. Or the analysis might indicate that media other than the printed word have been ignored. These "literatures" could be important, and the teacher might take steps to include them.

Evaluating a student's work against this sort of checklist might reveal that she is extremely reluctant to express responses, preferring the security of impersonal intellectual discussion. Other students might gladly talk about their feelings and opinions but shy away from the demanding work of reasoning about the texts they read or considering the ideas of others in the group. Neither extreme is desirable: each allows students to avoid an important aspect of the literary experience and of their own development. An evaluation scheme similar to Purves' checklists of content and behavior might reveal these imbalances in the literature program and in the growth of the students.

Of course, such an evaluation scheme would not have the comforting but false precision of testing programs based entirely on the content of the literature. Nor would it be easy to apply and grade. A teacher cannot, for example, give a ten-question multiple-choice test to judge the student's satisfaction in responding. That is a matter that she must assess continually, taking into consideration the interaction between the student and her classmates, how much the student seems to have liked the works read, and countless other variables. Still, it is worth assessing, because so much of the student's enjoyment of literature depends on her ability and willingness to respond to what she reads.

Hillocks analyzes the possible content of the literature program in a slightly different way, focusing on comprehension skills. He suggests that there is a hierarchy of skills, and that students who have trouble with questions at one level of the hierarchy will have a great deal more difficulty at the higher levels. The levels Hillocks proposes are these:

LITERAL LEVEL OF COMPREHENSION
1. Basic stated information—information that is prominent and important in the text.
2. Key detail—important to the plot, but less prominently presented.
3. Stated relationship—a relationship, often causal, between bits of information.

INFERENTIAL LEVEL OF COMPREHENSION
4. Simple implied relationships—relationships not stated in the text.
5. Complex implied relationships—require inferences drawn from many pieces of information.
6. Author's generalization—inferences about the author's vision drawn from the total work.
7. Structural generalizations—require an analysis of the work's structure, and an explanation of how it works.[3]

Hillocks proposes the hierarchy as an organizing principle for evaluation. He points out its obvious advantages over assessments using simplistic readability scores, observing that

Readability scores are universally based on measures of vocabulary difficulty and aspects of sentence length. They necessarily ignore what might be called the *inferential load* of a work.[4]

They make the further error of assuming that longer words are more difficult than shorter words, although it is obvious that words like "love," "peace," "justice," "honor," "good," and the like are more difficult than "television," "rocketship," "automobile," and "hamburger." Length and difficulty do not always correspond.

Hillocks suggests developing an inventory based on his hierarchy and administering it at the beginning of the school year. The results serve, he says,

to define and predict, in fairly specific terms, the comprehension levels of specific students and groups of students and, therefore, provide a guide for deciding how to begin the term's literature program.[5]

A second inventory given at the end of the term would indicate something about the progress made in between. On comparable inventories, students should presumably perform better at the end of the term than they did at the beginning, if we accept the hierarchy as our set of goals for instruction. But although Hillocks' scheme is excellent as far as it goes, it neglects important elements in reading. It assesses only the skills of comprehension and analysis, which are, of course, very important. The development of these skills, however, is closely tied to the student's capacity for responding to the work, which Hillocks' scheme does not examine.

Purves' taxonomy suggests attention to both the literary work and the student in testing—a balanced approach to a difficult task. Ginn's *Responding*, perhaps the most interesting and creative literature program available, applies such a taxonomy in its evaluation plan. Cooper and Purves use a content-behavior grid; in the cells created by the intersection of content and behavior they suggest strategies for assessment. Those strategies include traditional tests as well as a variety of other devices.

One, which they call "The Attitude-Sort," assesses students' attitudes on four factors—willingness to respond, value placed on books and writers, importance given to personal engagement with literary works, and willingness to analyze literature.[6] It consists of 32 statements, which the student is asked to judge according to how much they are like her own opinions. This activity yields a rough picture of the class's attitudes toward the study of literature, and might, if conducted at the beginning and at the end of a year or semester, indicate changes in those attitudes. A similar tool is the Likert-Scale, consisting of statements which the student evaluates on a five-point scale from "strongly agree" to "strongly disagree." Such instruments may be designed by individual teachers or school systems to reflect what they consider most important in literature instruction, or they may be borrowed from sources like *A Guide to Evaluation*.

Cooper and Purves also recommend various shorter assessments, including two for students' perceptions of a class period, several for their perceptions of the class as a whole, one for their perceptions of the teacher, and one for their observations about the work of a group.[7] Although most of these do not deal specifically with literature teaching, they may still be useful, especially if modified slightly to suit a particular course or lesson or perhaps simply recast to sound more like the teacher. If students are involved in evaluating the ongoing work of the class, they are more likely to commit themselves to the work.

THE UNIQUENESS OF THE DISCIPLINE

The teacher of literature has a problem. She works in a time when measurement is worshipped, objectivity is a virtue, and the educational system is under attack. She wants to defend her profession and its accomplishments, yet she cannot use the sorts of objective tools that yield proof acceptable to the public. Knowledge of literature is simply not testable in any of the traditional ways. To test it is to subvert it, forcing it into a mold that it does not fit.

Tests that deny the personal and idiosyncratic element in literary knowledge or patterns of evaluation that locate authority in the teacher rather than in the student or that presume to establish an objective standard for understanding or appreciating literature will inevitably do more harm than good. It is still possible, of course, to assess and evaluate. But if the evaluations are to have any value for the student, they must respect her autonomy and individuality.

NOTES

1. Alan Purves, "Competence in Reading," in *The Nature and Measurement of Competency in English*, ed. Charles R. Cooper (Urbana, Ill: National Council of Teachers of English, 1981), p. 75.

2. Alan Purves, "Evaluation of Learning in Literature," in *Handbook on Formative and Summative Evaluation of Student Learning*, ed. Benjamin S. Bloom, J. Thomas Hastings, and George F. Madaus (New York: McGraw-Hill Book Company, 1971), pp. 697–766.

3. George Hillocks, Jr., "Toward a Hierarchy of Skills in the Comprehension of Literature," *English Journal*, 69, No. 3 (March 1980), 54–59.

4. Hillocks, p. 59.

5. Hillocks, p. 59.

6. Charles R. Cooper and Alan C. Purves, *A Guide to Evaluation* (Boston: Ginn and Company, 1973), p. 22; this manual accompanies Ginn's Responding series.

7. They cite two sources for these instruments: Alfred H. Gorman's *Teachers and Learners: The Interactive Process of Education* (Boston: Allyn and Bacon, 1969), and Robert Fox et al., *Diagnosing Classroom Learning Environments* (Chicago: Science Research Associates, Inc., 1966).

Current Literary Theory 9

The approach to literature teaching sketched in the preceding pages draws its justification from several areas of scholarship. Most obviously, it draws on the large body of critical theory known as reader-response criticism; but it is also supported by recent research in reading, especially that research most influenced by the psycholinguists, and by studies of reading interest and response to literature. Even more general studies in adolescent psychology and the nature of learning substantiate it. In this chapter we will briefly review some of the current work that lends credence to response-based teaching of literature, in order to demonstrate that a substantial body of research and theory undergirds it, explore some of the issues it raises and the problems it addresses, and suggest the richness of the field for any who might wish to explore it further.

We will concentrate here on recent ciritical theory, which seems to be the richest source of pedagogic goals and practices. Much of this has already been discussed—Louise Rosenblatt, the best representative of modern response-based critical theory, has been cited often. She has served us as the speaker for a diverse group, many of whom disagree enthusiastically with one another. They share, however, as Mailloux points out, a basic epistemological assumption: "the object of knowledge can never be separated from the knower; the perceived object can never be separated from perception by a perceiver."[1] That assumption grants the reader—that is, the student —a very important place in our thinking about teaching and curriculum. If we accept that assumption, then our plans cannot involve only the details of literary history or the nuances of textual analysis. We must consider the nature of the student as well, which is, of course, what educational psychology has told us all along.

It is that basic assumption that makes reader-response criticism compatible with educational theory and potentially valuable in the classroom. For our purposes, the implications of that one shared assumption are much more significant than the differences among the critical theorists. The shift in emphasis from the text alone to the reader and his interaction with it implies new priorities and procedures for the classroom. It suggests that students should not be subordinate to the text and submissive to the teacher, but active, making meaning and significance for themselves out of the literature they encounter.

In contrast, the pedagogy inspired by New Critical theories that emphasized the single text, "the autonomous and autotelic nature of the single, lonely poem,"[2] was a pedagogy in which the students and their views were of little significance. Scholes summarizes the consequences of New Critical domination in the schools:

> This New Critical privileging of the integrity of the work in literary study led to a whole series of interpretive, pedagogical, and editorial gestures. Students were given poems to interpret with their titles removed, their author's names concealed, and their dates ignored. Anthologies were produced with the works ordered not by chronology but by the alphabet, with biographical information omitted or hidden in appendices, with no visible clues as to country or date of origin. In the name of improved interpretation, reading was turned into a mystery and the literature classroom into a chapel where the priestly instructor (who knows the authors, dates, titles, biographies, and general provenance of the texts) astounded the faithful with miracles of interpretation. The scandal at the heart of the New Criticism—and the source of its power—was this use of cultural codes by instructors who officially asserted that such material was irrelevant to the interpretive process. I am not suggesting conscious fraud, of course, but a myth of pedagogy that was believed because it gratified the pedagogues who believed in it. And the whole position was grounded in the notion of the bounded, self-sufficient work.[3]

Scholes complains of the neglect of the "cultural codes," revealing his bias as a semiotician, but a similar complaint could be raised by those more interested in the readings and responses of individuals, those who approach criticism focusing on the psychology of the reader. Bleich, whose theories of reading Mailloux characterizes as "psychological" rather than "social," also reacts strongly to the New

Critical concentration on the single work. The goal of Bleich's work, as Mailloux describes it, is:

> to reinscribe the organized discussion of literature within a discourse that aggressively advocates the freedom of the individual self in a pedagogical community. Bleich's approach to teaching places the individual student and his subjective response at the center of literary study.[4]

These two views illustrate the differences that have arisen within reader-response criticism. Bleich, with his stress on the freedom of the individual reader, represents the school of thought that seeks to understand the literary act by examining how individuals make sense out of literary works. Scholes, on the other hand, places less emphasis on the uniquenesses of individual readers, concentrating instead on the larger patterns and conventions in literature and culture that enable the work to communicate meaning.

Although the differences among the various critics may at times seem trifling and unimportant, they do represent different ways of looking at the work and the reader and different aspects of literary studies that might be emphasized, and thus they may suggest different teaching practices. Let us examine some of the differences of opinion within current reader-response criticism to see what possibilities they open up for literature teachers in the secondary schools.

Reader-response critics differ in the relative stress they place on three elements: the reader, the text, and the relationship between text and world. Let us consider several different schools of thought on the matter.

SUBJECTIVE AND TRANSACTIVE CRITICISM

At one end of the spectrum we find such theorists as Bleich and Holland. Although they disagee on several particulars, they both locate the source of meaning in the individual reader, and their method of study demands close attention to the actual readings of their students. Bleich, in his major theoretical work, *Subjective Criticism*, insists on a revision of the epistemological base for the study of literature. Knowledge is made rather than found, he argues—all but the simplest acts of perception are in fact intellectual acts of making symbols and then interpreting them.

He illustrates the point by noting that if we observe a beautiful landscape—Mount Rainier, in his example—and if the observation yields a moment of reflection, the perception was evaluative. We focus our attention on the mountain because "it was not simply 'Mt. Rainier' that I saw, but it was 'the magnificent Mt. Rainier'." When this happens, he says, we have "peremptorily converted the real mountain into a symbolic mountain," and then evaluated our symbolization, our "perceptual experience of the mountain," and not the real, tree-covered, snow-capped granite object.[5]

It is the same with literature, Bleich asserts—we read, we transform the text into symbols as our emotions and intellect direct us, and we interpret the symbols we have created. Thus, the study of literature must begin with response. The literary work exists in the mind of the reader. By itself it is simply ink on paper—not until it is read, and thus reformulated in the reader's mind, does it become an act of literature.

Bleich places heavy emphasis on the act of reformulation, so much so that he rejects Rosenblatt's notion of a transaction between the reader and the text. That notion implies a more active role for the text than he is willing to grant it:

> The subjective paradigm, in emphasizing the distinction between real objects, symbolic objects, and subjects (i.e., people), holds that only subjects are capable of initiating action. . . .[6]

Thus the text, an object, cannot act. It cannot constrain and direct the reader—the reader alone directs himself in the activity of reading. Where Rosenblatt sees a transaction between text and reader, each playing an active role, Bleich sees only the action of the reader. The reader makes symbols of the text, just as the observer makes a symbol of the mountain and in making those symbols creates meanings.

Bleich's conception of reading must seem especially alien to those trained in the New Criticism, which postulates a stable text in which meaning resides. Bleich rejects that stability and security. Relocating meaning in the reader's subjective response and reflection on that response seems to suggest that there can be no standard of correct interpretation, no way of asserting anything at all that is not a statement only about the self. He suggests, however, that if we cannot appeal to objective criteria for the validation of knowledge, we do at least have ways to reach agreement.

He calls the process "negotiation," and it is dependent on his notion of an "interpretive community." If we cannot directly grasp the literary work, we can at least respond to it, "resymbolize" it, and communicate our personal recreation of the work to other readers. We can then see what is shared and what is not. Knowledge is thus the result of sharing responses. Readers declare their responses to the work and then are enabled, presumably by common cultural background, to discuss those individual recreations, seeking similarities and differences, and construct a consensus which—for them, at that time, in those circumstances—is knowledge. Knowledge, in Bleich's critical theory, is what is declared to be so by the community.

This concept presents an epistemological problem. Bleich denies that the text can act on the reader—it is an object, and "only subjects are capable of initiating action." He rejects both Holland's notion of "transactive" reading, in which the reader is constrained by the text in certain ways, though more so by his own psyche, and Rosenblatt's notion of "transactional" reading, in which reader and text seem to shape one another:

> . . . there is often an illusion that a text acts on a reader, but it can hardly be the case that a text actually does act on the reader. . . . Therefore, discussion of the work must refer to the subjective syntheses of the reader and not to the reader's interaction with the text.[7]

The reader is left solitary—alone in his subjectivity. There seems, in Bleich's view, no hope of communication with the text, in the usual sense that suggests some understanding of another's meaning. The literature is not a source of knowledge, but only a stimulus to subjective meditation—the knowledge is formulated later, in the interchange among readers. Communication, for Bleich, resides not in the act of reading, but only in the aftermath, the discussion of the reading with others:

> The practice of formulating response statements is a means for making a language experience (hearing, speaking, reading, or writing) available for conversion into knowledge. A response can acquire meaning only in the context of a predecided community (two or more people) interest in knowledge.[8]

That is to say, two or more readers come together, with a common interest in knowledge of something they have read, and talk in such a way that knowledge is the result. Bleich is unclear about the criteria by which that knowledge is to be judged—presumably agreement is the deciding factor. If a community agrees on some proposition, then that proposition *is* knowledge for that community. Bleich points out that even when some principle is disputed by a member of the community, the accepted "knowledge" of the group establishes the context in which the dispute takes place:

> Like the infantile processes of language acquisition, subsequent contexts of knowledge formation are always communal, even if a particular individual forms knowledge in opposition to his community.[9]

The difficulty here is that an exchange between members of a community is no less verbal than the act of reading. When we meet to discuss our responses to a literary work, we speak; that is, we interact linguistically. An individual participating in the discussion is thus confronted with the words of his comrades. But is this not almost exactly the same situation he finds himself in when he reads a literary work? He then has the words of the text before him. If those words are inert, if they have meaning only insofar as he "resymbolizes" or reconstitutes them, then surely the spoken and written words of those in his community are also inert until resymbolized or reconstituted.

The difference between the reader sitting down with a novel and the student reading a classmate's response paper or hearing his comments is surely not so great that we may consider one but not the other to be a source of knowledge. The listener must, after all, act on the words of his colleagues just as the reader acts on the words of the text. In both cases, if we accept Bleich's premises, he must resymbolize and then work with the images and thoughts he has created. Like the text, the spoken word is inert and immobile—it must be heard by an active, thinking listener to become anything more than vibrations in the air. If the immediate verbal exchanges within the community, governed as they must be by the rules of language, can yield knowledge, then surely the verbal exchanges between writer and reader might also yield knowledge.

Bleich must acknowledge that at some point there is significant interchange between people, or he cannot possibly account for the frequent similarity in the responses of different readers to one text. To confine that significant interchange to members of a rather narrowly conceived interpretive community is to deny the obvious similarity between immediate, face-to-face communication and written communication over distance and time. Bleich allows interaction between individuals—interaction that is inescapably linguistic—but he rejects the possibility of interaction between reader and text, which is also linguistic. In both cases the individuals are either trapped within their subjectivity or they are not, and thus it seems that both situations might either lead to knowledge or not.

There seems to be no reason why the notion of community Bleich offers could not be extended to include the writer and his work. This is not to deny the communal context for the production of knowledge upon which Bleich insists, nor the subjectivity in which each of us is trapped. Still, all linguistic activities have both social and idiosyncratic dimensions, and both must be recognized. If we are to communicate at all, the words we employ must call to mind for each of us images or associations that are essentially similar. The word "mother," for instance, must suggest some image of a female who has borne children. But precisely what that image is will depend on what we think and feel about our own mothers, whether or not we happen to be mothers, and a multitude of other variables. You cannot know exactly what I mean by the word, nor can I know exactly what you mean.

Bleich's epistemology is a problem, but his critical theory in general does have the great virtue of focusing attention on individual readers. In his system, readers respond to a work, consider each other's responses, and finally assess the work and their comprehension of it as a community. This perspective is likely to lead to a pedagogy that respects the students. The teacher working from such a base will not fall into the patterns for which Scholes criticized the New Critical professors. Rather than performing miracles of interpretation for the class, such a teacher will more likely invite the students themselves to perform.

Further, he is likely to value learning about the self as highly as learning about the literature. In fact, he may not see the two as distinct. Learning about the literature without learning about the self would be pointless or impossible in a program founded on the principles Bleich develops. One of the undeniable implications of his theory is that students and their thoughts are the center of the curriculum.

Although Bleich's critical theory and the sort of research and teaching that emerge from it may give us some insight into the student's role in his own literary experiences, they do not tell us as much as we might like about the contributions of the literature itself. More moderate critics and teachers, however much they respect the reader's perspective, might feel uncomfortable with a theory that places so much weight on the students' shoulders, especially in the secondary schools. On the one hand, such an approach is likely to appeal to students. It does, after all, grant them and their opinions a central place in the classroom, and thus might motivate them to participate. On the other hand, too many students are inclined to value their own unconsidered opinions too highly already, and teachers may fear the potential for misunderstanding the subjective approach. If students assume that the invitation to express and examine their own feelings and thoughts is, in fact, an invitation to say whatever they please without bothering to think, then the classroom could become unmanageable. Although Bleich suggests some techniques for directing the work of the class, and we have discussed similar strategies in the first several chapters, the teachers' fear is likely to persist.

Bleich's critical theory also seems to offer little guidance for developing the literature curriculum. The directions a class will take are presumably to be found in the course of reading and discussion. Athough that notion is exciting and potentially powerful, since it suggests a natural movement for the course that would allow real growth and exploration, it offers little security. It requires the teacher to be unfailingly conscious of students' responses to the literature and each other, always looking for the next step. The prospect of maintaining that degree of vigilance would be intimidating enough under ideal circumstances, with small and fewer classes. For a teacher faced with 150 students of widely differing backgrounds and abilities, it may be overwhelming.

TRANSACTIONAL CRITICISM AND RECEPTION AESTHETICS

Teachers may seek a bit more structure than they find in Bleich's ideas, and if so they may tend to prefer theories that suggest a more active role for the literature, either in constraining or in directing the reader. Such theories, by focusing attention on the text, offer a more stable base from which to work. Rosenblatt represents a group which views reading as an interaction or transaction between the reader and the text. Iser and Jauss, both of the German school of critical thought known as reception aesthetics, also seem to maintain a balance, recognizing that the reader's unique perspective will greatly influence the shape a literary work takes in his mind but also granting that the work itself has power to affect his responses, guiding him in some directions and steering him away from others.

Rosenblatt argues:

"The poem" cannot be equated solely with *either* the text *or* the experience of a reader. Something encapsulated in a reader's mind without relevance to a text may be a wonderful fantasy, but the term "poem" or "literary work," in transactional terminology, would not be applicable to such a "mental experience" any more than to an entity apart from a reader.[10]

Her view is more moderate than Bleich's. Still, she argues:

> What each reader makes of the text is, indeed, *for him* the poem, in the sense that this is his only direct perception of it. No one else can read it for him. He may learn indirectly about others' experiences with the text; he may come to see that his own was confused or impoverished, and he may then be stimulated to attempt to call forth from the text a better poem. But this he must do himself, and only what he himself experiences in relation to the text is— again let us underline—*for him*, the work.[11]

Rosenblatt does not diminish the reader's role, but she insists that the reader must accommodate himself to the text. He must be in some ways guided, or he is fantasizing rather than reading. Iser makes a similar case. For him, also, the text is more controlling and confining than it is for Bleich or Holland, who view the reader as the source of meaning. It does, he says, several things. It establishes a perspective, it arouses—and frustrates—expectations, it guides the reader's imagination through the creative act of reading, and it provides gaps and uncertainties which the reader must fill in. The text, for Iser, is a much more active agent than it is for Bleich. Still, all of these actions imply equal participation by the reader. The text guides, but the reader realizes:

> ... a literary text contains intersubjectively verifiable instructions for meaning-production, but the meaning produced may then lead to a whole variety of different experiences and hence subjective judgments.[12]

The text supplies much, but not everything. Were it to offer everything, Iser argues, the reader would be bored and dissatisfied. His imagination and intellect must have work to do—details to sketch in, implications to elaborate, questions to answer—or he will find reading a monotonous and unchallenging activity. The fictional world, Iser insists, must leave much to the reader. He says, in his discussion of conflict:

> Generally, the nature of these conflicts is such that although possible solutions are adumbrated in the text, they are not explicitly formulated there. The formulation will

take place through the guided activity stimulated in the reader, for only in this way can it become part of the reader's own experience.[13]

He speculates that the emptiness of much escape literature results from the usurping of the reader's role:

> The more explicit the text, the less involved he will be, and in passing one might remark that this accounts in great measure for the feeling of anticlimax that accompanies so much of what is called "light reading."[14]

It is also possible, of course, for the text to demand too much and offer too little, frustrating the reader:

> In this process the text may either not go far enough, or may go too far, so we may say that boredom and overstrain form the boundaries beyond which the reader will leave the field of play.[15]

We may note that Rosenblatt's and Iser's conception of the literary text is slightly different from that of either Bleich or the group we have so casually categorized as New Critics. The New Critics see the text as the repository of meaning. Bleich sees the individual reader as the source of meaning. Rosenblatt and Iser, on the other hand, see the exchange between text and reader as a process yielding knowledge. The potential richness of the literary work thus exceeds its contents, because the work initiates emotional and intellectual responses that cannot be predicted from the text, and cannot be said to reside in the text, but are not purely and simply within the readers.

Reading is thus neither a search for the meaning of the work, as in the New Critical approaches, nor a self-contained journey into one's own mind, as in subjective criticism, but an opportunity to explore and create. The task is not finding clues and solving problems, but realizing potential. The question becomes not so much, "What does the work mean?" as "What can we do with the work?"

This can be a very productive question for literature teachers to raise, for it forces them to consider the perspective of their students and look on them as potentially active, thinking, creative individuals. Further, it broadens the possibilities for teaching, because it respects the potential of the work to generate thought that goes beyond the work itself. Students need not, in other words, be confined to interpretation, to discussing meaning or the author's techniques and intentions. Rather, they may explore the possibilities of transforming the work of fiction into a poem, or the poem into a play, or they may find that a work stimulates them to introspection. Iser's view implies respect for all these possible directions. The field in which the reader may play is larger, in Iser's conception of literature, than it is in the New Critic's, and the range of possibilities for the classroom is thus significantly broadened.

Still, despite these possibilities, the reader is not outside the control of the text. As Iser is careful to point out, the work structures and directs, and it is this fact that gives the work its significance. It provides a "structure that enables the reader to break out of his accustomed framework of conventions, so allowing him to formulate that which has been unleashed by the text."[16] The answer to our subjective isolation is clearer in Iser than in Bleich. It lies not in negotiation among readers but in the direct exchange between reader and text. The text takes its reader beyond the confines of his own prior experience, and it does so not by giving him new information but by providing him with material and experience from which to formulate the new. That material *is* new; it is something other than the reader, and thus by contrast with it the reader may define himself. The knowledge he gains is not something that the literary work has given him—it is something of his own that the work has enabled him to create.

This is likely to be a more comfortable and manageable epistemology than Bleich's. Knowledge in Bleich is a result of communal labor—the negotiations of a group working on its experiences of the literary work. Rosenblatt and Iser, on the other hand, allow for a knowledge-producing exchange between the reader and the work. Drawing heavily on Poulet's notion that the reader becomes the subject of the thoughts of the work, a notion that invests the work itself with something like consciousness, Iser describes the loss of self in reading. The reader thinks, for a time, the thoughts of another, abandoning his own perspectives, attitudes, and ideas. It is in that temporary loss of self that the individual profits from reading, for through it he is able to reformulate and see freshly:

> . . . there occurs a kind of artificial division as the reader brings into his own foreground something which he is not. This does not mean, though, that his own orientations disappear completely. However much they may recede into the past, they still form the background against which the prevailing thoughts of the author take on thematic significance. In reading, then, there are always two levels, and despite the multifarious ways in

which they may be related they can never be totally kept apart. Indeed, we *can* only bring another person's thoughts into our foreground if they are in some way related to the virtual background of our own orientations (for otherwise they would be totally incomprehensible).[17]

The confrontation with the new, in the form of the literary text, allows the reader to see aspects of himself that were previously hidden. Thus, much of the learning that results from the literary experience, in Iser's vision, is learning about the self:

> . . . a layer of the reader's personality is brought to light which had hitherto remained hidden in the shadows. . . . The significance of the work, then, does not lie in the meaning sealed within the text, but in the fact that that meaning brings out what had previously been sealed within us.[18]

The process is not just inference. It is not, that is, simply the task of tracking down the thoughts and perceptions underlying the text. It is instead an exploration: a process of discovering the self by introducing into it the alien thoughts and perceptions offered by the literary work, by submitting—momentarily and partially—to the control and direction of the text.

RECONCEIVING THE ACT OF READING

Iser's discussion suggests an interesting point about the act of reading. It reminds us that a literary work is not a thing, but a process. Often, perhaps especially in the secondary school classroom, the work is treated as a single unchanging entity. The experience of reading, however, refutes that. As we read, we find ourselves changing perspective, revising impressions, accumulating information and insight, and passing through a series of emotional states. Iser would have us consider the flux and movement of reading, something the less sophisticated reader may have difficulty doing.

Fish, who is perhaps even more interested in the temporal nature of reading than Iser, demonstrates the idea with a subtle analysis of several disputed points in Milton scholarship. He shows that one reading is possible, even probable, up to a certain point in the poem, but at that point another reading must be admitted into the picture. Traditional scholarship has disputed which meaning is the more likely, revealing its view of the literary work as a stable, meaning-bearing entity. Fish, however, argues that it is less appropriate to treat the work as a thing, with a demonstrable meaning, than as an experience with life and movement. He argues that the reader should observe the shift, accept it, and consider it part of the effect—and thus the meaning—of the poem:

> This moment of hesitation, of semantic or syntactic slide, is crucial to the experience the verse provides, but, in a formalist analysis, that moment will disappear, either because it has been flattened out and made into an (insoluble) interpretive crux, or because it has been eliminated in the course of a procedure that is incapable of finding value in temporal phenomena.[19]

Although the subtleties of Milton may be beyond most secondary school students, they can still gain from observing the evolution of their perspective as they read. In even so simple a work as *Killing Mr. Griffin*, discussed earlier, the shift in perspective is important. The first several chapters are told from the point of view of the students. For these characters, and thus quite likely for the reader, Mr. Griffin is harsh, demanding, and unfriendly. In about the fourth or fifth chapter, the reader is shown Mr. Griffin more directly, unfiltered by the minds of the students. Seen that way, he is a much more likable fellow, whose humor and goodwill are for the first time in clear view.

This shift in perspective almost demands an accommodation by the reader. He cannot retain his earlier sense of identification with the students. He must at the very least examine the new evidence; most likely his view of Griffin will be softened for the remainder of the book. The effect of the novel is to arouse an expectation and then frustrate it, to borrow Iser's terminology, and the reader is thus invited to participate in the process of learning, which is the process of continually revising one's perceptions and beliefs.

Fish would argue that the work's meaning lies in the process, not in a final, neat, completed statement that immobilizes it. We need not debate to a conclusion whether Griffin is vicious or kind. Rather, we might notice what effect the change in stance has on us as readers. We may feel chastened and cautioned, realizing that we have been comfortable with a premature judgment. If so, then that feeling, and perhaps a resolution to judge less hastily, will be part of the meaning of the novel for us. "It is the experience of an utterance—*all* of it and not anything that could be said about it, including anything I could say—that *is* its meaning."[20]

Awareness of the temporal nature of literature could have an obviously invigorating effect in the classroom, primarily because it raises interesting and provocative questions besides "What does it mean?" It may stimulate teachers to consider techniques for helping students watch themselves in the process of reading. It may suggest the simple virtue of changing one's mind, and reward that act above the rather dubious accomplishment of being "right." And it of course suggests the value of literature as experience, as an analogue of life itself, not simply a means to an obscure end like "appreciation of the cultural heritage."

Rosenblatt, Iser and Fish present us with a vision of literature as communication. The literary work is, or at least represents, another consciousness, giving the reader access to insights, experiences, and perceptions that would otherwise lie beyond his reach, and thus allowing him to reformulate his own consciousness. In Bleich's conception that communication seems possible only within a group actively conversing. In Iser's, it is possible in the encounter of reader and text. Both views acknowledge and respect the uniqueness of the reader. Bleich sees that uniqueness as almost inviolable—the individual is trapped within his subjectivity, freed from it only slightly through knowledge-producing discourse with friends or classmates. Iser has the individual overcome his isolation not through talk but through reading, which invites the reshaping of perceptions:

> The efficacy of a literary text is brought about by the apparent evocation and subsequent negation of the familiar. What at first seemed to be an affirmation of our assumptions leads to our own rejection of them, thus tending to prepare us for a re-orientation. And it is only when we have outstripped our preconceptions and left the shelter of the familiar that we are in a position to gather new experiences. As the literary text involves the reader in the formation of illusion and the simultaneous formation of the means whereby the illusion is punctured, reading reflects the process by which we gain experience.[21]

Clearly Iser believes the reader has contact with the visions offered by the text and can profit from them. We may go a step further, however, from the relationship between the reader and the text to that between the reader and the culture. We have mentioned the idiosyncratic element in language and literature. You and I cannot ever know precisely what the other means by a word. No word, even the simplest concrete noun, like "dog" or "house," will evoke identical thoughts in the minds of two people. But linguistic activity is not totally idiosyncratic. It also has a social dimension—we must

CURRENT LITERARY THEORY ✄ 241

share something, or language is no longer language, but simply random utterances that communicate nothing. If someone insists on thinking of furry, affectionate creatures when he hears the word "house," and structures used as dwellings when he hears the word "dog," then we can no longer talk with him. Not, at any rate, unless we are willing to share his redefinition of terms, in which case we again have shared meanings and have reestablished the social dimension of language.

So it is with literature. Although we have emphasized individual responses and have argued that response and interpretation cannot be adequately discussed without considering the reader, literature also serves a social purpose. It serves to integrate the reader into the culture, inviting him to define himself against the background of cultural expectations and to modify that background. Jauss, a proponent of reception aesthetics, argues [that the reader]:

> does not first have to bump into a new obstacle to gain a new experience of reality. The experience of reading can liberate one from adaptations, prejudices, and predicaments of a lived praxis in that it compels one to a new perception of things. The horizon of expectations of literature distinguishes itself before the horizon of expectations of historical lived praxis in that it not only preserves actual experiences, but also anticipates unrealized possibility, broadens the limited space of social behavior for new desires, claims, and goals, and thereby opens paths of future experience.[22]

Literature thus has a "socially formative function"[23]—it both shapes the individual so that he fits the culture and reshapes the culture in response to new visions. The idiosyncratic and the social are, then, the two aspects of literature's function. It trains the reader in the conventions of meaning peculiar to the society, giving the members of the group a common conceptual framework. And it reshapes that framework by bringing to bear on it what is unique in the writer and in the reader. Thus it forms the reader to fit his culture and reforms the culture to fit the reader.

This is a much more complete vision of the "cultural heritage" than that offered by the traditional literature curriculum, which often seems to see the cultural heritage as a stack of books or a list of great names. Here we begin to develop a sense of the dynamic relationship between the individual—reader or writer—and the culture. The individual assimilates the culture into himself, defines himself in relation to the norms of the culture, and presses for a redefinition of those norms. In the traditional curriculum, the task is much simpler and less interesting; it simply involves learning the culture, remembering its rough outlines and its major events and names, and accepting its values and customs. Jauss and others suggest a much more vigorous and healthy role for literature. They point out that its primary task is defining reality—clarifying and enriching our understanding of "love," "justice," "good," "right," "happiness," and the other great cultural issues.

STRUCTURALISM

The emerging changes in our view of the text, of the reader's role, of the act of reading, and of literature's place in the culture raise a related question about the nature of interpretation. Despite all the turmoil in current criticism, as several theorists have observed, interpretation has remained the unquestioned goal of literary studies. Culler, more strongly than anyone else, condemns this tendency:

> There are many tasks that confront criticism, many things we need to advance our understanding of literature, but one thing we do not need is more interpretations of literary works. It is not at all difficult to list in a general way critical projects which would be of compelling interest if carried through to some measure of completion; and such a list is in itself the best illustration of the potential fecundity of other ways of writing about literature. We have no convincing account of the role or function of literature in society or social consciousness. We have only fragmentary or anecdotal histories of literature as an institution: we need a fuller exploration of its historical relation to the other forms of discourse through which the world is organized and human activities are given meaning. We need a more sophisticated and apposite account of the role of literature in the psychological economies of both writers and readers; and in particular we ought to understand much more than we do about the effects of *fictional* discourse. . . . What are the ways of moving between life and art? What operations or figures articulate this movement? Have we in fact progressed beyond Freud's simple distinction between the figures of condensation and displacement? Finally, or perhaps in sum, we need a typology of discourse and a theory of the relations (both mimetic and

nonmimetic) between literature and the other modes of discourse which make up the text of intersubjective experience.[24]

Treating literature as experience, rather than simply as meaning-bearing text, requires us at least to reassess the nature of interpretation. Fish would redefine interpretation *as* experience. Culler would go further and have us abandon the notion that interpretation is the only critical task, or even the most valuable. The needs he lists for literary studies suggest the range of possibilities. Clearly, some are being addressed—Fish deals with literature's effects, Bleich and others with the "psychological economies," Jauss with its function in social consciousness. All of these approaches could begin to influence and reshape the literature curriculum in the secondary schools, offering us new structures, goals, and activities. This text explores some of the changes that might be inspired by the work of Rosenblatt and others; the studies that Culler and other structuralists propose would suggest many other possibilities.

The structuralists and semioticians concern themselves less with the individual reader, so central to our own argument, and less with the collective reader, important to Jauss; they concentrate instead on the systems that enable readers to obtain meaning from a text. Drawing much of their inspiration and methodology from linguists, whose focus on the structures of language parallels their own interest in the conventions of literature, the structuralist critics concentrate on how the literature means, rather than what it means. Discussing the research of Norman Holland, Culler says, "More interesting that the clichés of his readers' differences are the factors that make their perceptions and associations converge."[25]

Culler suggests that the convergence of response may be the result of an unarticulated knowledge of literary conventions, "an implicit understanding of the operations of literary discourse which tells one what to look for."[26] In a brief discussion of a Blake poem he identifies several of the conventions: the "rule of significance," which leads us to see the poem "as expressing a significant attitude to some problem concerning man and/or his relation to the universe"; the convention of "metaphorical coherence," which makes us look for consistency in the metaphors offered; and the convention of "thematic unity," which leads us to seek meaningful and consistent connections among the events and situations of the work.[27]

Culler's argument suggests the potential of structuralist approaches to literature. Such conventions, somewhat more fully explained and organized, might provide an alternative structure for the literature curriculum. At the very least, they suggest lines of inquiry beyond the historical issues that tend to dominate chronologically arranged courses.

Other structuralist studies have also produced interesting results. Andrews, in surveying the history of narratology, provides us with a convenient catalog of structuralist contributions. Studies have addressed type of action, subordination of actions, characters, character interrelations, type of discourse, subordination of tales, narrator, and narrative distance. Consider his comments on one category, character interrelations:

> Characters are interrelated by opposition (desire, hate), by reciprocation (to desire, to be desired), and by dissimulation (hating, while appearing to desire). The events of the tale force transformations within characters and among them according to a limited set of rules. . . . Todorov has constructed four axioms to account for all character transformations. Obviously these axioms appear ludicrously reductive. . . . For example, "Rule 1. Given A and B, two agents, and A loves B. Then A acts in such a way as to effect the reciprocal of this predicate (that is, the proposition 'A is loved by B')." . . . While this rule is doubtless universal, other rules are specific to eighteenth-century mores.[28]

What Todorov seems to be searching for in such analysis is a basic pattern that will explain some aspect of narrative, and so by extension some aspect of the human mind. The possibility of that extension is perhaps clearer in Lévi-Strauss's analysis of myth. As Culler describes it, "The investigation of myth is part of a long-term project which uses ethnographic material to study the fundamental operations of the human mind."[29]

Structuralists remind us that the individuality of the reader can be defined only against the background of society, in terms of its network of structures and concepts. We have been discussing such relationships from the first—that of the reader and the text, the reader and other readers, the text and other texts—and the discussion inevitably leads us to consider the broadest spectrum of relationships, those that constitute the culture. Ultimately, literature is the reservoir of mankind's efforts to cope with life, to impose some order on the chaos of experience. It allows the intelligent reader access to himself by giving him access to others, all those others who have written in a language he can read.

The studies of literature and literary theory touched on here have begun to reinstate the reader at the center of the literary experience, thus redefining literature's place in the culture. It becomes once again the possession of everyman, rather than of the scholarly elite, and it provides him with a touchstone by which to judge and revise his own conceptions of the world and his place in it. It thus merits a place at the center of the curriculum, as the most fundamental and significant of all the disciplines, for it is in the study of literature that we each build the conceptual world in which we live.

NOTES

1. Steven Mailloux, *Interpretive Conventions: The Reader in the Study of American Fiction* (Ithaca: Cornell University Press, 1982), p. 43.

2. Frank Lentricchia, *After the New Criticism* (Chicago: Univ. of Chicago Press, 1980), p. 3.

3. Robert Scholes, *Semiotics and Interpretation* (New Haven: Yale Univ. Press, 1982), p. 15.

4. Mailloux, p. 36.

5. David Bleich, *Subjective Criticism* (Baltimore: Johns Hopkins Univ. Press, 1978), p. 98.

6. Bleich, pp. 110–11.

7. Bleich, p. 111.

8. Bleich, p. 132.

9. Bleich, p. 133.

10. Louise M. Rosenblatt, *The Reader, the Text, the Poem: The Transactional Theory of the Literary Work* (Carbondale: Southern Illinois Univ. Press, 1978), p. 105.

11. Rosenblatt, p. 105.

12. Wolfgang Iser, *The Act of Reading: A Theory of Aesthetic Response* (Baltimore: Johns Hopkins Univ. Press, 1978), p. 25.

13. Iser, p. 46.

14. Iser, p .46.

15. Iser, "The Reading Process: A Phenomenological Approach," *New Literary History*, 3, No. 2 (Winter 1972), 280.

16. Iser, *The Act of Reading*, p. 50.

17. Iser, *The Act of Reading*, p. 155.

18. Iser, *The Act of Reading*, p. 157.

19. Stanley Fish, "Interpreting the Variorum," in *Is There a Text in This Class?* (Cambridge: Harvard Univ. Press, 1980), pp. 154–55.

20. Fish, "Literature in the Reader: Affective Stylistics," in *Is There a Text in This Class?* p. 32.

21. Iser, "The Reading Process," p. 295.

22. Hans Robert Jauss, *Toward an Aesthetic of Reception*, trans. Timothy Bahti (Minneapolis: Univ. of Minnesota Press, 1982), p. 41.

23. Jauss, p. 40.

24. Jonathan Culler, *The Pursuit of Signs: Semiotics, Literature, Deconstruction* (Ithaca: Cornell Univ. Press, 1981), p. 6.

25. Culler, p. 53.

26. Culler, *Structuralist Poetics: Structuralism, Linguistics, and the Study of Literature* (Ithaca: Cornell Univ. Press, 1975), p. 114.

27. Culler, *Structuralist Poetics*, p. 115.

28. J. Dudley Andrews, "The Structuralist Study of Narrative: Its History, Use, and Limits," in *The Horizon of Literature*, ed. Paul Hernadi (Lincoln: Univ. of Nebraska Press, 1982), p. 109. Andrews quotes Tzvetan Todorov from "Les catégories du récit littéraire," *Communications* 8 (1966), p. 136.

29. Culler, *Structuralist Poetics*, p. 40.

BOOKS ON LITERARY THEORY AND RELATED TOPICS

Applebee, Arthur N. *The Child's Concept of Story*. Chicago: Univ. of Chicago Press, 1978.

Bleich, David. *Readings and Feelings*. Urbana: National Council of Teachers of English, 1975.

———. *Subjective Criticism*. Baltimore: Johns Hopkins Univ. Press, 1978.

Bloom, Harold, ed. *Deconstruction and Criticism*. New York: Seabury Press, 1979.

Burke, Kenneth. *The Philosophy of Literary Form*. New York: Vintage Books, 1957.

Carlsen, G. Robert. *Books and the Teenage Reader*. 2nd rev. ed. New York: Harper & Row, 1980.

Cawelti, John G. *Adventure, Mystery, and Romance*. Chicago: Univ. of Chicago Press, 1976.

Culler, Jonathan. *The Pursuit of Signs: Semiotics, Literature, Deconstruction*. Ithaca: Cornell Univ. Press, 1981.

———. *Structuralist Poetics: Structuralism, Linguistics, and the Study of Literature*. Ithaca: Cornell Univ. Press, 1975.

Davis, Walter A. *The Act of Interpretation*. Chicago: Univ. of Chicago Press, 1978.

de Man, Paul. *Allegories of Reading: Figural Language in Rousseau, Nietzsche, Rilke, and Proust*. New Haven: Yale Univ. Press, 1979.

Dillon, George L. *Language Processing and the Reading of Literature.* Bloomington: Indiana Univ. Press, 1978.

Eco, Umberto. *The Role of the Reader: Explorations in the Semiotics of Texts.* Bloomington: Indiana Univ. Press, 1979.

Fagan, Edward R. *Field: A Process for Teaching Literature.* University Park: Pennsylvania State Univ. Press, 1964.

Favat, Andre. *Child and Tale: The Origins of Interest.* Urbana: National Council of Teachers of English, 1977.

Fish, Stanley. *Is There a Text in This Class?: The Authority of Interpretive Communities.* Cambridge: Harvard Univ. Press, 1980.

Fokkema, D. W., and Elrud Kunne-Ibsch. *Theories of Literature in the Twentieth Century: Structuralism, Marxism, Aesthetics of Response, Semiotics.* London: C. Hurst, 1978.

Fowler, Roger. *Literature as Social Discourse: The Practice of Linguistic Criticism.* Bloomington: Indiana Univ. Press, 1981.

Harari, Josué, ed. *Textual Strategies: Perspectives in Post-Structuralist Criticism.* Ithaca: Cornell Univ. Press, 1979.

Hartman, Geoffrey. *Criticism in the Wilderness.* New Haven: Yale Univ. Press, 1980.

———. *The Fate of Reading.* Chicago: Univ. of Chicago Press, 1975.

Hernadi, Paul, ed. *The Horizon of Literature.* Lincoln: Univ. of Nebraska Press, 1982.

———. *What Is Criticism?* Bloomington: Indiana Univ. Press, 1981.

———. *What Is Literature?* Bloomington: Indiana Univ. Press, 1978.

Holland, Norman. *The Dynamics of Literary Response.* New York: Oxford Univ. Press, 1968.

———. *5 Readers Reading.* New Haven: Yale Univ. Press, 1975.

———. *Poems in Persons: An Introduction to the Psychoanalysis of Literature.* New York: Norton, 1973.

Ingarden, Roman. *The Cognition of the Literary Work of Art.* Evanston: Northwestern Univ. Press, 1973.

———. *The Literary Work of Art: An Investigation on the Borderlines of Ontology, Logic, and the Theory of Literature.* Evanston: Northwestern Univ. Press, 1973.

Iser, Wolfgang. *The Act of Reading: A Theory of Aesthetic Response.* Baltimore: Johns Hopkins Univ. Press, 1978.

———. *The Implied Reader: Patterns of Communication in Prose Fiction from Bunyan to Beckett.* Baltimore, Johns Hopkins Univ. Press, 1974.

Jauss, Hans Robert. *Aesthetic Experience and Literary Hermeneutics.* Minneapolis: Univ. of Minnesota Press, 1982.

_____. *Toward an Aesthetic of Reception.* Minneapolis: Univ. of Minnesota Press, 1982.

Lentricchia, Frank. *After the New Criticism.* Chicago: Univ. of Chicago Press, 1980.

Lesser, Simon. *Fiction and the Unconscious.* Chicago: Univ. of Chicago Press, 1957.

Mailloux, Steven. *Interpretive Conventions: The Reader in the Study of American Fiction.* Ithaca: Cornell Univ. Press, 1982.

Miller, Bruce E. *Teaching the Art of Literature.* Urbana: National Council of Teachers of English, 1980.

Miller, G. Hillis. *Fiction and Repetition.* Cambridge: Harvard Univ. Press, 1982.

Norris, Christopher. *Deconstruction: Theory and Practice.* London: Methuen, 1982.

Pratt, Mary Louise. *Toward a Speech Act Theory of Literary Discourse.* Bloomington: Indiana Univ. Press, 1977.

Purves, Alan. *Literature Education in 10 Countries.* New York: John Wiley and Sons, 1973.

_____. *Literature and the Reader.* Urbana: National Council of Teachers of English, 1981.

Riffaterre, Michael. *Semiotics of Poetry.* Bloomington: Indiana Univ. Press, 1978.

Rosenblatt, Louise M. *Literature as Exploration.* 3rd ed. New York: Noble and Noble, 1968.

_____. *The Reader, the Text, the Poem: The Transactional Theory of the Literary Work.* Carbondale: Southern Illinois Univ. Press, 1978.

Scholes, Robert. *Semiotics and Interpretation.* New Haven: Yale Univ. Press, 1982.

Slatoff, Walter J. *With Respect to Readers.* Ithaca: Cornell Univ. Press, 1970.

Smith, Barbara Herrnstein. *On The Margins of Discourse.* Chicago: Univ. of Chicago Press, 1978.

Suleiman, Susan R., and Inge Crosman, eds. *The Reader in the Text: Essays on Audience and Interpretation.* Princeton: Princeton Univ. Press, 1980.

Todorov, Tzvetan. *Introduction to Poetics.* Minneapolis: Univ. of Minnesota Press, 1981.

Tompkins, Jane. *Reader-Response Criticism: From Formalism to Post-Structuralism.* Baltimore: Johns Hopkins Univ. Press, 1980.

Index

DATE DUE